D0758417

The Poet's Madness

A READING OF GEORG TRAKL

Francis Michael Sharp

CORNELL UNIVERSITY PRESS

Ithaca and London

Cornell University Press gratefully acknowledges a grant
from the Andrew W. Mellon Foundation that aided
in bringing this book to publication.

First published 1981 by Cornell University Press
Published in the United Kingdom by Cornell University Press Ltd.,
2–4 Brook Street, London W1Y 1AA.

International Standard Book Number 0-8014-1297-8
Library of Congress Catalog Card Number 80-23574
Printed in the United States of America
Librarians: Library of Congress cataloging information appears on the last page of the book.

For Winfried

Contents

Preface

The Austrian poet Georg Trakl has achieved a secure place on the lists of modern poets which are drawn up by literary critics and historians, yet he has in no way become merely historical. His poetry belongs to the present as well as to history. The fascination it continues to elicit in readers around the world hinges on what appears to be the essential otherness of the poet's experience, an otherness rooted in the poet's madness. Readers who grant this experience a reality apart from its reality in language encounter few familiar landmarks; they find a highly elusive world that alternately attracts and frustrates. One makes an uneasy peace with these poems.

This book claims no more than to have reached a truce with a poetry that seems to assert itself anew with each reading. My intent, moreover, has not been to gloss over the poetry's multiplicities and contradictions with a theory of the mind that pretends to explain the poet's madness. Rather, my readings attempt to reach directly to this otherness that is so alien, yet alluring. The antipsychiatry of R. D. Laing is an important model and guide for a constructive mediation between poet and reader. Because Laing has known and communicated the psychopathological experience so well and because he has refused to silence it either by therapy or by rigid theory, his approach is uniquely suitable for the examination of such poetry. His thought plays an essential role in restoring the visibility of the human aura in Trakl's verse, while assuring that this aura is not reduced to the common denominators of psychology. Although my readings are not directed toward the "person" of the poet behind the texts—antipsychiatry rests on the premise that it cannot *define* any person—they are directed toward activating the human presence within the texts, reinvesting them with a referential density that much of Trakl criticism denies.

In the fall of 1977, a group of Austrian and French Germanists gathered in Salzburg for a symposium commemorating the ninetieth anniversary of Trakl's birth. At one of the sessions a letter was read from an absent colleague in Germany, Hans-Georg Kemper, who wished the others success in imparting fresh impetus to Trakl scholarship. Kemper must have been disappointed, at least in part, for in the introductory pages of his own book on Trakl he had identified schizophrenia as a fundamental problem for any discussion of the poet. During the symposium, however, the topic appears to have been subject to an unspoken taboo. Only at one point during the long discussions of literary influence did evidence of this suppression rise to the surface. One participant, Brigitta Steinwendtner, complaining about the overemphasis on "syntactic models," noted the absence of reference to Trakl's "incredible sensitiveness in psychological matters." Joining this short-lived revolt, the writer Hilde Domin chided the academics for appearing to analyze Trakl's poems as mere mixtures of lines from the poems of predecessors such as Hölderlin and Rimbaud. Along with considerations of influence, she insisted, "we have to include Trakl's extremely labile personality and the extreme situation in general in which poems come about."[1] But the momentum of these remarks quickly dissipated in the ensuing discussion, whose course had been set as much by the unasked question as by those that had been posed.

This anecdote illustrates a general as well as a particular situa-

[1] *Salzburger Trakl-Symposion,* eds. Walter Weiss and Hans Weichselbaum, Trakl-Studien 9 (Salzburg: Otto Müller, 1978), pp. 101, 120–121.

tion among literary critics. The question of the role of psychopathology in literature often remains unraised, whether the justification for ignoring it is the supremacy of the text or the belief that the two topics are mutually exclusive. Much literary activity in the past few years, however, has seemed intent upon bringing the question into the open.

Thomas Bernhard, for example, one of the most acclaimed and powerful writers in the German-speaking literary world today, often exploits the electrifying tensions of psychopathological states in works of fiction. Heinar Kipphardt and Ernst Augustin, who are psychiatrists as well as writers, bring specialized training and insight to bear on fictionalized re-creations of these states. Other recent novelists have admittedly drawn on their own psychotic episodes as sources of their writings. Leo Navratil, an Austrian psychiatrist known for his theoretical works on psychopathology, art, and language, has published poetic texts by his patients which have earned the praise of several "sane" poets.[2] For these writers, psychopathology has various yet obvious roles to play in literature. The widespread and ready acceptance of the fact among creative minds will eventually, perhaps, persuade even the most resistant reader that the examination of these roles is justified.

A further obstacle in the path of this topic has been the traditional fear of psychology's reductionist tendencies, a fear, moreover, that has a real basis. Winfried Kudszus, who has worked extensively to mediate between textual criticism and psychological approaches to literature, has rightly noted that the text's "meaning and its energy cannot be contained within terminological networks."[3] Designed to calibrate the continuum of human behavior and experience, these networks are rough-hewn

[2]See Wolfgang Hädecke, "Der taube Lärm unterhalb der Geschichte: Das Thema Wahnsinn in der neuesten Literatur," *Der neue Rundschau,* 1 (1978), 120–130.

[3]Kudszus, "Reflections on the Double Bind of Literature and Psychopathology," *Sub-Stance,* No. 20 (1978), p. 33.

and clumsy tools for dealing with poetry. Extreme poetry, poetry that reflects the full force of the poet's human presence—whether we call this presence psychopathological or not—can easily fall in between the calibrations or entirely off the scale. It is in these uncharted areas, areas where Trakl's poetry often leads, that antipsychiatry holds an advantage over reductionist psychologies. While the latter tend to assert their own ordering systems, antipsychiatry enables the reader to follow the lead of the poem.

Translating poetry is in itself an act of interpretation. Although my translations of Trakl's poems are no exceptions, I made them only after I had formed my critical understanding of the originals. I leave it to the bilingual reader to judge their adequacy to Trakl's verse. In order to present the reader with the fewest possible impediments, I have chosen various ways to situate the poems in the book. Short poems are integrated into the text, presented in the German and followed by my translation. The long verse poems "Psalm" and "Helian," the prose poems, and the *Brenner* versions of "Passion" and "Abendland" appear in the Appendix, in German and in translation. The numbers in parentheses after quotations by or about Trakl refer to the two-volume historical-critical edition, *Georg Trakl: Dichtungen und Briefe* (Salzburg: Otto Müller, 1969), edited by Walther Killy and Hans Szklenar. Except where noted, all translations from the German are mine.

My sincere gratitude is extended to several people scattered in time and place throughout my life. My greatest debt is to my friend and teacher in Berkeley, Winfried Kudszus, whose presence in these pages is much too encompassing to be acknowledged in a few words. He guided the study from its beginnings, patiently read several manuscripts, and was always generous with ideas and encouragement. During the years I spent at Princeton, I was fortunate to work in a department alongside Theodore Ziolkowski and Victor Lange. Their influence is not easily measured, but I am especially grateful to Ted for advice on practical matters concerning the manuscript. Esther Breisacher typed several of its drafts with unfailing care and good humor. Theodore Fiedler's many suggestions for revision were always as persuasive as they were constructive. Their persuasiveness doubtless stemmed from his own close acquaintance with Trakl's works. The same is true of another reader, Herbert Lindenberger, whose book on Trakl is often in the footnotes of my own. Bernhard Kendler also has my thanks for his efficiency and his support.

My special thanks go to my wife and daughter, whose patience and sacrifice made these pages possible. To my brother and adviser, James Roger Sharp, I owe gratitude for encouragement and years of sage advice.

I am indebted to Otto Müller Verlag, Salzburg, for permission to quote and translate passages from the volume *Erinnerung an Georg Trakl: Zeugnisse und Briefe* (2d ed., 1959), and to Wesleyan University Press for permission to quote James Wright's "Echo for the Promise of Georg Trakl's Life" from *Collected Poems* (copyright © 1971 by James Wright). Excerpts from "Stanzas in Terza Rima" and "The Mine at Falun" by Hugo von Hofmannsthal, *Poems and Verse Plays,* ed. Michael Hamburger, Bollingen Series xxxiii, 2 (copyright © 1961 by Princeton University Press) are reprinted by permission of Princeton University Press. An earlier version of portions of Chapters 1 and 6 appears in the volume, *The Turn of the Century: German Literature and Art 1890–1915* (The Second McMaster Colloquium on German Literature), eds. Gerald Chapple and Hans H. Schulte (Bonn: Bouvier, in press).

Francis Michael Sharp

Stockton, California

The Poet's Madness

1

Psychopathology in Trakl's Life and Work

Trakl's Life (1887–1914)

Georg Trakl died in a psychiatric ward from an overdose of cocaine at the age of twenty-seven. Drug addiction, madness, and suicide threats not only attended his inglorious end, but ran like leitmotifs through his life. It is difficult to view Trakl's final days other than as the culmination of a grimly logical pattern. Although relatively little is reliably known about the factors that shaped this pattern, biographers with psychiatric knowledge as well as literary critics have formulated their accounts against the background of a progressively deteriorating personality.[1] The least—and perhaps the most—that can be said with certainty, however, is that Trakl's life clashed at many points with the norms of the social setting into which he was born.

According to these norms, moreover, the family history was tarnished long before Georg's birth. His mother, a Catholic, had divorced her first husband to marry the Protestant Tobias Trakl, by whom she had a child before the second marriage took place. Nothing is known about the fate of this child, but it is assumed that he or she died in infancy before the first of the legitimate

[1]For a list of biographical material available, see Christa Saas, *Georg Trakl* (Stuttgart: Metzler, 1974), pp. 5–7. A definitive biography has yet to appear although Saas reports the announcement of a new one by Alfred Doppler to be published by Otto Müller (p. 64).

Trakl children was born. Georg was born in Salzburg on February 3, 1887, as the fourth of these six siblings.

In the memory of Trakl's younger brother Fritz, their childhood home was a model of bourgeois ease and prosperity: "We were very well off. We had a large home and lived in that comfortable and self-evident affluence which no one can any longer imagine today."[2] The Trakl household reflected in many ways the material security in the Austro-Hungarian Empire at the end of the nineteenth century as it is described by Stefan Zweig in his reminiscences, *The World of Yesterday:*

> When I attempt to find a simple formula for the period in which I grew up, prior to the First World War, I hope that I convey its fullness by calling it the Golden Age of Security. Everything in our almost thousand-year-old Austrian monarchy seemed based on permanency, and the State itself was the chief guarantor of this stability. . . . In this vast empire everything stood firmly and immovably in its appointed place, and at its head was the aged emperor; and were he to die, one knew (or believed) another would come to take his place, and nothing would change in the well-regulated order. No one thought of wars, of revolutions, or revolts. All that was radical, all violence, seemed impossible in an age of reason.[3]

The prosperity of the Trakl family found its outward expression in the children's Alsatian governess and the large, comfortable house which looked out onto the most beautiful squares in Salzburg.

The social standing and affluence that the Trakl family enjoyed were primarily due to Georg's industrious father, Tobias. A successful businessman, Tobias had used the advantages of an era favorable to material progress to rise from the petite bourgeoisie into the most respected middle-class circles in Salzburg. Al-

[2]Otto Basil, *Georg Trakl in Selbstzeugnissen und Bilddokumenten* (Reinbek bei Hamburg: Rowohlt, 1965), p. 17.

[3]Zweig, *The World of Yesterday: An Autobiography* (New York: Viking, 1943), pp. 1–2.

though a solid and respectable figure who provided well for his family's material comfort, he seems to have been only a shadowy presence in Georg's emotional life. Neither the poet's letters nor the various sketches of his life contain any hint of Tobias' reaction to his son's increasingly bohemian existence. Erich Neumann has taken Trakl's biographers to task for stressing the family's physical comfort while ignoring the "catastrophic and lethally dangerous" familial atmosphere as well as the father's lack of active intervention in his son's crisis-ridden life.[4] The insubstantial part that Tobias had in Trakl's life may account for the secondary role which the father figure plays in his poetry. Moreover, this absence of involvement probably meant that the oedipal conflict failed to reach even its normal intensity, surely an exception in an age which produced more than its share of literary patricides. One factor that certainly influenced the relationship was Tobias' age—he was fifty when Georg was born and he died in 1910, just four years before his son. What biographers characterize as a lack of influence, Georg, it seems likely, felt as distance and indifference.

Maria Trakl, Tobias' second wife and fifteen years younger than he, must have presented a striking contrast to her even-tempered, well-adjusted husband. Outwardly, she had given up her Catholicism when she married Tobias, but an uncertainty about her religious faith remained even among her children, an uncertainty which suggests her extremely private and reserved nature.[5] Georg, who was christened as a Protestant, experienced the religious schism in the family in his earliest school days. He attended a Catholic school in the mornings and took part in Protestant religious instruction on certain afternoons.

[4]Neumann, "Georg Trakl: Person und Mythos," *Der schöpferische Mensch* (Zurich: Rhein, 1959), pp. 252–253. Neumann refers at this point to Theodor Spoerri, *Georg Trakl: Strukturen in Persönlichkeit und Werk* (Bern: Francke, 1954), and Wolfgang Schneditz, "Georg Trakl: Versuch einer Deutung des Menschen und des Dichters," *Georg Trakl: Nachlaß und Biographie: Gedichte, Briefe, Bilder, Essays,* ed. W. Schneditz (Salzburg: Otto Müller, 1949), III, pp. 66–126.

[5]Basil, pp. 19–20.

Collections of baroque furniture, precious glass, and fine porcelain occupied Maria Trakl's main attention. Fritz Trakl, the youngest of her sons, recalled that as the collections grew, more and more rooms in the house became taboo for the children:

> We were very attached to our French governess and our father. Mother worried more about her antique collection than about us. She was a cool, reserved woman; she cared well for us, but a warmth was lacking. She felt herself misunderstood by her husband, by her children, by the whole world. She was only completely happy when she remained alone with her collections—she then closed herself off for days in her rooms.[6]

Artistic interests other than antique collecting, especially music, also had a part in Maria Trakl's life. Most of the children's cultural education, however, was provided by their Alsatian governess, Maria Boring, who not only taught them French, but also escorted them to the musical and theatrical events in Salzburg.

Maria Trakl was quite unlike the maternal ideal of her culture and age. It is tempting to compare her with an older contemporary in Vienna, Amalie Freud, whose subsequently famous son credited much of his success in life to her partiality and lavish attention. Sigmund Freud—to his mother the "golden Sigi"—insisted throughout his life that it had been her doting love which had endowed him with an unshakable belief in himself and his capabilities. To a greater degree even than her husband, Maria Trakl appears to have stood aloof from the children. The psychiatrist Theodor Spoerri was struck by the driven, incalculable expression of her portrait and described her as self-willed and impenetrable.[7] She was addicted to drugs, as were four of her children. Georg's feelings toward her have best been described as torn between love and hate. Letters exist in which he expresses an attachment and concern for her, but he also once admitted to Ludwig von Ficker that he hated her so much that he could have

[6]Basil, p. 28 and p. 17.
[7]Spoerri, p. 42.

murdered her with his own hands. This ambivalent attitude is typical of Trakl, who was often at the mercy of inner conflicts.

Georg's younger sister Grete, the single most important figure in his life, was subject to many of the same conflicts. A gifted pianist, she has been variously depicted as aggressive, hysterical, and pathologically eccentric. While the two were together in Vienna in 1909, Georg helped her to obtain drugs, to which she became more and more severely addicted. A year later, still pursuing her musical training, she moved to Berlin, where in 1912 she entered into an unhappy marriage with a much older man. It was there that Georg saw her for the last time, just a few months before his death. In March 1914 he made a hasty trip to her bedside after she had suffered a near-fatal miscarriage. During the period following her brother's death in November of the same year, Grete's situation grew rapidly worse. Two unsuccessful drug cures and financial crises, combined with the unwillingness or inability of friends to help, brought her into dire mental and material straits. In 1917, while at a party with Herwarth Walden, publisher of the Berlin Expressionist journal *Der Sturm,* Grete suddenly disappeared into an adjoining room and shot herself.

To a greater or lesser degree, all of Trakl's biographers have been disturbed by the question whether their "incest" was actual or literary fiction. Theodor Spoerri claims to have access to proof that incestuous relations did take place, but in the book he published in 1954 he refrained from naming the source out of consideration for relatives who were still living.[8] Much that has been taken for biographical fact elsewhere, however, ultimately rests on passages extracted from the poetry. The editors of the first edition of Trakl's collected works (1919) were so convinced of its directly confessional nature that they omitted the early poem "Blutschuld" ("Incest") from the volume.

The most reliable sources for clarifying the matter of incest, the letters Georg and Grete exchanged, have been either lost or de-

[8]Spoerri, p. 41

stroyed. The suspicious curiosity which this loss naturally aroused was compounded by the extremely guarded attitude of the surviving relatives and the persistent denials of Erhard Buschbeck. Buschbeck, one of Trakl's earliest and closest friends—who himself probably had a short affair with Grete in 1912—always denied in conversations that any incestuous act had taken place. These anxious attempts to keep Trakl's memory free of the stigma of incest may not be convincing—and Spoerri has apparently invalidated them once and for all—but they volubly attest to the strength of the taboo itself. And, whether the transgressions against it occurred in fact or fancy, it was a taboo with which Trakl struggled throughout his life and in his poetry.

The attraction to his sister was a physical and spiritual fact for the poet. A close friend of Trakl's, Franz Bruckbauer, reported that early in his gymnasium days, Trakl spoke of her as "the most beautiful girl, the greatest artist, the most unusual woman."[9] One of the poet's last requests to Ludwig von Ficker was that his sister should inherit everything he had in case of his death. He made a few excursions to brothels in his youth, and reportedly was drawn into a platonic relationship with an old and wrinkled prostitute, but there was really no woman in his life other than his sister. The inner struggles to deny or come to terms with this attraction were also facts of the poet's life. They found their expression as an evolving central theme in the poetic work.

The memories of Trakl's relatives and oldest acquaintances do not yield a consistent picture of his early years. Erhard Buschbeck remembers him at their first meeting as shy and inhibited, while to others he seemed robust and more than willing to take part in juvenile pranks. Three obscure and variously interpreted incidents from these years are usually mentioned in order to establish a pattern of aberrant behavior. On one occasion, Trakl allegedly threw himself in front of a frightened horse. At another point early in his life, apparently prompted once more by an

[9] Basil, p. 76.

abhorrence of rapid motion, he stepped into the path of a moving train. The circumstances and aftermath of these two events are not recorded. The third event has been interpreted both as absent-mindedness and as an "expression of a psychotic situation."[10] Sometime between the ages of five and eight, Trakl walked directly into a pond until he disappeared under water. His hat floating on the surface provided his rescuers the only indication where he could be found, and he was pulled to safety. Mainly on the basis of this incident, Erich Neumann saw in Trakl's childhood the seeds of psychosis.

In school Trakl was an indifferent pupil. After his elementary education, he attended a humanistic gymnasium, the appropriate preparatory school for the university and for a professional career that would satisfy family expectations. The first indication that these were to remain unfulfilled came in the fourth class, which Trakl had to repeat because of bad marks. His indifference grew to outright disdain and cynicism until at the end of the seventh class he failed again and was forced to leave school for good. In a letter written in either August or September 1905 (I, 469), Trakl tells a classmate about his strenuous preparation for the exams he failed and the exhaustion caused by cramming and drugs. His remark that he "unfortunately" had "once more" to resort to chloroform to calm his nerves was not youthful bravado. It indicates that by the time he left the gymnasium his drug habit was already established. He had, in fact, carried a flask of chloroform with him since he was fifteen and regularly dipped his cigarettes into an opium solution. At one time or another in his life, he also used morphine, Veronal, and the fatal cocaine. This self-destructive habit probably began in part as an imitation of Baudelaire, whose drug-induced *paradis artificiels* were part of a fashionable decadence admired by the aspiring poet.

Although the possibilities of a profession based on a conventional university education were now closed to him, Trakl was left

[10]Spoerri, p. 23. Neumann, p. 251.

with an attractive alternative. With the six years of education at the gymnasium that he already had completed, three years of apprenticeship and four semesters of university study, he could become a pharmacist. This choice seemed all the more inviting to Trakl since it offered the promise of easy passage to the already familiar inner journeys. By the fall of 1908, Trakl had completed his apprenticeship at a pharmacy in Salzburg and was enrolled for the final phase of his studies at the university in Vienna.

His earliest poetry was written about 1904. These beginnings seemed harmlessly eccentric to the family, for whom his work remained alien. But with sympathetically inclined friends he began to discuss literary topics of the day and to read aloud poems of his own. These readings and discussions gradually grew into the regular monthly meetings of a literary club, which was christened "Apollo" and later became "Minerva." The members shared an interest in Baudelaire, George, and Hofmannsthal as well as an enthusiastic devotion to Nietzsche and Dostoyevsky. According to Bruckbauer, Trakl's contributions, many of them prose pieces, were at once the most numerous and the most peculiar (II, 518). In a letter written many years later, after the war had destroyed the manuscripts in his possession, Bruckbauer unwittingly contrasted the individuality of the lost prose pieces with the fashionably decadent mixture of passion and penance in an early poem that has survived (I, 254).

During early adolescence, Trakl began to go through changes of appearance and personality that were noticeable to his friends. He let his hair and sideburns grow long, he smoked and drank immoderately, and he began to dress in a fashionable, dandified style. Bruckbauer recalls him as often appearing "sullen, testy, arrogant, self-conscious and tired of life."[11] He became more withdrawn, and sudden switches in temperament and mood became commonplace. These changes have been variously described by biographers as either sudden or gradual, but always as

[11]Basil, p. 56.

outside the normal range of adolescent behavior. Yet even an expression of suicidal depression during this time was casually taken by one of his friends at less than face value. One day when he threatened to kill himself, his companion turned to him and said: "But please not when I am with you."[12] The element of false pathos and pretense in Trakl's behavior seems to have been quite clear to his friend. Many of his actions in these years should be seen in terms of pretense: as a cover-up for a failed education and as the mask of a *poète maudit*.

In 1905, Trakl became acquainted with the local *poète maudit,* Gustav Streicher, a dramatist and prose writer who is almost entirely forgotten today. Streicher encouraged the young poet in his dramatic efforts by recommending to the director of the city theater that two short plays of Trakl's be staged. On two separate occasions in 1906, *Totentag* (*All Souls' Day*) and *Fata Morgana* were performed. The mixed critical reception given the first was followed by the unanimous rejection of the second piece. Although Trakl afterward destroyed them both, skeletal versions of their contents are preserved in newspaper reviews (II, 511–517). *Totentag,* a one-act playlet, is of particular thematic interest. Subtitled a "dramatic mood piece," it dealt with the tragic love of a blind protagonist for an unfaithful female figure named Grete. As the review recounts it, Grete's infidelity finally drove the youth to madness and suicide. The *Salzburger Volksblatt* cited Ibsen's *Ghosts* as the playlet's clearest dramatic forebear and during the years 1906–1909 occasionally engaged Trakl to write short lyrical pieces.

After completing his apprenticeship in 1908, Trakl enrolled at the university in Vienna for the four semesters of pharmaceutical studies. Following his graduation two years later, he spent yet another year in the city, from the fall of 1910 to the fall of 1911, on active military duty. Especially at the beginning of his sojourn there, Trakl's antipathy toward cities came out in harsh state-

[12]Basil, p. 59.

ments about Vienna and what he perceived as the false conviviality and "unpleasant bonhomie" of its inhabitants (I, 473). Salzburg and Innsbruck became objects of similar negative appraisals at other periods of his life.

In Vienna he had few contacts until his good friend Buschbeck arrived from Salzburg in the fall of 1909 to study law at the university. Buschbeck immediately began to involve himself in the lively literary and artistic circles of the city and attempted to draw Trakl into his activities as well. One of his few successes was to introduce the reticent poet to Hermann Bahr, the critic who had exercised a strong influence on Viennese literary tastes since the 1890s. Trakl's hopes were high, but Bahr's initial interest faded and the only positive result was that three of his poems were published in the highly reputable *Neue Wiener Journal*. Buschbeck's attempts to promote his friend's poetry continued, however, and he sent a collection of it to a publisher in December 1909. These efforts also failed. Not until 1939 did Buschbeck manage to find a publisher for this earliest collection that then appeared under the title, *Aus goldenem Kelch* (*From the Golden Chalice*). Trakl later rejected all but two of these poems, which he then in 1913 included in his first published volume, *Gedichte*.

In spite of the new contacts with journalists and poets which Trakl made through Buschbeck, he probably spent a great deal of time during 1909–1910 with Grete, who was in Vienna for the year to study music. He seemed to prefer his old Salzburg friends Franz Schwab and Karl Minnich as drinking companions. According to the reports of friends and Trakl's own letters, drinking marathons often took place during these years. On May 20, 1911, Trakl wrote: "Schwab was in Vienna for fourteen days and we have never before caroused and squandered the nights so absurdly. I think we were both completely crazy" (I, 482). The habit lasted for the rest of his life, and in later years he often began a day's drinking early in the afternoon, once sleeping the following night in the snow in front of a friend's house. Although he consumed prodigious amounts of alcohol, one of his closest friends insisted that he could not become intoxicated and that he "was always *awake,* indeed the most wide-awake of all men."[13] In a letter to the journalist Karl Kraus, dated December 13, 1913, Trakl sent one of his most delicate lyrical productions along with a description of its origins during "days of delirious drunkenness and criminal melancholy . . ." (I, 530).

Difficulties in financing such an immoderate drinking habit and a constant supply of drugs became noticeable even while Trakl was in military service during 1910–1911. It was the first symptom of economic problems which never ceased to plague him. The end of his military service and the changed circumstances at home—his father had died in June 1910, shortly before Trakl passed his university examinations—brought him face to face with the necessity of becoming more financially independent. He tried to do so for the first time in the fall of 1911 by returning to his old job at the pharmacy in Salzburg. The steady exposure to the demands of customers, however, proved overly taxing to Trakl's fragile nervous system, and he soon quit.

The economic problem gradually grew into a frantic search not only for financial security, but for professional identity as well. In April 1912, with military reactivation as his goal, he began a period of probationary service in the pharmacy at the garrison hospital in Innsbruck. Even though he was accepted for active duty after the six-month trial period, he immediately petitioned for reserve status. Then in 1913–1914, until the outbreak of the war put an end to any wavering, he repeatedly tried through the influence of friends to be taken back into active service. During this period he also tried to obtain information about military medical service in Albania, and he wrote once to the Dutch Colonial Office to inquire about employment as a pharmacist in the Dutch East Indies (II, 725–726).

On three separate occasions during 1912–1913 he applied for

[13]Karl Borromäus Heinrich, "Die Erscheinung Georg Trakls," *Erinnerung an Georg Trakl: Zeugnisse und Briefe,* 2d ed. (Salzburg: Otto Müller, 1959), p. 108.

employment in the Viennese bureaucracy. Each time that he was successful he resigned shortly after beginning work, the first assignment being of especially short duration. On December 31, 1912, he reported for his new post in the Ministry for Public Works, left after two hours, and wrote his resignation the following day. On the other successful occasion, in July/August 1913, he stayed but a few days at the War Ministry. Regarded in light of other events in his life at the time, Trakl's arbitrary actions gain a certain plausibility. During the period from December 1912 to January 1913, Trakl was writing his long poem, "Helian," and Karl Borromäus Heinrich probably expressed the poet's own feelings when he noted that "the impossibility of completing a 'Helian' in Vienna drove him back to Innsbruck."[14] In July 1913, Trakl had just taken up his new post at the War Ministry when he received a copy of his first volume of poetry from the publisher. Shortly thereafter he reported sick and subsequently resigned. Both occasions demonstrate the wavering and ambivalence that surfaced in his poetry as well. One facet of his personality pushed him into a search for stability—possibly as an escape from the pain that writing entailed—while another facet impelled him away from such stability—possibly sensing an incompatability with his poetry.

Trakl countered the demands of his job at the pharmacy in the fall of 1911 with a life of wild excesses in the company of a new friend, Karl Hauer. They had become acquainted through their common association with the Salzburger Literatur- und Kunstgesellschaft Pan (the Pan Society of Literature and Art in Salzburg). Hauer was a skeptic and cynic of great intellectual gifts who had earlier contributed to Karl Kraus's journal *Die Fackel,* until Kraus himself began to write all of his own material. Not only did Hauer attack contemporary society and culture in print, but he lived a life of defiant dissoluteness. Trakl was easily won over to his critical attitudes and bohemian life style.

[14]Heinrich, p. 102.

The year 1912 brought not only continued financial worries—in its early months Trakl was forced to sell much of his private library—but also the fateful introduction into the inner circle of the periodical *Der Brenner*. Buschbeck once again played a mediating role. Through a friend he was able to get a Trakl poem published in the journal and to arrange for a meeting with its publisher, Ludwig von Ficker. The meeting took place in May 1912 at the Café Maximilian in Innsbruck, where Ficker normally spent the afternoons with friends and colleagues. Only gradually did he become aware of the poet, who had seated himself at a distance across the room. Eventually overcoming his timidity, Trakl had his card delivered to Ficker by the waiter. Ficker's invitation to join them at his table marked the beginning of a relationship which was as significant for Trakl personally as it was for his poetry. From October 1912 to July 1914 no issue of *Der Brenner* appeared without Trakl's work.

Trakl's publisher became a generous friend and patron as well. In the two short years that remained of his life, the poet often found periods of stability at the homes of both Ficker and Ficker's brother, where the doors were always open. Trakl's own words in a letter of February 23, 1913, best summarize the meaning that Ficker and the *Brenner* circle held for him. The letter was sent from the family home in Salzburg, where Trakl had gone to be present at the events surrounding the liquidation of the family business: "I feel more and more deeply what *Der Brenner* means to me—home and refuge in the circle of a noble humanity. Haunted by unspeakable emotions which are intent on either destroying or perfecting me, despairing of all my beginnings and facing a pitiably uncertain future, I feel more deeply than I can say, the good fortune of your magnanimity and kindness, the forgiving understanding of your friendship" (I, 504). To this idyllic security and mutual understanding, Trakl contrasted in the next lines the reality of his own family, where he felt an "inexplicable hatred" growing toward him. From the family's viewpoint if not from their prodigal son's, this antipathy probably had a logical explanation. They may well have had reason to suspect his sudden interest in the family business, especially at just the time when it was being dissolved.

From the end of May 1912, Trakl spent much of his time in the company of the regular contributors to *Der Brenner*—most of whom have long since been forgotten. His contacts widened to include men outside the circle, men instrumental in the shaping of Austrian culture at the time, such as Karl Kraus, the architect Adolf Loos, the artist Oskar Kokoschka, and the writer Peter Altenberg, among others. Now aided by the influential Ficker, Trakl's ambivalent search for a professional position continued. His poetry, however, benefited to an even greater extent from the connection with *Der Brenner*. Once lauded by Kraus as the "only honest review" in Austria and Germany, it provided invaluable exposure for the relatively unknown poet.[15] While Buschbeck was still unsuccessful in capturing a publisher's interest, the poetry in *Der Brenner* attracted the attention of Franz Werfel. A reader for the Kurt Wolff publishing house, Werfel requested Trakl to send him a collection which he considered publishable in book form. After some initial difficulties about the format and number of poems, which Ficker helped to resolve in Trakl's favor, a volume entitled *Gedichte* appeared in July 1913. A planned second volume, which Trakl meticulously revised, came out in 1915 under the title *Sebastian im Traum* (*Sebastian Dreaming*) only after his death.

The newfound sympathies of the *Brenner* group and the beginning of his success as a poet were the brightest spots in Trakl's life during his last two years. The unhappy marriage of his sister, on the other hand, doubtless cast the broadest shadow across them. On one occasion in June 1913, he had expected her to visit the family in Salzburg, but she had without warning remained in Berlin. In Vienna a month later, Trakl's presence and behavior were the subject of a letter written by Franz Zeis, a casual ac-

[15] Basil, p. 10, n. 2.

quaintance of the poet. Zeis wrote to a woman friend: "He is a dear person, silent, reserved, shy, entirely turned inward. Looks strong, powerful, but at the same time sensitive, sick. Has hallucinations, 'raves' (Schwab says)" (II, 713–714). A few lines further on, Zeis describes Trakl's habit of standing in the aisles of trains since sitting in a compartment forced him to face other passengers. He was apparently unable to bear the inquisitive scrutiny of a stranger for a prolonged period of time and unwanted physical contact was, as Buschbeck reports, an abomination to him.[16]

Ficker related an otherwise mysterious crisis in the poet's life in November 1913, to Grete's marital problems and pregnancy. Trakl had written to him in vague terms about his life being "unspeakably broken apart," leaving only a "speechless pain" without "bitterness." In the last paragraph, he wrote:

> Perhaps you could write me a few words—I no longer know in from out. It is such an indescribable disaster when one's world breaks apart. Oh my God, what a judgment has broken over me. Tell me that I must have the power to live on and to act truthfully. Tell me that I'm not insane. A stony darkness has broken in. Oh my friend, how small and unhappy I have become. [I, 530]

The pathos and vocabulary relate this letter, like many others sent to Ficker, more closely to the poetry than to the bulk of Trakl's correspondence. Typical too of his letters to his fatherly friend is the confessional attitude, an attitude which this time falls short of revealing the source of despair.

Trakl returned to Innsbruck at the end of November 1913. With the exception of his trip to Berlin in March 1914, he remained there until he departed for the Eastern front with his military unit in August 1914. From Berlin he wrote to Ficker:

> My poor sister is still quite ill. Her life is of such a heartrending sadness and bravery at the same time that I sometimes appear to

[16]Spoerri, p. 31

> myself very small in comparison. And she deserved it a thousand times more than I to live in a circle of good and noble people as it was granted me in such overly rich measure in difficult times.
>
> I intend to stay a few more days in Berlin, for my sister is alone the whole day and so my presence is of some use to her. [I, 534]

In contrast to the self-centered despair in the letter of the previous fall, there is here a self-deprecating flow of sympathy for his sister, whose lot he senses to be more desperate than his own.

Several months after his return to Innsbruck, Trakl's financial situation appeared to take a turn for the better. In July, shortly before the outbreak of World War I, he received through Ficker a grant of 20,000 crowns from a benefactor with whom neither the poet nor Ficker was personally acquainted. This small fortune proved to be part of a larger paternal inheritance which Ludwig Wittgenstein wished to give away to deserving Austrian artists. Ficker, who also allotted the same sum to Rilke, was given the authority by Wittgenstein to divide the money as he saw fit. Trakl, however, had little chance to use his share. On the one occasion when he went with Ficker to the bank to make a withdrawal from his account, he was overcome by anxiety and ran from the building drenched in his own perspiration. Nor did the poet ever meet his philosopher-benefactor, although wartime circumstances nearly brought them together. The opening phases of the war found them in close proximity on the Eastern front. One of Trakl's last postcards was a request to the philosopher to visit him in the hospital at Cracow—Wittgenstein, however, was unable to make the short journey until three days after Trakl's death.

Like many others, Trakl was initially caught up in the widespread enthusiasm for the war which Austria-Hungary declared on the recalcitrant Serbia on July 28. He volunteered shortly after its outbreak and left Innsbruck with his field-hospital unit in late August. By the beginning of September they had moved to Galicia, a province in Austrian-occupied Poland. At Grodek, commemorated in one of Trakl's last poems, the unit saw actual battle for the first time.

Here in the aftermath of a bloody defeat, Trakl was placed in charge of ninety badly wounded soldiers. He lacked all means and skill to relieve or alleviate the suffering of his charges. When one of them ended his misery by shooting himself in the head, Trakl's emotional limits were reached. He rushed from the barn which housed the wounded only to witness a second macabre scene compounding the horrors of the first. Hanged partisans dangled from the branches of the surrounding trees, a dance of death rivaling the most terrifying of Expressionist visions. He learned later—or he may have been present at the scene—that the last man had tied the rope around his own neck. A few days later, sometime during the chaotic general retreat, Trakl stood up and announced to his comrades at the evening meal that he could no longer live and that he must shoot himself. He hurried off but was caught and forcibly disarmed. Fourteen days later he was transferred to the Cracow garrison hospital, not for duty as a pharmacist as he had expected, but for psychiatric observation.

Trakl personally recounted these events to Ficker, who had traveled from Innsbruck to Cracow after learning of the poet's hospitalization.[17] During his two-day visit, Ficker tried in vain to obtain Trakl's release from circumstances which he knew were bound to aggravate his depressed condition. He felt that the dismal realities of institutional life could only intensify Trakl's fears and uncertainties. The windows of the narrow room that he shared with a disagreeable lieutenant suffering from delirium tremens were fitted with bars like a prison cell. The hospital garb of the patients reminded Ficker of prison uniforms. Furthermore, Trakl's belief in his culpability for his actions was strengthened by the uncertainty about the length of his stay. At one point he had been convinced that he would soon be released to his unit again, but during Ficker's visit he felt that the doctors were evading the issue altogether. In Ficker's view, a possible reason for the prolonged observation was the interest that one of the doctors

[17]Ludwig von Ficker, "Der Abschied," *Erinnerung an Georg Trakl*, pp. 181–204.

had in Trakl as a case of "genius and madness." The doctor had come upon this idea while reading some of his poetry in the course of censoring the mail. Whatever the truth of this conjecture may be, Ficker felt that Trakl was the victim of a coercive psychiatric treatment which would inevitably compound his mental distress. His last efforts in his friend's behalf were to rescue him from the hospital, where, as Ficker recounted it, the shrieks of the insane resounded in the brutal, prisonlike atmosphere. Possibly anticipating his failure and fearing the outcome, he asked Trakl if he still had drugs in his possession. Answering that he had, Trakl smiled and added: "Would I still be alive otherwise?"[18] Scarcely more than a week before his death, he saw drug intoxication not as a release from life, but as a buffer against an increasingly hostile world. As Theodor Spoerri noted, however, the question of intentionality in Trakl's death can never be completely resolved. And Spoerri may be correct when he interprets Trakl's last act as an intentional flight into a border zone between life and death where the poet left the final decision to chance.[19]

On November 11, one week after Trakl died, his older stepbrother Wilhelm wrote a letter of inquiry to the Cracow hospital. The reply from the military officials came within four days. With an air of finality it reported that following treatment for a mental disturbance, Trakl had committed suicide by taking an overdose of cocaine. The official parenthetically appended at this point the medical designation: "*Dement. praec.*"—a psychiatric syndrome today more familiar as schizophrenia (II, 736–737). There is no record of the Trakl family's reaction to the letter, but it was probably accepted in the same spirit that it was sent: as a military-medical document placing the official seal on a life run through with intoxicants, suicide threats, and erratic behavior.

This diagnosis appears to have been supported by a hospital

[18]Ficker, p. 194.
[19]Spoerri, pp. 34–35.

report which first came to light in 1967.[20] It was written by three doctors who attended Trakl during his last weeks. The first doctor recorded an incident which Trakl failed to mention to Ludwig von Ficker and which may more fully explain the atmosphere of delinquency that Ficker felt during his visit. While being transferred to the garrison hospital, Trakl had made an abortive attempt at desertion. This incident gives greater substance to his fear that he might have to stand trial for cowardice in face of the enemy—a fear that Ficker considered delusional. Yet if this was not truly delusional, other aspects of Trakl's behavior were clearly abnormal. His several attempts to be sent to the front lines as an infantryman before the battle at Grodek, while perhaps not unusual in themselves, were remarkable in their persistence and vehemence. On the day of the battle, the first doctor wrote that it took six men to disarm and stop him. He also noted that Trakl did not practice his profession in civilian life, but—he emphasized the irregularity with quotation marks—"wrote poetry."

Another physician recorded the following:

> From time to time since his childhood he has had visual hallucinations. It seems to him that a man with a drawn knife stands behind his back. From 12 to 24 years of age, he saw no such apparitions. For three years now he has again been suffering from these optical illusions and, moreover, he often hears bells ringing. He did not believe that his father was his own, but rather imagined, that he descends from a cardinal and that in the future, he will become a great man. [II, 730]

Such observations were certainly the decisive ones for the final diagnosis. Along with his erratically vacillating emotional states, Trakl's grandiose delusions and his visual and auditory hallucinations were central symptoms of *dementia praecox* as it was then understood. Emil Kraepelin, a German psychiatrist, had first dif-

[20]Johann Adam Stupp, "Neues über Georg Trakls Lazarettaufenthalte und Tod in Galizien," *Südostdeutsche Semesterblätter,* 19 (1967), 32–39. Reprinted in the historical-critical edition: II, 728–730.

ferentiated it as a distinct pathological entity in 1896. The name he gave it designated what, for him, was its most fundamental characteristic—an inexorable process of mental deterioration. More than a diagnosis, it was a prognosis as well, and one in which no allowance was made for the possibility of recovery. It is ironic that the poet generally considered to be the Cassandra of Austrian poetry should finally have had this Cassandra label of psychiatry attached to him. Unlike Cassandra, however, *dementia praecox* possessed credibility because of the stature of psychiatry as the science of the psyche. Its modern descendant, schizophrenia, still draws credibility from this powerful source.

In his book published in 1954, Theodor Spoerri wrote that he had found insufficient evidence to prove that Trakl had suffered from schizophrenia, yet he considered it probable.[21] The hospital report which came to light in 1967 apparently strengthened Spoerri in his opinion. To one of Trakl's biographers, he wrote in 1968: "The diagnosis has indeed become problematic for me again, and I believe that on the basis of this documentation a type of schizophrenia must be seriously considered."[22] Yet whether in 1914 Trakl's mental disturbances were properly diagnosed or whether even today they might be properly termed schizophrenic are questions of relatively little value. Psychiatry's growing disagreement on the nature of the "disease" itself represents an insurmountable obstacle for such a diagnosis. The extremes run from those who relate schizophrenia to organic pathology to those who call its very existence a myth.

To admit that these disturbances cannot be neatly bundled together under a psychiatric rubric is one thing, however. To leave out of account their effect on Trakl's work, on the other hand, severs the poetry from a vital source. While schizophrenia may indeed be a myth, in that it cannot be pinpointed like an organic disease, the radical changes in behavior and experience that an

[21]Spoerri, pp. 107–108.

[22]Cited in Johann Adam Stupp, "Georg Trakl der Dichter und seine südostdeutsche Abkunft," *Donauschwäbisches Schrifttum,* 14 (1969), 22.

individual who has been labeled schizophrenic undergoes are the starkest of realities.

The Pathology of the Poetry

The pathology in Trakl's life has been only infrequently tied explicitly to his poetry. If one considers the wide range of psychiatric opinion about schizophrenia and the modern disinclination to combine biography and textual interpretation, it is understandable that few attempts have been made to link schizophrenia directly to Trakl's poetic work. Among those who have pointed to such a link, the Jungian Erich Neumann sees the poetry as the product of a heroic creative effort which was made in spite of a diseased and endangered existence.[23] From a Freudian-influenced viewpoint, Theodor Spoerri, on the other hand, does not pit life against work as counterforces, but discovers in both an increasing disengagement from empirical reality.[24] In the most recent affirmation of the inseparability of Trakl's madness and his poetry, Maire Kurrik traces the poetic language ultimately "to naked primary process where there is no longer any directing idea to control the play of involuntary pathological associations and complexes."[25]

Far more often, oblique suggestions of pathology have been made in the language of literary criticism. The translation of vocabulary from psychiatry into the critical idiom is most transparent in comments such as those of the critic Emil Staiger: "There is no doubt that this poet no longer knows how things belong together." And further: "Georg Trakl surely stands outside the circle which encloses that world common to all men."[26] Such

[23]Neumann, p. 256.

[24]Spoerri, p. 106: "In his life as well as his work, the relation to the reality of the outer world becomes more and more tenuous." Basil claims to find a "progressive alienation from reality" and the formation of "a purely autistic world of expression" (p. 98).

[25]Kurrik, *Georg Trakl,* Columbia Essays on Modern Writers, 72 (New York: Columbia University Press, 1974), p. 3.

[26]Staiger, "Zu einem Gedicht Georg Trakls," *Euphorion,* 55 (1961), 282 and 279.

statements plainly echo Spoerri's discernment of a break with reality—the ultimate stage of schizophrenic alienation. Already in 1915, Rilke had laid the foundation for this characterization of Trakl's work: "I imagine that even the initiate experiences these outlooks and insights as an outsider pressed against panes of glass: for Trakl's experience occurs like mirror images and fills its entire space, which is inviolable like the space in the mirror."[27] It is impossible to measure accurately the effect which such pronouncements have on readers of Trakl's poetry. The direction of their underlying argument, however, is easier to determine. They encourage the notion that Trakl's poetic world is closed, his poetry an insoluble riddle, in a curious parallel to the closure of his life by psychiatry's diagnosis.

A half century after Rilke, Walther Killy's influential critical formulations brought this line of thought to its logical conclusion. Through his interpretive essays and as coeditor of the historical-critical edition, Killy had helped deflect Trakl scholarship away from theologically and philosophically oriented studies. He appeared to have undermined their basis by postulating that the meaning of the poems could not be reduced to conceptual thought. During the period of examining the variants and drafts while preparing the definitive edition, Killy became further convinced that the genesis of the poetry was as incomprehensible as the final product: "This poetry is not really intended to be understood in content."[28] Killy's viewpoints have dominated the great bulk of Trakl criticism during the past twenty years. They are the justification of a secondary literature which has largely resigned itself to formal and aesthetically oriented studies.[29]

The experiential factor which Rilke perceived but despaired of

[27]From a letter to Ficker in February 1915 reprinted in *Erinnerung an Georg Trakl,* p. 11.

[28]Killy, *Über Georg Trakl,* 3d ed. (Göttingen: Vandenhoeck & Ruprecht, 1967), p. 34.

[29]See Hans-Georg Kemper, "Trakl-Forschung der sechziger Jahre: Korrekturen über Korrekturen," *Deutsche Vierteljahrsschrift,* 45, Sonderheft (1971), 496–571.

reaching has receded ever further into the background of critical endeavor. Especially since Killy put forward the thesis that Trakl's poetry does not somehow reflect a versified body of conceptual thought, scholarship has largely responded to the poems as abstract language constructs. Studies that limit the poetry to its musical structure, or that characterize it as kaleidoscopic mosaics of images, ultimately reduce it to its lowest linguistic denominator. From this critical perspective, it appears to have a nonpoetic parallel in the realm of psychopathology, the so-called "word salad" of the acute schizophrenic. These jumbled and apparently meaningless utterances are the outward signs of a disordered process of association which Eugen Bleuler, a pioneer in schizophrenia research, considered central to this particular mental derangement. Pure pleasure in verbalization is still, for conventional psychiatry, a hallmark of schizophrenic speech.[30]

The apparent absence of ordering principles within Trakl's poems is in turn related to the theme of decay and dissolution which predominates in the single images. Disintegration permeates Trakl's poetry much as the inexorable sense of falling dominates the accounts of his life. Echoes of the terminal negativity of *dementia* have in various guises found their way into the language of Trakl critics. For example, in a study of the variants, Hans-Georg Kemper discerns a deteriorating development in the later poems, especially the prose poetry of 1913–1914. From a planned neutralization of values in the poems of *Sebastian im Traum,* where a balance is held between negative and positive images, Trakl, according to Kemper, succumbed to the overpowering negative imagery of decay, misery, pain, and horror.[31] The pattern of Trakl's poetry appears to fall into neat congruence with the pattern of his life.

[30]Silvano Arieti, "Language in Schizophrenia," *Interpretation of Schizophrenia,* 2d ed. (New York: Basic, 1974), pp. 249–266.

[31]Kemper, *Georg Trakls Entwürfe: Aspekte zu ihrem Verständnis* (Tübingen: Max Niemeyer, 1970), p. 179.

The Poetry of Pathology?

There is indeed madness in Trakl's poetry, a madness which like all others, pursues its own lines of reasoning—which, in turn, the reader must pursue. It resists capture or exhaustion by the conceptual framework of psychiatry. Specifically the term schizophrenia, with its burden of pejorative overtones, can profitably be replaced by the broader and less categorical concept of metanoia. Metanoia too denotes a fundamental change of mind, a shift in the ontological center of the self, but is free of the burdens that the term schizophrenia today bears. In addition to its neutral semantic value, metanoia has the further advantage of being a nodal term where poetry and madness have often met.

The modern roots of this fertile conjunction reach back to the German Romantics and French Symbolists, poets who were often on intimate terms with variously induced changes of mind. Further removed in time, Plato wrote that "a poet is a light and winged thing, and holy, and never able to compose until he has become inspired, and is beside himself, and reason is no longer in him. So long as he has this in his possession, no man is able to make poetry or chant in prophecy."[32] Rimbaud cultivated the disarray of sensory experiences as an essential step in his poetic practice. Influenced by Freud, the Surrealists endeavored to infuse their creations with the metanoia of dreams and madness, an attempt which, incidentally, earned them only the scorn of their mentor. Countless poets have tried to alter what Paul Celan called their particular "angle of inclination" toward the object world to gain access to a unique reality through a change of mind.[33] Poets differ in their metanoia from madmen principally in the ability to

[32] "Ion," *The Collected Dialogues of Plato Including the Letters,* eds. Edith Hamilton and Huntington Cairns, trans. Lane Cooper (Princeton: Princeton University Press, 1961), p. 220.

[33] In talking about the poet's particular existential posture toward the world, Celan used the term "Neigungswinkel" in a letter to the Librairie Flinker in Paris in 1958. The letter is reprinted in the introduction to *Über Paul Celan,* ed. Dietlind Meinecke (Frankfurt am Main: Suhrkamp, 1970), p. 23.

return at least to a minimal social functioning on the periphery of the common mind. Yet the art of the insane also appears to signify for the madman the desire for this return.

Psychiatry has often attempted to describe and delineate the boundary between sane and insane creative efforts. Opinions have ranged widely, from the view of Lombroso, who in *The Man of Genius* tried to identify genius with insanity, to Ludwig Binswanger's rejection of any kind of compatability.[34] Similarities and differences have been sought in the creative process as well as in formal characteristics. Poets, according to some, resemble schizophrenics in the degree of access which they have to the mechanisms of primary process—the mode of functioning of the unconscious system in Freudian thought—and their use of cognitive media which derive from it. What divides them, on the other hand, is the final triumph of secondary process mechanisms—the mode of functioning of the preconscious-conscious system—in the product of the sane poet.[35] In the light of his own extensive studies of schizophrenics and their art, Leo Navratil has returned a sense of relativity to the topic of psychopathology and art, which had threatened to ossify into the question, psychopathology *or* art. He has found that essential characteristics of so-called schizophrenic art are consonant with the work in certain manneristic periods of sane artists. Navratil, in fact, is led to conclude that there is no basic difference between schizophrenic and sane artists, in either the creative process or its results.[36]

In its relationship to the psychopathological process, however, the art of psychotics is peculiar in its implied promise that the

[34]Cesare Lombroso, *The Man of Genius* (London: Scott, 1891). Ludwig Binswanger, *Drei Formen mißglückten Daseins: Verstiegenheit, Verschrobenheit, Manieriertheit* (Tübingen: Max Niemeyer, 1956).

[35]Arieti, p. 370. Also Ernst Kris, *Psychoanalytic Explorations in Art* (New York: Schocken, 1964). For a concise discussion of primary and secondary process, see J. Laplanche and J.-B. Pontalis, *The Language of Psycho-Analysis*, trans. Donald Nicholson-Smith (New York: Norton, 1973), pp. 339–341.

[36]Leo Navratil, *Schizophrenie und Sprache: Zur Psychologie der Dichtung*, 2d ed. (Munich: Deutscher Taschenbuch, 1968).

alienation from the common mind may not be permanent or irreversible. It signals an attempt at recovery, an attempt to reconstitute the broken world of psychosis.[37] At the beginning of a process of restitution, the art works of psychotics are the forays of minds in search of community. Prior even to the interpretive aids of Freudian psychoanalysis, psychiatry had begun in the last quarter of the nineteenth century to perceive the correlation of this outer evidence to inner orientation.[38] These products of rearranged minds have since told receptive listeners much about the unique order of their sources.

Beyond these initial bridges through art, a change in the relationship between therapist and patient has allowed a more penetrating look into the so-called schizophrenic mind. While Freud considered schizophrenics beyond the reach of his therapeutic method dependent on transference, Harry Stack Sullivan, an American psychiatrist renowned for successful therapy with these patients, pioneered in changing the role of therapist from detached to participant observer. Representatives of sanity have since yielded their distance and strict rational control in favor of a flexible openness to the extent that even the utterances once regarded as "word salads" are being increasingly understood as tortuous communicative detours.[39] In therapy with schizophrenics, some therapists have relinquished the indisputable claim to know truth and reality and the associated claim that their patients' illness is to perceive this truth and reality incorrectly. Others have pondered the ramifications of considering schizophrenia a successful attempt to avoid adjustment to a dysfunctional social reality.[40] The term *dementia* has long since given way to the

[37]Navratil, p. 161.

[38]See Margaret Naumburg's survey: "A Survey of the Significance of Psychotic and Neurotic Art, 1876–1950," *Schizophrenic Art: Its Meaning in Psychotherapy* (New York: Grune & Stratton, 1950), pp. 3–34.

[39]R. D. Laing gives an enlightening and convincing reinterpretation of the "nonsense" of one of Emil Kraepelin's patients in *The Divided Self: An Existential Study in Sanity and Madness* (Harmondsworth: Penguin, 1971), pp. 29–31.

[40]R. D. Laing, *The Politics of Experience* (New York: Ballantine, 1968).

Freudian concept of regression in characterizing the negative component of the schizophrenic process. Beyond this, however, innovative research has shifted perceptibly away from asking why people regress to more infantile levels of integration to the question why all of them do not go through their madness to realize entirely new relationships with themselves and their world. Increasing attention is being paid to familial, societal, and institutional factors which effectively block the *natural* course of a process that points ultimately past the initial break with reality toward psychic reintegration on a new level.

The Polish psychiatrist Kazimierz Dabrowski has theorized that psychoneurotic and psychotic symptoms are quite often "an expression of the developmental continuity. They are processes of positive disintegration and creative nonadaptation." In contrast to Freud, he stresses the potential rather then the morbidity of psychic conflict:

> The conception of Freud, stressing the morbidity of conflict between libido and reality, and between the id, ego and superego, is not a full explanation of the dynamics of normal and pathological development. In my opinion, the conflict within the inner psychic milieu, especially in its multilevel structure, is one of the most important dynamisms in the positive development of personality.[41]

Dealing explicitly with what he calls the "schizophrenic episode," Gregory Bateson describes its negative aspect as merely the first stage in a more encompassing process:

> Once begun, a schizophrenic episode would appear to have as definite a course as an initiation ceremony—a death and rebirth—into which the novice may have been precipitated by his family life or by adventitious circumstance, but which in its course is largely steered by endogenous process.
>
> In terms of this picture, spontaneous remission is no problem. This is only the final and natural outcome of the total process. What

[41]Dabrowski, *Positive Disintegration,* ed. Jason Aronson (Boston: Little, Brown, 1964), pp. 13 and 104.

> needs to be explained is the failure of many who embark upon this voyage to return from it.[42]

Although psychiatry has not solved the riddle of schizophrenia, a diagnosis no longer carries with it the forecast of a deteriorating mind. Dabrowski and Bateson, in fact, represent a prognostic view that stands diametrically opposed to the one originally put forth by Kraepelin.

If indeed madness does reside in Trakl's poetry, it is even more evident that poetry suffuses his madness. Yet the two elements exist in a relationship of interdependence, an interdependence where the disjunctive psychopathology *or* art is inappropriate. They enforce each other by mutually supporting a proclivity to break through what Dieter Wellershoff has called the readers' "practical rule over reality,"[43] a proclivity he terms necessary to the poetic effect. Both the poetry and the madness contribute to a temporary disruption in the continuum of the reader's constant awareness of making sense of his perceptions. To such a conjunction, a formalistic response is necessary, but only partially sufficient. Such a response exhausts itself on the linguistic surface of the poem. The discussions of the poems in the following chapters shift the response to Trakl's madness, but with the knowledge that the two elements are indissolubly bound together. One cannot be lifted out for examination without attention being given to the other.

Psychiatry has taken long strides toward understanding schizophrenic language as validly expressive of psychotic experience. Poetry which incorporates flights of metanoia into its fabric is still, however, largely measured by a static reality of consensus which inevitably terms it negative. It has been pointed out in

[42] *Perceval's Narrative: A Patient's Account of his Psychosis 1830–1832*, ed. Gregory Bateson (Stanford: Stanford University Press, 1961), p. XIV.

[43] Wellershoff, "Transzendenz und scheinhafter Mehrwert: Zur Kategorie des Poetischen," *Literatur und Lustprinzip: Essays* (Cologne: Kiepenheuer & Witsch, 1973), p. 43.

Trakl criticism that the negative categories developed by Hugo Friedrich in *Die Struktur der modernen Lyrik,* categories tremendously influential in shaping the critical image of modern poetry in general, have been used as a kind of controlling agency by which a work is measured and censured.[44] In the most blatant misuse of these categories, critics have overlooked the presupposition of an intact metaphysical order that adheres to them, but which has little if anything more to do with modern poetry.

Trakl's poetry is a unique coincidence of aesthetic and psychopathological impulses that can be generically located as a type of dynamic poetry in search rather than in imitation of reality. It belongs to a poetic modality to which Paul Celan ascribed the task not of reflecting reality, but of seeking and conquering it.[45] For Trakl, this search proceeded primarily in the mind space anterior to language and only secondarily in language itself. That is, the experimental nature of the poetry, a nature shared by much of modern poetry, is grounded less in its linguistic contortions than in the metanoiac flights anterior to linguistic expression. Trakl's compulsion to revise and refine, a process well documented by the multiple variants, is the most visible remaining sign of a search for expression. These revisions have been called an "inquiry after the essence of things," an appropriate observation if essence is understood not as adhering entirely to things-out-there, but as the result of the interaction between the given of phenomena and the structuring forms of consciousness.[46] While eschewing the deeply rutted paths of linear and traditional poetic discourse, Trakl attempts to chart unique experiential patterns in a recalcitrant language.

The notion of the work existing at the meeting point of poetry and madness connects, one may suspect, with the awe in which

[44]Eckhard Philipp, *Die Funktion des Wortes in den Gedichten Georg Trakls: Linguistische Aspekte ihrer Interpretation* (Tübingen: Max Niemeyer, 1971), p. 84.

[45]*Über Paul Celan,* p. 23.

[46]Philipp, p. 76.

Trakl was held by many among the *Brenner* group. These earliest reactions stemmed from a belief that he had prophetic insight into a reality more profound than that of ordinary consciousness. Yet this aura need not again be projected onto the poetry and the once controversial topic of genius and madness need not be resuscitated. What is, however, worthy of note is the willingly suspended desire of those early readers to see a reality mirrored back at them approximating their own. In contrast, when later readers did not find the boundaries of their own universe affirmed there, they denied the poetry ontological status in terms other than as empty linguistic structures. This denial amounts to an invalidation of the right of every madness to modify reality. For the psychology of madness has to do with the radical realignment of the filter of perceptual apparatus with which the individual imprint of the universe is formed. When adjectives such as unreal, fanciful, fantastic, grotesque, and absurd are used in connection with Trakl's poetry, the writer reveals little except his degree of involvement in consensus reality.

The metanoia of this poetry prescribes its own terms of access in two distinct stages. To assume its perspectives temporarily is the initial ideal, to resubstantiate it in terms of the lingua franca of sanity, the ultimate and only partially realizable goal. Reading it is an exercise in letting one's self be pushed beyond the edges of the common mind into the mind of the poem or what can be called the lyric consciousness. Instead of pointing to a congress between poet and reader in a generally valid symbolical system or even within a private mythology, the poems require the reader to be drawn into their hallucinatory world. Immersing himself in it while holding the schemata of his sane existence in abeyance, the reader becomes actively involved in meeting it more than halfway. One critic, who argued against the value of the poetry as art and warned against its infectiousness, touched unintentionally upon the source of its real strength.[47] For its effectiveness—the

[47]Hanns Haeckel, "Verfall und Verfallenheit: Anläßlich eines Deutungsversuchs an einem Gedicht Georg Trakls," *Zeitschrift für deutsche Philologie*, 78 (1959), 369–394.

intensity of effect it exercises—depends largely on the degree to which it can "infect" or inculcate the reader with its optics and structures. A decrease in distance from the altered perspectives of experience in the madness of Trakl's poetry brings with it an increase in understanding.

For the reader to match the lyric consciousness perfectly in its flights of freedom from convention is as unrealizable as to mediate the entirety of its utterances into communal sense and the prose of interpretation. A great deal remains irretrievably lost, a factor which contributes to the impression of a kaleidoscopic poetry of loose ends—that is, of infinite ambiguity and polyvalence. The word "irretrievable" is perhaps too strong, since the poems may become more accessible as human sensibilities change into more receptive configurations. Even now much can be retrieved, for there exists a sliding rather than a fixed boundary between metanoia and the communal sense.

Sanity has as little right to be called mind per se as insanity has to be called mindlessness—a circumlocution for the fact that they share a common essence and differ in degree rather than in kind.[48] The aim of the reader-as-intermediary is to place what is presently retrievable upon a broader spectrum of understanding. In answer to the poetry's appeal for active participation, the following readings of reconciliation attempt to situate the cast of mind behind the linguistic surface on the range of human possibilities. In this attempt at reconciliation they try furthermore to follow and articulate the impulse toward reintegration of a madness finally not of perdition, but of transition.

Transition and search express two aspects of the same change-of-mind process that underlies much of Trakl's poetry from beginning to end, but especially of the last two years. The

[48]Their relatedness has been graphically demonstrated in recent years by a psychiatrist working from studies of drug-induced psychoses. He has charted a "perceptual-hallucination continuum" which ranges from meditative through normal, creative, and schizophrenic states, and finally extends to ecstatic states of consciousness (Roland Fischer, "A Cartography of the Ecstatic and Meditative States: The Experimental and Experiential Features of a Perception-Hallucination Continuum Are Considered," *Science*, 174 [1971], 897–904).

process involved a move of the self away from its position of experiential adjustment in the direction it sensed might bring relief from ingrained guilt and self-recriminations. The poems show the self's increasing sense of a false adjustment, one with which it could no longer live. This phenomenon, a result of distorted socialization, has been described in the literature of psychiatry as the assumption of a false cloak of self, a shell formed by familial and societal norms with which a hidden "true self" must ultimately clash.[49] Disloyal in its experience and actions to this repressed core of genuine needs and wants, the "false self" presents a facade which appears harmonious with its environment. A psychological crisis arises when this schizoid split can no longer be hidden and maintained. The breakdown is often identified as schizophrenic, but rarely recognized as the cleansing process it can become, an elimination of the overlay of haze and mystification imposed on the true self by family and society. The adjusted false self literally dies as it undergoes a process of disintegration, a process which, however, even in the disintegrative stage contains the embryo of reintegration. In Laingian terms: "Madness need not be all breakdown. It may also be breakthrough. It is potentially liberation and renewal as well as enslavement and existential death."[50]

One aim of this study is to bring the dynamics of the healing process into visible relief against the background of decay and disintegration which has tended to obscure it. It might be said, as Sullivan once remarked about schizophrenics, that although Trakl's poems often proclaim death, they are clearly "not through with life."[51] The signs of breakthrough beyond a nadir, signs present even in the last poetry, call for a reconsideration of the apparently unambiguous curve of descent in Trakl's life and

[49]See Laing, *The Divided Self*, pp. 94–105.

[50]Laing, *The Politics of Experience*, p. 133.

[51]Harry Stack Sullivan, *Conceptions of Modern Psychiatry* (New York: Norton, 1953), p. 152.

its reflection in his poetry.[52] They bring a disturbing, but genuine complexity to the contrived harmony of critical constructs.

[52]On the basis of a similar theoretical reinterpretation of schizophrenia, Winfried Kudszus has suggested that Hölderlin's madness might be understood as what he terms a "necessarily ambivalent" beginning ("Versuch einer Heilung: Hölderlins spätere Lyrik," *Hölderlin ohne Mythos*, ed. Ingrid Riedel [Göttingen: Vandenhoeck & Ruprecht, 1973], p. 32).

2

The Poetry until Late 1912

The Beginnings in Tradition

Trakl's earliest poetry, much of it included in the volume *Aus goldenem Kelch* (1939), reflects a stability of perspective largely controlled by literary convention. Contrary to the habits of other major German poets, Trakl left little evidence apart from a single short book list about his connections to literary and intellectual forebears (II, 727). His letters rarely even suggest reflection on predecessors or poetic method, yet the ties of tradition are often overly visible in the poetry itself. The conscious *poète maudit* who sought the bohemian elements in life and lyrical expression is plainly evident. The instances of splitting, the distortions, the challenges to conventional social and moral norms depend heavily during this period on models which Trakl found fashionable in German and French poets of the *fin de siècle* and their predecessors. Even where the theme of multiple selves appears to foreshadow the later poetry, there is plainly detectable manipulation taking place that draws its reason and guidance from convention. The toying with the limits of subjective and objective reality occurs within a language and mode of thought which Trakl found preformed and ready for use. Only gradually does this posing yield to the imperative of his own poetic voice.

The underlying lyricism in Trakl's early playlets finds its counterpart in the dramatic qualities of a number of poems. Among these, the early sonnet "Das Grauen" ("Horror"—I, 220) depicts an inner sequence played out by two opposing possibilities of the self, the tension between the two forming the basis of the drama:

Ich sah mich durch verlass'ne Zimmer gehn.
—Die Sterne tanzten irr auf blauem Grunde,
Und auf den Feldern heulten laut die Hunde,
Und in den Wipfeln wühlte wild der Föhn.

Doch plötzlich: Stille! Dumpfe Fieberglut
Läßt giftige Blumen blühn aus meinem Munde,
Aus dem Geäst fällt wie aus einer Wunde
Blaß schimmernd Tau, und fällt, und fällt wie Blut.

Aus eines Spiegels trügerischer Leere
Hebt langsam sich, und wie ins Ungefähre
Aus Graun und Finsternis ein Antlitz: Kain!

Sehr leise rauscht die samtene Portiere,
Durchs Fenster schaut der Mond gleichwie ins Leere,
Da bin mit meinem Mörder ich allein.

I saw myself going through deserted rooms.
—The stars danced chaotically on the blue firmament,
And in the fields the dogs howled loudly
And in the treetops the wind wailed wildly.

Yet suddenly: Quiet! Fever's dull glow
Sends poisonous flowers blooming from my mouth.
From the branches falls, as if from a wound,
Pale shimmering dew, and falls and falls like blood.

From the deceiving emptiness of a mirror
Rises slowly, and as if into near resemblance,
From horror and darkness, a face: Cain!

The satin curtain rustles very quietly.
Through the window the moon peers as if into emptiness,
Then with my murderer I am alone.

Trakl transforms the familiar biblical clash, which taps emotional and religious responses, into a drama of the psyche. The slain brother meets his slayer in his own mirror image.

The curve traced by the mounting and subsiding tension also belongs to the poem's dramatic nature. After the identity of the alter ego is revealed, a point of peripety is reached, the poem loses its charged intensity and tapers off in the final tercet in an atmosphere of quietly rustling curtains. The tension arises in the pandemonium of nature in the first quatrain and becomes internalized in the next two strophes. The aftermath of its resolution is projected back onto an outer reality in the final three lines. In this movement from externality to internality and back again, Trakl attempts to evoke an interpenetration of the subject of the poem with its environment. Yet there are several factors which prevent it from becoming a convincing poetic statement about the intermingling of objective and subjective realities.

In the second quatrain, its "poisonous flowers" an allusion to Baudelaire's *Fleurs du mal,* the fever of nature is transferred inwardly. The metaphorical language used to convey this transfer suggests, however, less of an interpenetration than a narrative about the process. The correspondence of natural and human attributes in the figures of speech evokes an artificial and contrived suffusion, an effect partially due to what Gottfried Benn saw as one of the hallmarks of a premodern tradition of poetry—the use of the connectives "as if" and "like".[1] Furthermore, Trakl carefully and conspicuously motivates the inner events of the poem with a fever, a physical cause in explanation of the hallucinations. "Das Grauen" is not only an outdated attempt to parallel the emotions of the poem's speaker with his surroundings, but attests as well to Trakl's distance from the perspective of this *I.* Here as elsewhere in the early poetry, he makes use of the first-person pronoun, but it is distinctly artificial, a role which conceals more than it reveals.

[1]Benn, "Probleme der Lyrik," *Essays, Reden, Vorträge: Gesammelte Werke in 4 Bänden,* ed. Dieter Wellershoff (Wiesbaden: Limes, 1959), I, 504.

The split of the poem's speaker between murderer and victim reflects the recurring theme of multiple souls residing in one breast, souls which are often starkly alienated from one another. The fragmentary puppet play *Blaubart* (*Bluebeard*—I, 435–445) presents a radical clash of contraries within one character. Bridegroom, murderer, and penitent all within the duration of a few short moments, the protagonist of this fragmentary work emerges at the play's end from the bridal chamber dripping with the blood of his fifteen-year-old bride. He hurls himself down in front of a crucifix and utters a final exclamation: "God!" The roots of Trakl's fascination with the moral perversity of Bluebeard can be partially traced to the profligacy in the lives and works of such well-known decadents as Baudelaire, Verlaine, Rimbaud, and Oscar Wilde, and still further to Dostoyevsky's saintly sinners, those frequently encountered fictional characters torn between barbarity and piety. Sonja, the morally pure prostitute in *Crime and Punishment* appears by name in two of Trakl's later poems.[2] A less known influence has also left its mark here and on other related early works of Trakl. Otto Weininger's book *Geschlecht und Charakter* (1903), an antifeminist work which proclaimed the bisexuality of all life, had considerable repercussions in literature around the turn of the century in Austria.[3] Weininger viewed Eros as antithetical to reason, and in the chapter "Erotik und Ästhetik," he pointed repeatedly to the relationship of the sexual act and murder.

Splitting of characters occurs along temporal as well as moral lines in Trakl's early poetry. In "Naturtheater" ("Nature's Theater"—I, 241) and "Andacht" ("Devotion"—I, 221), a clearly defined present self is juxtaposed to a clearly defined past self. In the first of these, the present self finds itself in a country

[2]"Verwandlung des Bösen" ("Transformation of Evil"—I, 97–98) and "Sonja" (I, 105).

[3]Alfred Doppler, "Georg Trakl und Otto Weininger," *Peripherie und Zentrum: Studien zur österreichischen Literatur*, eds. Gerlinde Weiss and Klaus Zelewitz (Salzburg: Das Bergland-Buch, 1971), pp. 43–54.

landscape viewing its idyllic past replayed before its eyes. It becomes the private audience of animated memories:

Ich steh' vor einer grünen Bühne!
Fang an, fang wieder an, du Spiel
Verlorner Tage, ohn' Schuld und Sühne,
Gespensterhaft nur, fremd und kühl!

Zur Melodie der frühen Tage
Seh' ich da oben mich wiedergehn,
Ein Kind, des leise, vergessene Klage
Ich weinen seh', fremd meinem Verstehn.

I stand before a green stage!
Begin, begin again, you drama of
Lost days, without guilt and penance,
Only ghostlike, strange and cool!

To the melody of those early days
I see myself above once more walking,
A child, whose soft, forgotten lament
I see crying, beyond my comprehension.

The same feeling of estrangement and discontinuity between the former and the present self is found in "Andacht":

Ich seh' mich träumend still die Hände falten
Und längst vergessene Gebete flüstern,
Und frühe Schwermut meinen Blick umdüstern.

I see myself dreamily quiet folding my hands
And whispering long forgotten prayers,
And early melancholy darkening my glance.

A particularly Austrian sensitivity for the inconstancy and evanescence of life is evident in these two poems. It becomes even more apparent in a poem entitled "Confiteor" (I, 246):

Die bunten Bilder, die das Leben malt
Seh' ich umdüstert nur von Dämmerungen,
Wie kraus verzerrte Schatten, trüb und kalt,
Die kaum geboren schon der Tod bezwungen.

Und da von jedem Ding die Maske fiel,
Seh' ich nur Angst, Verzweiflung, Schmach und Seuchen,
Der Menschheit heldenloses Trauerspiel,
Ein schlechtes Stück, gespielt auf Gräbern, Leichen.

Mich ekelt dieses wüste Traumgesicht.
Doch will ein Machtgebot, daß ich verweile,
Ein Komödiant, der seine Rolle spricht,
Gezwungen, voll Verzweiflung—Langeweile!

The colorful images which life paints
I see only overshadowed by twilights,
Like crinkly twisted shadows, opaque and cold.
Scarcely born, they are subdued by death.

And as the mask fell from every thing,
I see only fear, despair, outrage and disease,
Man's tragedy played without hero,
A wretched play performed on graves and corpses.

This desolate vision disgusts me.
Yet a despotic order commands that I linger,
A buffoon who speaks his role,
Constrained, filled with despair—Boredom!

The central images of "Confiteor" recall the rich medieval and baroque inheritance which has retained its vitality among many German-speaking poets, especially in Austria. The cry of Andreas Gryphius (1616–1664), "Vanitas! Vanitatum Vanitas!" distantly echoes in Trakl's depiction of life's images destined to be mere fleeting shadows. The final response of the poetic speaker to the transient surface and hideous underside of life is, however, distinctly modern. The introductory poem of Baudelaire's *Fleurs du mal* entitled "To the Reader" concludes after an excursion into life's seaminess:

> But in this den of jackals, monkeys, curs,
> Scorpions, buzzards, snakes—this paradise
> Of filthy beasts that screech, howl, grovel, grunt—
> In this menagerie of mankind's vice
>
> There's one supremely hideous and impure!
> Soft-spoken, not the type to cause a scene,
> He'd willingly make rubble of the earth
> And swallow up creation in a yawn.
>
> I mean *Ennui!* who in his hookah-dreams
> Produces hangmen and real tears together.
> How well you know this fastidious monster, reader,
> —Hypocrite reader, you—my double! my brother![4]

Trakl's early works show contemporary strains of influence common to Hofmannsthal's poetry, influences tying him to the widespread literary, philosophical, and scientific skepticism of *fin-de-siècle* Austria. In literature this skepticism frequently took the form of a problematic relationship of the poet to language. As has been remarked, however, the crisis of language which became so acute at the turn of the century in Austria and Germany reached out beyond these national boundaries and beyond literary activities to become a characteristic of twentieth-century culture in general.[5] A passage from a fragmentary drama, *Don Juans*

[4]Charles Baudelaire, *The Flowers of Evil,* eds. Marthiel and Jackson Mathews, trans. Stanley Kunitz, rev. ed. (New York: New Directions, 1962), p. 2. Copyright © 1958 by Stanley Kunitz and reprinted from *The Poems of Stanley Kunitz 1928–1978* by permission of Little, Brown & Co, in association with the Atlantic Monthly Press, and of Martin Secker & Warburg Ltd.

[5]Theodore Ziolkowski not only sketches the extent of this crisis of language among poets before and after 1900, but alludes as well to its sources and more recent reverberations in other fields. "James Joyces Epiphanie und die Überwindung der empirischen Welt in der modernen deutschen Prosa," *Deutsche Vierteljahrsschrift,* 35 (1961), 594–600.

Tod (*Don Juan's Death*—I, 449–453), attests to Trakl's involvement in this intellectual atmosphere:

> Dem Unfaßbaren hascht das träge Wort
> Vergeblich nach, das nur in dunklem Schweigen
> An unsres Geistes letzte Grenzen rührt.
>
> Straining futilely after the ineffable,
> The sluggish word touches only
> In dark silence the furthest bounds of the spirit.

Trakl's lament about the insufficiency of language, the inability of the "sluggish word" to break the silence of the "ineffable" is a variation of the experience at the heart of Hofmannsthal's famous Lord Chandos letter. This letter, ostensibly written by a literary figure at the beginning of the seventeenth century, is actually a depiction of Hofmannsthal's own struggle with language. The fictitious Lord Chandos writes to his historical friend and admirer Francis Bacon to apologize and to find understanding for his renunciation of further literary activity. He has lost his trust in language and is no longer capable of using its abstractions about the objects and occurrences of empirical reality. Even the judgments and opinions of everyday life have become impossible since the necessary abstract terms "crumbled in my mouth like mouldy fungi."[6]

The problematical relationship to language is conditioned in Lord Chandos by a deeper-lying change of consciousness toward the world and his own identity. He attributes his literary silence to a loss of feeling at one with his surroundings, to the disappearance of that unmediated relationship to the world which Hofmannsthal elsewhere called pre-existence. An alienation has occurred which cannot be bridged by the dead concepts of abstract language, concepts which now stand between him and the truth of

[6]Hugo von Hofmannsthal, *Selected Prose,* trans. Mary Hottinger and Tania and James Stern (New York: Pantheon, 1952), p. 134.

the world. Chandos describes in the letter a further estrangement from his earlier works and from the self which created these works, an estrangement which Hofmannsthal frequently cast into lyrical expression:

> This is a thing that mocks the deepest mind
> And far too terrifying for lament:
> That all flows by us, leaving us behind.
>
> And that unhindered my own self could flow
> Out of a little child whom now I find
> Remote as a dumb dog, and scarcely know.[7]

The poetic expressions of the world's flux and the mutability of personal identity were more than isolated echoes of an older literary tradition. They were commonly held intellectual property of poets, scientists, and philosophers in Vienna around the turn of the century. An influential disseminator of such ideas was Ernst Mach, the father of modern scientific positivism with whom Hofmannsthal had been in direct contact at the university in Vienna. Trakl was doubtlessly exposed indirectly to this theoretician of the "irrecoverable ego" ("das unrettbare Ich"), whose thoughts were "found everywhere, almost in his own formulations."[8] In his teachings, Mach contended that neither the ego nor physical objects had a reality independent of the sensations in the mind by which they appear to exist. They are fictitious constructs which are easier to live with than to live without. Mach's thought provided wide-reaching roots for the prevailing skepticism about the existence of a solid, immutable self and the existence of a fixed and constant outer reality.

With regard to Hofmannsthal's early works, one critic has suggested that the altered experiential perspective implied in this

[7]Hugo von Hofmannsthal, "Stanzas in Terza Rima," *Poems and Verse Plays*, ed. and trans. Michael Hamburger (New York: Pantheon, 1961), II, 29.

[8]Gotthart Wunberg, *Der frühe Hofmannsthal: Schizophrenie als dichterische Struktur* (Stuttgart: W. Kohlhammer, 1965), p. 28.

skepticism can be encompassed by the psychiatric term depersonalization.[9] This term is used to describe the initial feelings of alienation which a latent schizophrenic has toward himself and his accustomed environment prior to a more radical break. The many examples of depersonalization in these texts have led the same critic to speak of their schizophrenic structures, structures which he divests, however, of any biographical implications.

In Trakl's early poetry, the splitting of characters, the extreme alienation of the partial selves, the intermingling of inner and outer realities and their inconstancy all point in the same direction as the similar themes in Hofmannsthal's poetry. And the reservation about biographical implications holds as well. For this early poetry is not shaped by a personal dilemma of language or consciousness in which the poet is critically involved, but by the intellectual fashion of the age. In a sense he transcends these problematical issues as he laments and articulates them—an articulation more fully and poetically done in Hofmannsthal's lyrical productions. Trakl's poetry, in its early stages, plays against the backdrop of a norm-attuned consciousness with its perspectives aligned by convention.

Incest as Theme

"Blutschuld" (I, 249), the poem omitted from the first edition of Trakl's collected works apparently because of its taboo subject matter, has frequently and understandably been read in light of the poet's biography. What appears, however, to be an unabashedly direct treatment of a socially offensive theme is filled with a sense of posing and does not penetrate behind the mask of *poète maudit*. The cries of guilt and the pleas for forgiveness of the two-dimensional poetic personae are a stylized treatment of a decadent topic, a topic in which the poet revels:

[9] Wunberg, pp. 12–15.

Es dräut die Nacht am Lager unsrer Küsse.
Es flüstert wo: Wer nimmt von euch die Schuld?
Noch bebend von verruchter Wollust Süße
Wir beten: Verzeih uns, Maria, in deiner Huld!

Aus Blumenschalen steigen gierige Düfte,
Umschmeicheln unsere Stirnen bleich von Schuld.
Ermattend unterm Hauch der schwülen Lüfte
Wir träumen: Verzeih uns, Maria, in deiner Huld!

Doch lauter rauscht der Brunnen der Sirenen
Und dunkler ragt die Sphinx vor unsrer Schuld,
Daß unsre Herzen sündiger wieder tönen,
Wir schluchzen: Verzeih uns, Maria, in deiner Huld!

The night threatens at the lair of our kisses.
Somewhere there is whispering: Who will relieve you from guilt?
Still trembling from the sweetness of vile lust
We pray: Forgive us, Maria, in your grace!

From the flowers' cups climb lecherous aromas,
Caressing our brows pale from guilt.
Exhausted under the breath of sultry breezes
We dream: Forgive us, Maria, in your grace!

Yet more loudly roars the fountain of the sirens
And more darkly towers the sphinx before our guilt,
That our hearts again resound more sinfully,
We sob: Forgive us, Maria, in your grace!

The poem centers on the refrain in the concluding line of each stanza, the repeated plea of the sinful lovers for deliverance from guilt and a return of innocence. Some intensification of the degree of emotion in these pleas is sought by varying the manner in which Maria is addressed, yet even the despair of the lovers' final sobs cannot undo the alleviating countersense of rigid formal elements. The refrain, the regular alternating rhyme with the recurring identical rhyming words in each stanza, and the strongly punctuated iambic rhythm give the poem a chantlike quality which does not match the emotional dilemma. These formal elements appear to hold the poem together when, according to its content, it should break apart.

Not only does the authenticity of the suffering seem compromised by this mismatch; the guilt itself is not as destructively oppressive as it appears. A planned play on the intermingling of pleasure and guilt enters the poem as side by side with the overt pursuit of absolution there runs a perverse delight in the forbidden act. The question in line 2 is asked less for a response than to intensify the degree of evil. The appeals to Maria are left unanswered less for tragic effect then to underscore the enormity of the crime. While the personified night seems to threaten the illicit lovers with an indeterminate punishment, it actually serves to heighten the erotic pleasure, a pleasure intensified by the taboo and its threat of retribution. The forbidden liaison leaves them feeling far from contrite when in its aftermath they still savor the "sweetness of vile lust." The imagery of the second and third stanzas lends a further intensifying element, an exoticism culminating in the figures of the sirens whose irresistible but menacing nature captures the poem's dialectic of desire and danger.

In her immovability and apparent deafness to the lovers' pleas, Maria becomes for them an enigma, the image of the sphinx underlining the distinction between her and the traditionally all-embracing, all-forgiving Mother of God. Nor is she approached in an attitude of humility and contrition. Passions are still aroused just prior to the pleas in the first and third stanzas and the lovers dream of "sultry breezes" as they call on her in the middle stanza. The tarnish clinging to the holy figure here becomes corrosive in another poem of the same early period entitled "Metamorphose" (I, 252):

> Ein ewiges Licht glüht düsterrot,
> Ein Herz so rot, in Sündennot!
> Gegrüßt seist du, o Maria!

Dein bleiches Bildnis ist erblüht
Und dein verhüllter Leib erglüht,
O Fraue du, Maria!

In süßen Qualen brennt dein Schoß,
Da lächelt dein Auge schmerzlich und groß,
O Mutter du, Maria!

An eternal light glows darkly red,
A heart so red, in sins' distress!
Greetings, O Maria!

Your pale image is blooming
And your veiled body glows,
O woman Maria!

In sweet torment your womb burns,
Then your eye smiles sadly and greatly
O Mother Maria!

The blasphemous tendency in "Blutschuld" is here carried further as Maria is metamorphosed from sanctity to earthly passions and finally to motherhood. Otto Weininger's differentiation between two extreme feminine types, the prostitute and the mother, neither of which in reality ever appears in pure form, has left its mark on these poems. A variant of the fourth line of "Blutschuld" further suggests that Trakl may not have limited his blasphemy to religious implications. At one point, he wrote: "We pray: forgive us mother Maria in your grace." Parallel to the transformation of the holy figure into an earthly motherhood with its passion and pain in "Metamorphose," a more mundane element seems to have found its way into the Maria-figure in "Blutschuld." A reference to Trakl's own mother, who shared the name and the remoteness of the religious figure, may also be concealed in its connotations.

The Poet's Multiple Eyes–Toward Anonymity

Trakl's years in Vienna and later, up until the time when he became a regularly published poet as a member of the *Brenner* circle, were years of poetic maturation during which literary tradition and fashion were assimilated and molded into perspectives uniquely his own. A letter accompanying a revised version of the poem "Klagelied" ("Elegy"—I, 280) and sent to Erhard Buschbeck in the fall of 1911 discloses a concern which points ahead in his own development to the uniqueness of "Helian" as well as laterally to a common poetic quandry. It reads in part:

> Included the revised poem. It is just that much better than the original as it now is impersonal and bursting full of movement and visions.
>
> I am convinced that it will say and mean more to you in this universal form and manner than in the limited personal [manner] of the first draft.
>
> You can believe me that it is not easy nor will it ever be easy for me to subordinate myself unconditionally to that which is to be presented and I will have to correct myself again and again to give to the truth what truth is. [I, 485–486]

The letter and its wording are problematic. It has been cited by one critic as evidence of his theory regarding the entirety of Trakl's works, a theory which asserts that the language of the poetry is largely a preformed one, the poems a conglomerate of "quotations, references, and allusions" all gathered from the works of predecessors.[10] The aim of this borrowing was to aid the poet in eliminating personal elements from his poetry. These elements, however, even in a straightforward autobiographical sense, return again and again in the later poetry. Especially the prose poems reveal a more acutely experienced personal truth

[10]Rudolf Dirk Schier, *Die Sprache Georg Trakls* (Heidelberg: Carl Winter, 1970), pp. 23–24.

than such superficially autobiographical poems as "Blutschuld" in which Trakl hides self-truth under the cover of literary attitude.

Even if Rilke's *Neue Gedichte* (*New Poems*) had not been included on the list of books that Trakl left behind, the dichotomy expressed in the letter would invite comparison. This group of poems signified an important change of direction in Rilke's lyrical development, a turning away from an earlier impressionistic phase toward a conscious restraint of inwardness subsequently expressed in the guise of images and objects. In Paris under the influence of Rodin he learned to restrict the direct inroads of subjective elements so strongly expressed in his earlier poetry and subjugate these to the "thing" to be portrayed. These poems are not intended to be totally impersonal, however, and their self-revelation occurs indirectly through the central object or image, the poet renouncing the use of the first-person pronoun as a point of central reference. The Trakl poem, on the other hand, the poem for which in the accompanying letter he claims an impersonal orientation, retains the first-person form and suggests the distinctly different significance which the dichotomy of personal and impersonal had for him at this stage:

Die Freundin, die mit grünen Blumen gaukelnd
Spielt in mondenen Gärten—
O! was glüht hinter Taxushecken!
Goldener Mund, der meine Lippen rührt,
Und sie erklingen wie die Sterne
Über dem Bache Kidron.
Aber die Sternennebel sinken über der Ebene,
Tänze wild und unsagbar.
O! meine Freundin deine Lippen
Granatapfellippen
Reifen an meinem kristallenen Muschelmund.
Schwer ruht auf uns
Das goldene Schweigen der Ebene.
Zum Himmel dampft das Blut
Der von Herodes
Gemordeten Kinder.

The beloved, who conjuring with green flowers
Plays in lunar gardens—
O! what is glowing behind the yew hedges!
Golden mouth which touches my lips,
And they ring out like the stars
Over the brook of Kidron.
But the star-fogs sink over the plain,
Dances wild and unspeakable.
O! my beloved, your lips—
Pomegranate-lips
Ripen on my crystalline mussel-mouth.
The golden silence of the plain
Weighs heavily upon us.
To heaven fumes the blood of
The children murdered
By Herod.

Although the original version of "Klagelied" has been lost, it is clear from the letter that in Trakl's eyes this latter version has gained in quality by becoming what he terms "impersonal and bursting full of movement and visions." It has gained a "universal form and manner" in contrast to the "limited personal" manner of the first version. These key words indicate Trakl's reference is to a change in the method of the poem, to its form and structuring elements and not to a restraint of subjective, emotional impingements in the sense of Goethe's classical attitude or in the Rilkean sense. Trakl's concern here is with the limits in connotation that are set to a personally expressed poem not from the autobiographical point of view, but from a formal psychological point of view. If a poem reflects and reaches only to the boundaries of the structuring self as expressed in a poetic speaker, it is limited. In an age in which a vital intellectual current professed a conception of inner and outer reality with extremely malleable boundaries, Trakl proposed that the traditional bounds of the self were constricting factors in poetic expression. He attempted to overcome these in "Klagelied."

Thematically, the poem traverses familiar ground: a forbidden love, a blend of exotic, erotic, and religious imagery, a silent higher authority expressing its condemnation by its very silence and the self-righteous pathos toward the injustice. And as in "Blutschuld," the poet reveals himself less in the themes than in the structure. Central to this structure are the apparently unmotivated changes of focal points, the movement to which Trakl refers in the letter and the basis of the poem's multiplicity. The poem has what appear to be multiple perspectives or different types of eyes through which the reader is visually guided onto its loosely connected scenes. The splitting no longer takes place on the thematic surface of the poem, but has shifted so that it now seems to occur within the speaker's self. What the reader experiences as changes of focal points is the result of the poet's transferral of the multiple-selves theme into a way of writing and for the reader, into a way of reading.

The success of the attempt to escape the psychological limits of the personal by appearing to fragment the speaking self is at this point conditioned by a marked degree of inauthenticity. In "Klagelied" the various focusings are ultimately embraced by a coherent meta-self, a gathering point at a further remove where there is stability and a kind of self-base to which all the split-off perspectives refer. From here the apparently chaotic fragmentation of perspective reveals its method: the perceptual modes vary from the simple seeing of the beloved in lines 1–2 to a metaphorical seeing in lines 3–6 and then to a visionary seeing in lines 7–8 which develops gradually from the preceding stage. The latter half of the poem repeats this sequence. A simple seeing or meeting of the beloved in line 9 passes over into a metaphorized kiss in lines 10–11 which in turn gives way to a final extended vision.

In "Seele des Lebens" ("Soul of Life"—I, 36), a poem probably written a short time after "Klagelied," Trakl combines the technique of multiple perspectives with one of his most frequently encountered themes:

> Verfall, der weich das Laub umdüstert,
> Es wohnt im Wald sein weites Schweigen.

Bald scheint ein Dorf sich geisterhaft zu neigen.
Der Schwester Mund in schwarzen Zweigen flüstert.

Der Einsame wird bald entgleiten,
Vielleicht ein Hirt auf dunklen Pfaden.
Ein Tier tritt leise aus den Baumarkaden,
Indes die Lider sich vor Gottheit weiten.

Der blaue Fluß rinnt schön hinunter,
Gewölke sich am Abend zeigen;
Die Seele auch in engelhaftem Schweigen.
Vergängliche Gebilde gehen unter.

Decay, which gently overshadows the foliage,
In the forest lives its broad silence.
Soon a village appears to incline ghostlike.
The sister's mouth whispers in black branches.

The lonely one will soon slip away,
Perhaps a shepherd on dark paths.
An animal steps gently from the arcade of trees,
While its eyelids part widely before the deity.

The blue river runs beautifully downward,
Clouds appear in the evening;
The soul too in angelic silence.
Transient images go under.

Decay is the common denominator of all the images, those of both man and nature, a common effluvium flowing through and effacing life's boundaries. Subject and object within the poem converge by means of their mutual participation in this all-embracing process. It is the "Soul of Life." The "sister's mouth" whispering in the branches exemplifies in one image Trakl's development of poetic technique in which the narrative about the process of convergence has been superseded by direct statement.

Paradoxically, decay lives in each of the images as a force of dissolution while at the same time it binds them into a thematic unity. Moreover, while the poem's perspective seems to have undergone a parallel dissipation, all of the multiple eyes focus on similarly "transient images." The high degree of formal structure deepens the imprint of a withdrawn, but cohesive meta-self of the poem's speaker. The clearest indicator of this cohesion and control is the frame formed by the poem's initial and final lines, statements that subsume the intervening series of concrete images under a higher order of abstraction. The identical rhythmic patterns of each stanza: two lines of iambic tetrameter followed by two lines of iambic pentameter; the consistent use of feminine rhyme; the analogous rhyme patterns with the diphthong "ei" recurring in all these patterns as well as internally—all of these formal elements run counter to the poem's theme. Dissolution is further opposed by the transitional words "perhaps" and "while," words which smooth over the otherwise punctuated breaks between lines and carry an image over from one line to the next. The end effect of the combination of the theme of decay within the confines of strict form does not evoke dissonance, but rather a typical portrait of beauty in decay so often a subject of *fin-de-siècle* poets.

Structurally, then, Trakl's early poems counter the impulses toward both anonymity and dissolution. Moreover, on the thematic level alone, dissolution is at times only one moment of what approaches a dialectical shift. The transcending moment of this shift is, however, never more than a premonition which points toward a vague goal lying beyond the time and circumstance of the poetic world. In "Melancholie des Abends" ("Evening Melancholy"—I, 19), a flight of wild birds, one of Trakl's favorite images, embodies this movement beyond:

> —Der Wald, der sich verstorben breitet—
> Und Schatten sind um ihn, wie Hecken.
> Das Wild kommt zitternd aus Verstecken,
> Indes ein Bach ganz leise gleitet
>
> Und Farnen folgt und alten Steinen
> Und silbern glänzt aus Laubgewinden.

Man hört ihn bald in schwarzen Schlünden—
Vielleicht, daß auch schon Sterne scheinen.

Der dunkle Plan scheint ohne Maßen,
Verstreute Dörfer, Sumpf und Weiher,
Und etwas täuscht dir vor ein Feuer.
Ein kalter Glanz huscht über Straßen.

Am Himmel ahnet man Bewegung,
Ein Heer von wilden Vögeln wandern
Nach jenen Ländern, schönen, andern.
Es steigt und sinkt des Rohres Regung.

—The moribund expansion of the forest—
And shadows enclose it like hedges.
The animal comes trembling out of concealment,
While a stream very quietly flows

And follows ferns and old stones
And glistens silvery from entangled foliage.
One soon hears it in black gorges—
Perhaps also that stars already shine.

The dark plain seems without measure,
Scattered villages, marsh and pond,
And something seems to you a fire.
A cold brightness flits over the streets.

In the heavens one portends movement,
A host of wild birds wander
Toward those lands, those beautiful ones, those others.
The stirring reed rises and falls.

The forest in the opening lines literally "expands deathlike," an oblique allusion to the growing shadows which it casts and which finally enclose it in evening's darkness. Following this envelopment of the forest in its own shadows, an animal ventures out of its concealment. Its motion carries it in the reverse direction, away from its enclosure. The next image reverses the process once again: the stream flows until it is confined by the black gorge. A similar principle appears to govern each of the images: at one end is extension or movement, while containment marks the opposite limit.

In contrast to this principle and the more obvious formal structures of the poem's meter and rhyme, the imagery of the third stanza depicts a landscape both vast in dimension and without measure in the sense of structure. The villages, marsh, and pond are randomly scattered, their cohesion threatened further by the fire and lightninglike illumination. The entire poetic landscape seems on the verge of flying apart. The centrifugal impulse is extended in the image of the migrating birds in the final stanza. Their flight carries them away from the poetic landscape toward lands that are only vaguely specified. Yet while the outline of these lands is vague, they are at the same time literally "other," that is, located within a set of coordinates separate from those of the poetic landscape. As the projected endpoint of the birds' wandering, these lands echo the containment pole of the poem's initial images, yet in their "otherness," they exist in the unknown beyond the land of the flight's beginning, the world of the poetic speaker. In the image of the final line, his vision returns to the cyclical motion of his surroundings as he looks down from the movement in the skies to the regular rising and falling of the reed.

However worn by literary usage the image of the migrating birds may be, flight was for the unstable Trakl more than a borrowed poetic metaphor and more than a literary pose. "Perhaps I will also go to Borneo," he wrote to Buschbeck in April 1912, a short-lived plan that may to some degree have been formulated after the model of Rimbaud's adventures.[11] In the same breath that he proposes a journey to this distant land, however, he writes of the storm threatening his inner life: "Somehow the storm gathering in me will soon break. Let it happen, and even if it

[11]Herbert Lindenberger believes that Trakl here "hints at wanting to follow in Rimbaud's steps" ("Georg Trakl and Rimbaud: A Study in Influence and Development," *Comparative Literature*, 10 [1958], 22).

[breaks] into sickness and melancholy." Flight and the foreboding of mental crisis are two facets of a single train of thought. Borneo is less a concrete goal mentioned in imitation of a literary forebear than simply that "other" land whose significance lies in its unfathomable distance from Trakl's familiar physical and mental realities. Trakl's work and life became increasingly less imitative as they became increasingly responsive to the imperative building within him. The tone of openness toward such radical flight in the letter rapidly gives way to a reassertion of control: "Nevertheless, I'm enduring these shattering experiences [das Zerfahrene] rather calmly and not without maturity" (I, 488). This sober gesture of resolution strikes a chord similar to the lowered eyes at the end of "Melancholie des Abends," eyes which sink from the open skies and come to rest upon the bobbing reed.

The Self-Disclosure of Anonymity

A great mass of evidence has accumulated in the critical literature that points to Arthur Rimbaud (1854–1891) as a key figure—one critic calls him *the* key figure—in Trakl's poetic development.[12] Trakl had learned the basics of the French language from his governess as a child, although the decisive acquaintance with Rimbaud probably came through a German translation published in 1907 by Karl Klammer, an Austrian army officer who wrote under the pen name K. L. Ammer. Stefan Zweig contributed a substantial biographical sketch as an introduction to this widely read translation. In Rimbaud, Trakl discovered a great poet whose break with past and present conventions was as extreme in his poetry as it was in his life. The multiple borrowings found in Trakl's vocabulary are but the most apparent sign of a profound influence that reached a peak during 1911–1912. Even while its

[12]Reinhold Grimm, "Georg Trakls Verhältnis zu Rimbaud," *Zur Lyrik-Diskussion*, ed. R. Grimm (Darmstadt: Wissenschaftliche Buchgesellschaft, 1966), pp. 271–313. Christa Saas's volume gives a complete bibliographical account of Trakl/Rimbaud literature.

factual existence is beyond doubt, the precise modality of the influence remains problematic. In a matter of such consuming importance to him as his poetry, however, Trakl could only have been receptive to an influence that strengthened tendencies already evident in his own work or crystallized those that still lay latent. Rimbaud's function in Trakl's life and work was nearer that of a catalyst than an overwhelming poet-father figure. Trakl's indebtedness to his predecessor as well as his own maturing poetic method emerge clearly in a poem entitled "Psalm" (I, 55–56) written in September 1912 (see Appendix).

The example of Rimbaud's free verse undoubtedly contributed to Trakl's own departure in "Psalm" from the conventions of meter and rhyme. The basic motives behind this formal innovation were, moreover, of a similar nature in both poets. Free verse held out the promise of a relatively unencumbered exploration of the heights and depths of poetic sensitivity, an exploration not forced into and distorted by traditional rhymes and meters. The release from the mechanics of convention facilitated the plumbing of these fallow recesses. In the process, it also allowed a strong undertone of ambivalence to surface which permeates the poem's structure and imagery. Even while the verse in "Psalm" is free, ambivalence echoes in the voice of the poetic speaker. Paradoxically, as the opening strophe of the poem illustrates, it becomes a mainspring rather than a debilitating factor in Trakl's work:

> There is a light which the wind has extinguished.
> There is a tavern on the heath which a drunk leaves in the
> afternoon.
> There is a vineyard, burnt and black with holes full of spiders.
> There is a room which they have whitewashed with milk.
> The madman has died. There is a South Sea island
> To receive the sun god. They strike the drums.
> The men perform warlike dances.
> The women sway their hips in liana and fire flowers
> When the sea sings. O our lost paradise.

"Psalm" begins with a series of five disconnected images. Only with the last of these does the poetic speaker reach firm enough ground to depict an extended scene. The axial image—"The madman has died"—is at precisely the midpoint of the strophe. Regardless of its puzzling content, it is the first image left to stand unmodified in its original assertiveness. Each of the images in the preceding assertions is retracted or modified: the light said to exist in the first line has been extinguished; the tavern has been abandoned by the drunk; the image of the vineyards is disfigured; the room has been mysteriously whitewashed. The speaker in these four lines haltingly overcomes a compulsion to dismantle or at least significantly modify his initial utterances. Only with the image of the madman does he surmount this retarding impulse to poetic vision and construct a sustained scene. Yet much as he retracts the existence of the light in the first line, he retracts the entire scene with his final words: "O our lost paradise." Throughout the strophe the speaker takes back as much as he has given.

The striking yet apparently simple declarative technique in the opening lines of "Psalm" is directly traceable to the section of Rimbaud's *Illuminations* entitled "Enfance." Similarly constructed lines appear later in "Psalm" as well as in the conspicuous opening lines of another poem from the same time period, "De Profundis" (I, 46).[13] Trakl used this borrowed sentence structure in a manner already characteristic of his own poetry. It is an intensified form of the serial listing of images with no apparent transitions. Each repetition of "There is . . ." sharply delimits the connection to the preceding imagery and emphasizes the independence of the fragment. The preponderance of these forms at

[13] Es ist ein Stoppelfeld, in das ein schwarzer Regen fällt.
Es ist ein brauner Baum, der einsam dasteht.
Es ist ein Zischelwind, der leere Hütten umkreist.
Wie traurig dieser Abend.

There is a stubble field into which a black rain falls.
There is a brown tree which stands alone.
There is a whispering wind which circles empty huts.
How sad this evening.

the beginning sets the basic method of the entire poem. It is intimately related to Trakl's previous attempts to create an unmotivated shift of focus, a shift that intends to mute and even shut out the presence of a cohesive and limiting self. The poet actively resists the focusing effect of the controlling self and the poem becomes like the reflection of a prismatically divided beam of light which is cut off from its source of convergence. Its single units of lines and short scenes seem to lie on the parallel lines of a psychic spectrum without referring back to a unified origin. The structuring consciousness is to be so radically fractured that it approaches nonexistence. In the act of writing a poem like "Psalm," Trakl appears to abandon the age-old quest of poets for the answer to "Who am I?" by replying: "I am not." Yet the poet's answer might better be phrased: "The I is not," a reply similar to Rimbaud's pronouncement: "I is someone else" (*Je est un autre*).[14] Rimbaud wrote the following to Paul Demeny in the remarkable letter known as the *Lettre du voyant:* "If old imbeciles had not discovered only the false meaning of the Ego, we would not have to sweep away those millions of skeletons which, for time immemorial, have accumulated the results of their one-eyed intellects by claiming to be the authors!"[15] Rimbaud laments the past narrowness of egoically-limited poets and calls for destruction of the ego by any and all means, by the "rational *derangement* of *all the senses.*"[16] Trakl left no such statement of his poetics, yet his poetry vividly records the same struggle against the "one-eyed intellect," a struggle abetted by alcohol and drugs and increasingly by the metanoia of his madness.

The opening four lines of the second strophe of "Psalm" extend the vision of the fallen state or the paradise lost at the end of the first strophe:

> The nymphs have left the golden woods.
> They bury the stranger. Then a glistening rain begins.

[14]*Rimbaud: Complete Works, Selected Letters*, trans. Wallace Fowlie (Chicago: University of Chicago Press, 1966), pp. 304–305.

[15]*Rimbaud*, p. 307.

[16]*Rimbaud*, p. 307.

> The son of Pan appears in the form of a laborer
> Who sleeps away the noon by the glowing asphalt.

The strophe's first line predates by exactly ten years T. S. Eliot's laconic comment in *The Waste Land:* "The nymphs are departed."[17] Nature's mythological inhabitants have abandoned or perhaps been driven from their home in both poems. The "son of Pan" in "Psalm," whose progenitor in mythology was the personification of nature, sleeps away the midday hour like his father, yet far from his native fields and woods. Trakl's choice of the son over the father follows Rimbaud's celebration of the "fils de Pan" in "Antique," a short prose poem from *Les Illuminations.* Here the bisexual figure plays the main role in a "parable of birth and evolution," the metamorphosis of the poet as the son of Pan from his animal ancestors.[18] In Trakl's other use of the image in "Helian," the figure again sleeps in an alien environment:

> The steps sound quietly in the grass. Yet the son of Pan
> Still sleeps in the grey marble.
>
> [4–5]

In both instances, the figure appears outside its context in mythologized nature, a fitting companion for the nymphs who have also abandoned their native habitat. Trakl, however, does not here or elsewhere build a coherent antimyth that attempts to embrace modern man's "fallen" state within a demythologized nature or wasteland. Perhaps the most that can be said of Trakl and Rimbaud alike is that their poetry knows "the intermeshing of a paradisiacal and a depraved realm."[19] Such imagery in Trakl's poetry, woven with strands of conflicting poetic impulses, has its deepest roots in the soil of ambivalence.

[17]Eduard Lachmann first noted this similarity in *Kreuz und Abend: Eine Interpretation der Dichtungen Georg Trakls,* Trakl-Studien 1 (Salzburg: Otto Müller, 1954), p. 136.

[18] Wallace Fowlie, *Rimbaud* (Chicago: University of Chicago Press, 1965), p. 159.

[19]Bernhard Böschenstein, "Wirkungen des französischen Symbolismus auf die deutsche Lyrik der Jahrhundertwende," *Euphorion,* 58 (1964), 394.

The tenuous continuity established between the first two strophes comes to an end with the fourth line of the second strophe, and a new series of images commences:

> There are small girls in a court in dresses of heartrending poverty!
> There are rooms filled with chords and sonatas.
> There are shadows which embrace in front of a blinded mirror.

Each of these lines corresponds to lines in both the third and fourth strophes, yet the connections are frail ones. Their very nature is to remain tentative. The terse phrase in line 26, for example, "Final chords of a quartet," gives the impression of being a kind of splinter image of the musical imagery in line 15. One of the themes most consistently repeated is that of childhood. With a glance ahead in time to the mono-thematic prose poems and a sidewards glance to Trakl's structural model—Rimbaud's "Enfance"—the repeated allusions to children seem less arbitrary. Moreover, the shadows (Schatten) embracing in front of a "blinded mirror" (16) and those damned shades (Schatten) descending to the "sighing waters" (35) contain the embryo of later variations of doubles. Both images present figures without substance, empty of lifeblood. In front of a mirror that gives no reflection, the insubstantiality of the first shadows is further intensified. The shades of the damned later in the poem descend to the water's reflective surface, but they are without discernible intent or purpose.

Of all the thematically corresponding lines and images within "Psalm," those in the final two lines of the second strophe (17–18) and the first two lines of the fourth strophe (28–29) correspond most closely:

> At the windows of the hospital the convalescents warm themselves.
> A white steamer bears bloody pestilence up the canal.

> There is an empty boat which makes its way down the canal in the evening.
> Human ruins decay in the gloom of the old asylum.

Structurally, these lines form a kind of frame around the entire third strophe and in effect highlight its opening scene:

> The strange sister appears again in someone's evil dreams.
> Resting in the hazelbush she plays with his stars.
> The student, perhaps a double, gazes long after her from the window.
> Behind him stands his dead brother or he descends the old winding stairs.

These four lines stand out not only as the beginning of a framed strophe, but also because they form the third and last of the poem's extended scenes. Even more notable, the series of previously anonymous images is interrupted by these brother and sister figures whose relationship is far from unambiguous, but sufficiently spelled out to evoke intimacy and guilt. The mysteriously whitewashed room in line 4, where the poem's anonymity was earlier broken by a personal pronoun, now appears to belong to this constellation of images indirectly alluding to the incestuous act and its aftermath.

Incest makes its appearance far more obliquely, yet at the same time more authentically in "Psalm" than in "Blutschuld." No longer formulated as a pleasurable revel in sinful acts, the forbidden passion is subject to the same ambivalence that runs throughout the poem. The "perhaps" in line 21 and the "or" in line 22 as well as the enigmatic "someone" in line 19 point to a wavering attitude, an attitude which cannot opt for one formulation or the other, but must keep its choices open. A variant of line 19 shows a capitalized "Someone," a variant that Trakl rejected in the final version in favor of a less obtrusive small letter. The relationships of the sister, the "someone," the student, the double, and the dead brother are essentially open ones which the poet hesitates to close. A direct statement about incest is not made, but the sibling pair is sufficiently intertwined within a constellation of evil and intimacy to call forth its presence.

As the poet dissipates the impression of a central focusing

source in "Klagelied," "Seele des Lebens," and "Psalm," he seems to recede further from the poems. Yet paradoxically this dissipation worked as a release and in conjunction with Trakl's increasing abandonment of literary selves and conventional forms, it worked to effect a more authentic involvement of the poet in his poetry. He was seldom more startlingly literal about his involvement than in a line from the poem "Ein Herbstabend" ("An Autumn Evening"—I, 61) written a short time later than "Psalm":

> Doch immer ist das Eigne schwarz und nah.
>
> Yet always the Self is black and near.

The black self in "Ein Herbstabend" is no longer the cosmetic facade of decadent literary fashion as it was earlier. And as the self becomes less literary, it becomes at the same time more authentically the poet's and hence more poetic. In the fragments of "Psalm," this authentic self makes its presence most distinctly felt in the poem's pervasive ambivalence.

One critic has attempted to dissolve this ambivalence by tracing a "movement upwards" which he sees reflected in Trakl's use of the leitmotif gold.[20] From the exit of the nymphs out of the golden woods in line 10 to the search of the children in line 25 for "heaven's gold" to the final line where God opens his golden eyes on the Golgotha of the world, he sees replayed the familiar pattern of paradise/paradise lost/paradise regained. A promise of transcendence is implied by the very presence of God and by his beginning awareness of man's misery. Understated and invalidated in this interpretation of the imagery is the countering silence of God, a silence made more awesome by its accentuated position at the beginning of the line: "Silently above Golgotha

[20]Albert Hellmich, *Klang und Erlösung: Das Problem musikalischer Strukturen in der Lyrik Georg Trakls,* Trakl-Studien 8 (Salzburg: Otto Müller, 1971), p. 65.

God's golden eyes open." Before deciding on this final line, Trakl weighed two other endings:

> Wie eitel ist alles!
>
> O how vain everything is!
>
> Immer über der Schädelstätte tanzen magnetene Monde.
>
> Magnetized moons dance forever over Golgotha.

The first line quoted closes an earlier version of "Psalm." This version is in essence the same poem as the final version up to line 22 where it begins to move in a direction much more clearly negative. The less ambivalent direction is clearly expressed a few lines later:

> Es ist der Untergang, dem wir zutreiben.
>
> It is the abyss toward which we steer.

The line quoted second was discarded by the poet while writing the poem's final and published version. The contrasts between the variant lines and the line finally chosen and between the first and second versions of the poem suggest that the poet himself was uncertain about the direction which the ending should take. It finally ends on a note of ambivalence expressed by the silent god becoming aware of man's fallen state. The poem resists patterns of expectation implied in the movement from paradise lost to paradise regained, and like Rimbaud's poetry, it seems to exhibit an imagery composed of traces of a paradisiacal condition intertwined with those of a fallen state. Behind these poetic compromises is an ambivalence, a fragility of attitude that may opt in either direction without great cause or motivation.

"Psalm" appeared in the first October issue of *Der Brenner* in 1912. It was a productive period in Trakl's life, not many months after he had first met Ludwig von Ficker whose journal regularly published his poetry for the next three years. Trakl dedicated "Psalm" to another recently made friend, Karl Kraus, who acknowledged the dedication in his own journal with a short parable about "seven-month children."[21] Brought into the world too early, Kraus wrote, these children thereafter feel cheated of the lost time in the security of the womb. Trakl, flattered by the response, sent Kraus a telegram in return thanking him for a "moment of most painful clarity" (I, 492).

[21] *Die Fackel,* Nos. 360–362 (7 November 1912), p. 24.

3

On the Soul's Landscape

"Helian"—Demise as Prelude

From his refuge in Innsbruck among the *Brenner* circle, Trakl wrote late in January 1913 to Buschbeck about his precarious state of mind following his short-lived attempt to hold a job in the Viennese bureaucracy: "My condition is still not the best, although I have it better here than anywhere. Perhaps it really would have been better to have let it come to a crisis in Vienna." In the same letter he adds: "In the next few days, I will send you a copy of Helian. To me it is the most precious and the most painful thing that I have ever written" (I, 500–501). Precisely how Trakl understood the interplay of his emotions toward this poem is uncertain. Judging from the mass of variants and numerous shorter poems out of which "Helian" (I, 69–73) finally evolved, however, the poem apparently underwent a tortuously complicated conception.[1] And, according to a diary kept by Karl Röck, a frequent companion of Trakl's during 1912–1914, Trakl held special admiration for poets who "bled" in their works and disdained those like Goethe who, he imagined, "even as a young

[1]See Walther Killy, "Entwurf des Gedichts: Über den *Helian*-Komplex," *Über Georg Trakl,* 3d ed. (Göttingen: Vandenhoeck & Ruprecht, 1967), pp. 52–83. Killy pointedly limits his interpretation of "Helian" to its "musical" aspects—the recurrence of configurations that contain certain images, modes of perception, and directions of movement. For the reactions of Trakl's friends to the poem, see Karl Borromäus Heinrich, "Die Erscheinung Georg Trakls," *Erinnerung an Georg Trakl,* pp. 100–104, and Ficker's letter to Trakl, II, 760. For critical studies, see Saas, p. 22.

man did not write neurasthenically."[2] Yet as evidence of a theoretical cast of mind, Trakl's pronouncement is doubly impugned—as a memory of a conversation reported by a second person and by the circumstances of its origin in the alcoholic haze of an Innsbruck bar. Although Trakl may have intermittently held vague notions about a productive relationship between suffering and creativity—notions passed down from time immemorial by poets and finally codified by psychoanalysis—his poetry knows more of its method than anything the poet ever said about it.

As tradition retreated to a less overt role in Trakl's poetry—a development at least partially explicable by his increasing recognition as a poet—he moved toward a more genuine confrontation with resources closer at hand. The richest as well as the most painful of these was the labile psychic organization precariously contained by what one critic has called the "shell of convention, habit and circumstance" comprising the empirical self.[3] The act of writing brought Trakl into increasingly intimate contact with the stress points of this shell and was an act that was bound to bring crisis as well as poetry in its wake. The growing impersonality of Trakl's verse was a direct expression of the vanishing "person" that the shell had defined. Yet, at the same time, the poetry delved more deeply and searchingly into the fissures and shifting structures of this shell.[4] "Helian" reflects the probing of this amorphous self-entity.

"Who may he have been?" Rilke once rhetorically asked about

[2]Hans Szklenar, "Beiträge zur Chronologie und Anordnung von Georg Trakls Gedichten auf Grund des Nachlasses von Karl Röck," *Euphorion,* 60 (1966), 227.

[3]Michael Hamburger, *The Truth of Poetry: Tensions in Modern Poetry from Baudelaire to the 1960s* (New York: Harcourt Brace Jovanovich, 1969), p. 147.

[4]Herbert Lindenberger is one of many critics to have noted an increasing impersonality in Trakl's poetry: "Trakl's mature verse shows an extreme reticence to engage in overtly personal utterance." Even though he accounts for it in terms of literary technique and influence, Lindenberger notes, however, the basic paradox when he writes several lines later with regard to "Helian": "He had now found a way of writing poetry that allowed him to explore the intricacies of the self more fully than any of his earlier poetic modes could do" (*Georg Trakl* [New York: Twayne, 1971], p. 77).

the author of *Sebastian im Traum.*[5] Readers of "Helian" have repeatedly posed a parallel question about the poem's title figure, but without Rilke's knowing sense of futility. Among those identities which have been suggested are Helios, the sun god; Lélian, Verlaine's name for himself in *Les Poètes Maudits; Heliand,* an Old Saxon poem; and Heiland, a German word for savior.[6] Neither singly nor together do these names suffice to identify Trakl's Helian, who appears by name only once toward the end of the poem. The contention, moreover, that Trakl fragmented "his protagonist among a large number of guises" assumes that he had in mind a bridging identity for the various figures in the poem.[7] Helian's identity, however, is precisely as indeterminate as that of the poet's.

Trakl's longest poem in verse begins with a relatively high degree of structure in comparison to its later parts. The series of scenes that make up the first of its five major sections is held together by a reflection of seasonal progression:

> In the lonely hours of the spirit
> It is beautiful to walk in the sun
> Along the yellow walls of summer.
> The steps sound quietly in the grass. Yet the son of Pan
> Still sleeps in the grey marble.
>
> Evenings on the terrace we got drunk on brown wine.
> The peach glows reddish in the leaves.
> Soft sonata, happy laughter.
>
> The night's tranquillity is beautiful.
> On the dark clearing
> We encounter shepherds and white stars.
>
> When it has become fall

[5]*Erinnerung an Georg Trakl,* p. 11.

[6]Reinhold Grimm, "Die Sonne: Bemerkungen zu einem Motiv Georg Trakls," *Deutsche Vierteljahrsschrift,* 35 (1961), 237–238. See also Lindenberger, *Georg Trakl,* p. 76.

[7]Lindenberger, *Georg Trakl,* p. 76.

Sober clarity emerges in the grove.
Calmed, we wander along red walls
And the rounded eyes follow the flight of the birds.
In the evening the white water sinks in the funeral urns.

In bare branches the heavens celebrate.
In pure hands the peasant bears bread and wine
And the fruits ripen peacefully in the sunny chamber.

O how solemn is the face of the beloved dead one.
Yet the soul enjoys just contemplation.

This first section of "Helian" falls with noticeable ease into two parts nearly equal in length. Within the eleven lines of the initial part, three further divisions are clearly marked by the physical grouping of the lines into miniature scenes of a landscape in late summer. Their references to times of day link them in a temporal sequence and an impressionistic, idyllic air pervades them all. Lines 6 through 8 are particularly rich in their appeal to the senses, and the larger scene is twice praised for its beauty by the poetic speaker. There is, moreover, a sense of completion and rounding off in the imagery that begins with a walk and ends with a meeting, a familiar course of events in Trakl's poetry. The meeting with the "shepherds and white stars" introduces the first traces of metaphysical elements into the poem.

The past tense in the sixth line along with the reference to the generalized "evenings" runs counter to the impressionistic quality of the scene. The poem's voice shifts abruptly as if memory had suddenly vaulted to the forefront of consciousness drowning out the preoccupation with the present. The aesthetic effect is to modify the sense of time conveyed by the other verbs as well. Their reference to a present reality seems equivocated by the elegaic tone of the past tense.[8] Their presentness may be a func-

[8]Ludwig Dietz calls "Helian" the "first poem to which we must give the name 'Elegy'" (*Die lyrische Form Georg Trakls,* Trakl-Studien 5 [Salzburg: Otto Müller, 1959], p. 133).

tion of the strength of past memories—that is, they express a past so vividly that they are perceived by the speaker as present.

While even the images that refer to the present may be interpreted as a past reality, the larger scene is not insulated from threat, not the idyll of a paradise lost. The "reddish" glow of the peach suggests overripeness and the approach of fall. The allusion to drunkenness poses the disquieting threat of revelry and dissolution. In its present context, the image of the "son of Pan" also represents a latent disturbance to the idyll's serenity. The steps in line 4 "sound quietly" as if taking heed not to wake him and arouse the legendary shout which is said to send those into "panic" terror who hear it. This scene of late summer, then, does not exist in the perfectly idyllic terms of a lost paradise, its beauty untainted and shielded from inevitable decay. It is rather a foil for the poem's increasingly destructive imagery and dissolving structure.

The multiple appeal to the senses and their intoxication in the summer landscape yields to the "sober clarity" (13) of the autumnal atmosphere, a juxtaposition echoing Hölderlin's creative state of intoxicated sobriety. The image of the peasant bearing the elements of the Eucharist amid the peaceful images of a bountiful fall strengthens the echo of Hölderlin's presence in this multilevel poem. Walls again figure prominently in the imagery as the speaker moves beside them once more, this time in the company of an unspecified figure. It is the third and last time in the poem that the first-person plural form is used. The close relationship implied in this *We*-perspective dissolves into a more distant, narrative perspective. The complement of the speaker's unspoken *I* is displaced onto a series of figures designated in the third person.

A simple, conventional piety marks the attitude toward the fall as the final phase of nature's cycle. The apparent acquiescence to the gathering signs of decay and death is tempered, however, by the ambiguity of the last two lines of the section. Readings of "der teueren Toten" (20) as a single female figure and as a plurality of figures are both grammatical possibilities. The singular forms of "face" and "soul" seem to favor the first possibility, however. Yet this soul can also be construed as that of the speaker himself, which is uplifted by the sight of death. This interpretation agrees with the prevailing tone of assent toward death and cannot be entirely discounted because of the directness in which the speaker involves himself. Later in the poem, he clearly admonishes himself in a manner even more direct: "Let the song also remember the boy" (77). The more persuasive reading, however, imputes "just contemplation" to the soul of the deceased and by implication, its absence in the souls of the living. Neither autumn nor death is greeted as a terminus to life, but as a transition—in a way not totally defined by recourse to Christian beliefs—to a reality of the soul inherently more equitable. The familiar image of the migrating birds in line 15 strengthens the sense of autumn as a season of passage within a longer, more encompassing journey.

As the year progresses beyond fall's temperate period of harvest and further toward winter, the process of life's cessation loses its overlay of serenity. What was depicted as peaceful maturation (19) in nature changes to devastation (22) and destruction (33) in the second major section of "Helian":

> The silence of the devastated garden is powerful,
> As the young novice garlands his brow with brown foliage,
> His breath drinks icy gold.
>
> The hands touch the age of bluish waters
> Or in cold night, the white cheeks of the sisters.
>
> Quiet and harmonious is the walk past friendly rooms
> Where there is solitude and the murmur of the maple,
> Where perhaps the thrush still sings.
>
> Man is beautiful and manifest in the darkness
> When astonished he moves arms and legs
> And in crimson sockets his eyes silently roll.
>
> At vespers the stranger loses his way in the black destruction of
> November,

Under decaying branches, along walls full of leprosy,
Where in former times the holy brother had gone,
Lost in the gentle string music of his madness.

O how lonely the evening wind ceases.
Dying, the head bows down in the darkness of the olive tree.

The striking quality of the opening line stems from its attribution of intensity (powerful) to an absence of sensory perception (silence).[9] In one of the apparent sequences in "Helian," which is in turn closely tied to the seasonal progression, silence represents nature's withdrawal of her claims on the senses. Its power then must resonate inwardly on a scale only indirectly attached to perceptual reality, a scale which registers the "silence of winter" at the end of the following section as well. Together with indicators from the preceding section—the sudden shift of tense and the possibly direct involvement of the speaker in the final line—this evidence of an operative inner scale indicates the mingling of landscape and mind-scape in the poem's images.[10]

Oblique and distorted allusions to biblical events as well as references to quasi-religious rituals are woven conspicuously into

[9] Trakl used the same elements of imagery in a slightly altered configuration in the opening strophe of "Verklärter Herbst" ("Transfigured Fall"—I, 37), a poem written a few months before "Helian":

Gewaltig endet so das Jahr
Mit goldnem Wein und Frucht der Gärten.
Rund schweigen Wälder wunderbar
Und sind des Einsamen Gefährten.

Powerfully the year ends
With golden wine and fruit of the gardens.
Round about, the forests are wonderfully silent
And are the lonely one's companions.

[10] In an excellent introduction to her translations, Lucia Getsi points to the flow of "landscapes... into inscapes" in Trakl's mature poetry: "In Trakl's early poetry this rupture [between self and 'other'] and the resulting tension is manifested as the one common to most Western cultures, between the perceiving 'I' and the external world of objects. However, in Trakl's mature poetry the tension between external and internal reality becomes so tightly knit that landscapes flow into inscapes" ("The Poetry of Georg Trakl," *Georg Trakl: Poems* [Athens O.: Mundus Artium Press, 1973], p. 3).

the poem's imagery, yet are no more than strands in its larger fabric. The image of the conjuring hands over the waters in line 25 touches lightly on Christ's conversion of water into wine. Equally delicate—and equally askew—is the connection of the image in the next line to his miraculous laying of hands upon the dead. The bowed head under the olive tree in the final lines of the section suggests Christ's reconciliation with his crucifixion on the Mount of Olives. Tangentially connected to this image is the novice who at the beginning of the section places the autumn foliage on his brow. By this action as well as his inhalation of the "icy gold" in the following line, he appears to take upon and into himself nature's signs of impending death. However, by dint of associations with nature worship, pagan overtones here predominate over Christian ones. At such points, Trakl's imagery seems to seek the most fragilely distinct echoes of biblical events while, just as distinctly, it seeks to deform their familiarity by entwining them with extraneous material.

In the onrush of scenes of intensifying destruction, the idyllic "quiet and harmonious" walk in lines 27–29 functions as a structural countercurrent, a reversal of the situation in the first scene in which the idyll is undercut by latently threatening images. Although the following unit (30–32) returns to the poem's mainstream, the lines create their own sense of discord. The heart of this discord lies in the conjunction of "beautiful"—an adjective still resonating from its repeated use in the preceding section—with a general pronouncement on man's condition during an intense, almost frightening experience. Together with the parallel modifier "manifest," however, it characterizes the aesthetic response of the speaker-observer as one primarily of marvel at the existential state exhibited by man. One critic has interpreted the experience in these lines as a birth of sorts, an interpretation that captures the sense of profound change taking place.[11] But within the context and considering the choice of

[11]Grimm, "Die Sonne," p. 236.

vocabulary, the change more nearly approximates the onset of death or insanity.[12] Facing the impending end of consciousness, man becomes manifest or evident (*erscheinend*) to himself, gaining a heightened self-awareness at the moment of his demise. When set off against its approaching absence, man's presence to himself becomes a matter of astonishment (31). The experience whereby life becomes magnified in the face of its loss is the converse of that barren death-in-life existence characteristic of the protagonist in the later prose poems.

At one point in the complex creation and shifting of variants that finally crystallized into the finished poem, the "stranger" in line 33 was called the "sick novice," an apparent continuation of the religious overtones in lines 23–24. In the final version these overtones are muted, yet the setting of the scene at vespers when the "stranger" repeats the fate of a "holy" predecessor does not allow them to become entirely lost. Channels drawing from sources other than religious ones inform the images of this scene with further echoes. Hölderlin, his madness, and his poetry most obviously had an influence on the figure of the "holy brother." Just as obviously, this influence does not exclude other sources; the figure has been interpreted as a composite of Hölderlin, Rimbaud, and Trakl's friend Karl Borromäus Heinrich.[13] This "holy brother," cast out of the community of man by his music and madness, had in a previous time walked a path along walls marked by leprosy, the disease of outcasts. The other figure, also an outcast in his role as stranger, "loses his way" along these very walls. The richness of "Helian" and the poverty of any translation becomes evident in the German reflexive verb *sich verlieren,* translated here as "loses his way." It also contains the sense of dispersing or disappearing. As a literal depiction of madness, the stranger's dispersing or disappearing self metaphorically

[12]Two variants of line 30 support this reading: "O how beautiful dying man is and manifest in the darkness" and "O how pale in madness man is and manifest in the darkness" (II, 453).

[13]Dietz, p. 134, n. 38.

describes the manner in which the stranger follows the mad "holy brother." The meaning levels of "Helian" blend almost inextricably into one another as individual images and scenes are multiply determined and connected like those in a dream. They reflect the splintered and overlapping voices of the poet's empirical self whose brittle shell had begun to loosen and shift.

From the gentleness of the gesture in line 38 to the "shattering" apocalyptic vision at the beginning of the poem's third main section is a startling transition. The focus of the poem shifts as well from a miniature scene to one of macrocosmic proportions:

> Shattering is the demise of the race.
> In this hour the eyes of the beholder fill up
> With the gold of his stars.
>
> In the evening a carillon sinks that no longer rings.
> The black walls on the square crumble.
> The dead soldier calls to prayer.
>
> A pale angel,
> The son enters the empty house of his fathers.
>
> The sisters have gone far away to white old men.
> At night the sleeper found them under the pillars of the hall,
> Returned from sad pilgrimages.
>
> O how their hair stiffens from filth and worms,
> As he stands in it with silver feet,
> And deceased, they step out of barren rooms.
>
> O you psalms in the fiery rains of midnight,
> As the servants beat their soft eyes with nettles;
> The childlike fruits of the elder
> Bow down astonished over an empty grave.
>
> Quietly, yellowed moons roll
> Over the fever linens of the youth,
> Before the silence of winter ensues.

Translation again acts to muffle the full reverberations of the original, particularly in line 39. The English "shattering" attempts to capture the primary emotional connotations of the German *erschütternd* while preserving a literal meaning of violent convulsion appropriate to the physical dimension of the catastrophe. As an emotional response, "shattering" once again points to that aspect of "Helian" as a mind-scape of a directly involved speaker. The greater difficulty in translating line 39, however, involves the German word *Geschlecht*. It is a highly flexible word with a broad field of meaning and particularly sensitive to its context. It can mean both sexual and grammatical gender, species, genus, lineage or clan—thus, a group of people of common descent—as well as race in the sense of human race. When the context itself is made up of various strata of signification, each of these activates that aspect of the word commensurate with its own particular meaning. In "Abendländisches Lied" ("Song of the Occident"—I, 119), a poem written a year later than "Helian," the initial stanzas are concerned with the Occident as a broad cultural designation for an identifiable group of human beings. Yet the "demise" in the last stanza has primarily to do with the metamorphosis of lovers of the opposite sex into resurrected beings of the same sex:

> O, die bittere Stunde des Untergangs,
> Da wir ein steinernes Antlitz in schwarzen Wassern beschaun.
> Aber strahlend heben die silbernen Lider die Liebenden:
> Ein Geschlecht. Weihrauch strömt von rosigen Kissen
> Und der süße Gesang der Auferstandenen.
>
> O, the bitter hour of demise,
> As we behold a stony face in black waters.
> But beaming, the lovers lift their silver lids:
> One sex. Incense streams from rosy pillows
> And the sweet song of the resurrected.

In "Helian," the English "race" for *Geschlecht* suggests the intertwining of sociocultural and metaphysical facets of the imagery which follows. The central image where these facets converge is the image of the "son" in line 46 who enters into a home without "fathers."

In its entirety, the poem's third section moves toward an endpoint in the sequence of seasons that finally issues into the dormant silence of winter. A dialectical impetus, latent in this larger movement and increasingly encountered in Trakl's images of catastrophe and death, is exhibited on a smaller scale in each of the section's opening scenes. A "beholder" or a figure identified only as one who sees is the first figure on the poetic landscape. His vision—expressed in terms of eyes that "fill up"—pointedly occurs "in this hour" and in a kind of literal answering motion to the "going down" (*Untergang*) of the race. The imagery of "Abendländisches Lied" traces an identical rhythmical motion from "demise" (*Untergang*) to the lifting of the lovers' eyes onto a new reality. The crumbling walls in line 43 of "Helian" are encased between an image that announces the end of the bells' ringing and the sound of a dead soldier's call to prayer. It is often, as it is here, only the purely formal characteristic of a dialectical motion that joins one image to another, the second image appearing to refuse the terminality that the first declares.

The image of the walls and the reference to winter (59) are structural elements already familiar from their repeated occurrences in the poem's previous sections. Up to this point, the walls had served as a means for giving direction to the various wanderers, as a guide for channeling movement in a specific direction. In this section, after the fall of the "race," the walls crumble and fall into ruins. The seasonal motif recurs, but at a distance of several lines from the walls, and the motion along the walls is entirely lacking. Not only have the walls fallen, but on a formal level, the structural unit consisting of walls/season/wanderer has itself been fragmented. None of the fragments carry over beyond the third section; the poem seems to have charted the dissolution of its own structural backbone.

Thematically, this section suggests a loss parallel to that of the disintegrated structural unit. Christianity appears to be denied its claim as a valid metaphysical structure. The images that admit to a degree of Christian content are ones that uniformly refer to events after the crucifixion. They attach themselves to the strand of imagery that ended in the preceding section with the bowed head under the "olive tree". As a "pale angel," the son has ascended to a paternal home which he finds empty (45–46). Several lines later (53–56), this thread of the poem's imagery is continued in a cryptic scene of the suffering and amazement at the site of the "empty grave." Biblical overtones sound plainly in the "psalms" being sung and in the acts of despairing self-flagellation by the servants. At one point in the poem's genesis, Trakl removed from the lines which follow a more explicit reference to the risen Christ. The "fever linens" had once been "death linens," a distinct allusion to a shroud. According to Christian orthodoxy, the empty tomb signifies the triumph of the metaphysical over the physical world. Christ transcends worldly bonds through resurrection and returns to an otherworldly home. But the emptiness of this home in the poem undermines the foundation of this orthodoxy. Though the *deus absconditus* is hardly startling as a philosophical insight since Nietzsche, Trakl's vision of it is nevertheless unique in its poetic literality.

Yet the imagery of lines 45–46 belongs to another, more worldly level of the poem. Religious implications blend with familial, probably autobiographical ones, especially in the context of the immediately following lines (47–52). Trakl's own father had died over two years before "Helian" was begun, but the family business was dissolved early in 1913. Trakl returned to Salzburg on February 1 of that year to be on hand for the business proceedings, but must have known for some time about the imminence of the plan. A few months before Trakl began "Helian," his sister Grete, then in Berlin, had met and married a much older man, Arthur Langen. There seems little doubt, in spite of the pluralization, that echoes of this painfully repressed occurrence in Trakl's life become audible in line 47.[14] Variants that Trakl finally discarded tend to confirm the autobiographical substratum of these lines:

> The house towered blackly on the old square.
>
> Mighty is the gloom in the house.
> Locked up the dark gate.
> [II, 128]

In the dream of the sleeper (48–49), the departed sisters return, tainted by their unholy sojourn with the white old men. In a variant of these lines, they appear to search for the sleeper's purifying powers:

> Their heavy hair seeks his silver feet;
> It stiffens from filth and worms.
> [II, 129]

In these discarded lines, the sisters' impulse to seek expiation had been more explicit, an impulse projected onto them by the dreamer himself. Trakl's fantasy in life, the return of a contrite sister from her wayward path, remained unfulfilled. In spite of this, the late poetry reflects a relationship of reconciliation and marked idealization of the sister figure. The drama of return and expiation in "Helian" culminates with a passage through death and a departure from the sterile rooms (52). The poem's levels merge with one another, oblique autobiographical fragments blending with equally oblique biblical fragments. Allusions to atonement through death bind them together. The imagery in lines 45–46 belongs to both levels of the poem, yet exclusively to neither. It displays a salient characteristic of Trakl's imagery in "Helian"—a resistance to being pinned down, an oscillation be-

[14]Spoerri believes this to be "unquestionably" the case (p. 39).

tween various strata of the poem and a resultant multiplicity of meaning.

The final three lines of the poem's middle section strike a gentle and muted concluding note. Absent from the "silence of winter" is the awesome power of fall's silence. The "yellowed moons" suggest the leavening effects of time's passing, a long, healing interval after the destruction and suffering of the preceding images. What follows in the fourth section of the poem are tentative responses of renewal which are largely without the elements of sequence and structure of the early portions of the poem:

> A sublime destiny ponders down the Kidron
> Where the cedar, a tender creation,
> Evolves under the blue brows of the father.
> At night a shepherd leads his herd over the meadow.
> Or there are cries in sleep,
> When a brazen angel in the grove approaches man.
> The flesh of the holy one melts away on the glowing grate.
>
> Around the mudhuts climb purple grapes,
> Ringing bundles of gilded grain,
> The bees' buzzing, the crane's flight.
> In the evening those risen from the dead meet on rocky paths.
>
> In black waters lepers mirror themselves;
> Or they open their filth-stained robes
> Crying to the balmy wind which blows from the rosy hill.
>
> Slender servant girls grope through the night streets
> Seeking the loving shepherd.
> Saturdays, gentle singing sounds in the huts.
>
> Let the song also remember the boy,
> His madness, white brows and his departure;
> The mouldering one who opens his eyes bluishly.
> O how sad this reunion is.

An initially constructive momentum in the images of this section counters the previously overriding sense of destruction. As if swept along by the motion of the Kidron's current, the "sublime destiny"—a distinct countering vision to the "demise of the race"—hangs suspended in an abstract form above the stream waiting for concrete fulfillment. Overtones in the German *hinabsinnen* (to "ponder down") of contriving or inventing, insinuate themselves into these lines. They support the sense of a new creation beginning its evolution in the imagery of lines 60–62. The speaker here more explicitly assumes the role hinted at earlier in the poem, that of conjurer whose gaze passes beyond mundane reality toward the threshold of a "sublime destiny."

Yet this vision is even more fragile than the idyll of the poem's earliest lines. The speaker's assertive, fate-creating attitude is temporarily suspended by the nightmarish interlude in lines 64–66. The shrillness, the terror, and the dissolution in the single images momentarily block any resonance from the initial vision. The suspension ceases just as rapidly, however, as the following lines (67–70) shift to a landscape of vitalized nature. In the poem's most explicit language, the resurrected figures affirm the abrogation of death's terminality. Nature, in its abundance, mature colors, sounds, and movement supersedes the wintry silence into which the seasonal sequence had progressed. The poem has moved through nature's period of dormancy, yet neither into spring nor, for that matter, into any season identified by name. This lack of designation—a lack magnified by the contrast with earlier repeated mention of specific seasons—and the static, descriptive use of the verbs convey a timeless, preternatural quality.

From this peak of constructive resolve, the following two scenes add figures whose actions are ambiguous, the results open-ended. Whether the lepers find the healing response in nature which they apparently seek is left open. The "black waters" appear particularly incapable of reflection or response. The servant girls "grope" uncertainly for the love of a guardian and protector while the site of the search—"through the night streets"—casts some doubt on the purity of their purpose. And the uncertainty of the outcome is considerably more pronounced in the German subjunctive construction of line 75 than in the translation.

The gentle self-imperative of the poem in line 77 reasserts the flagging pose of conjuration assumed in the opening lines. Here the process is a conscious act of remembrance whereby the speaker enjoins himself to allow a memory to emerge which then takes on concrete form on the poetic landscape. As earlier in the poem, past becomes present when the figure of the boy gains a life of its own in line 79. The sadness in the final line can be attributed either to the boy or to the speaker or simultaneously to both. From either perspective, it can express regret at the renewal of the boy's suffering, a sadness about the memory's new life. For the boy's part—he comes to life in the poem by opening his eyes—the sadness can also be read as a reaction to "seeing again," a literal translation of the German "Wiedersehn" ("reunion"). The memory brought to life appears to unfold further in the poem's final lines:

> The steps of madness in black rooms,
> The shades of the old men under the open door;
> Then Helian's soul looks upon itself in the rosy mirror
> And snow and leprosy fall from his brow.
>
> On the walls the stars are extinguished
> And the white forms of light.
>
> The remains of graves descend from the tapestry,
> The silence of fallen crosses on the mound,
> The sweetness of incense in the purple night wind.
>
> O you shattered eyes in black mouths,
> As the grandson in gentle derangement
> Ponders the darker end in solitude,
> The quiet god lowers his blue lids over him.

The "boy" who in the previous section emerged from the speaker's memory (77–78) and gained an independent poetic existence (79), apparently assumes the identity of the poem's title figure in the final section. In other words, lines 77–80 function as a kind of introduction to Helian's appearance. Since Helian—the "boy"—is a memory, however, it is both for him and for the speaker a reappearance, a reenactment of his past madness in the present tense of the poem.

The steps, rooms, the door and mirror, the walls and tapestry all function as interior images on two levels. As elements of a physical setting, they situate the scene within a house and invoke the familial aspects of "Helian" once more. The gaze of Helian's soul upon itself situates the scene in a psychic interior as well. On this inner landscape, the "steps of madness" become synonymous with an inward passage into the mirror of the soul and juxtaposed to a passage through the "open door" leading out among the "shades of the old men." The absence of light in the "black rooms" and the absence of verbs in both the first lines convey the stifling atmosphere which compels Helian's movement from them. Instead of going out of the "black rooms" of his mind, Helian turns inward to the "mirror" of the soul and finds a reflected image from which the marks on his brow have fallen away. For this moment of the poem, Helian's inward gaze discovers a self free of blemish. Anticipating imagery of healing in the prose poems, the "rosy mirror" reflects an image cleansed of the marks of madness—the mad boy was first introduced into the poem with "white brows" (78)—and leprosy. The association of leprosy and madness not only ties Helian to the lepers who also seek their cure through self-reflection in the "black waters," but expresses a relationship which Michel Foucault has shown to be historically valid. Foucault sees the modern madman as the unfortunate heir to the moral stigma and isolation once attached to the leper in medieval Europe.[15]

There is, moreover, at this point in the poem, a flickering insight into the regenerative possibilities of a madness that chooses

[15]Foucault, *Madness and Civilization: A History of Insanity in the Age of Reason,* trans. Richard Howard (New York: Vintage, 1973), p. 7.

to go down deeper into itself rather than escape its darkness by opting for the easier passage through an "open door." For although it is the easier choice, crossing that threshold would lead Helian out of his own mind among the insubstantial "shades of the old men." It is a fleeting option for the painful yet curative journey inward into the true self over the self-denying journey out of his mind into a false self. At least through the poetic figure of these lines, Trakl was able "to let it come to a crisis" (I, 500).

The moment of Helian's healing inner vision is short-lived, however. The following lines (85–89) explicitly extend the imagery of the house's interior and implicitly carry with them the psychic level of the section as well. Helian's fall into madness assumes sinister dimensions with the generation of a chaos void of light and form. Death no longer figures in the imagery as a process of transition: the graves yield no signs of resurrection, only the bones of the dead. The poem's last image of silence in line 88 lacks any hint of imminent or dormant life. The speaker retreats from Helian's propitious vision and abandons the poem's constructive momentum with the image of the dissipating incense.

The final lines of the poem begin with a linguistic gesture repeatedly used in "Helian" and so familiar from Trakl's other poems that it borders on a mannerism.[16] With the vocative "O," the speaker indirectly addresses the "grandson" in the next line. His words, however, are first directed to an altered state of mind which—after the figure is named—is paraphrased as "gentle derangement." The grandson's perceptual faculties intermingle. They are fragmented and multiple. "Shattered eyes" suggest disjointed vision through shattered lenses, lenses which no longer mediate a focused, unified image of the world. And conversely, the "mouths" are the source of the pluralized voices from this fractured perspective. Yet this metanoia is "gentle," a cogitative

[16]In his tabulation of Trakl's vocabulary, Heinz Wetzel lists "O" as the ninth most frequently occurring word (*Konkordanz zu den Dichtungen Georg Trakls*, Trakl-Studien 7 [Salzburg: Otto Müller, 1971], p. 813).

state of mind in express contrast to the "darker end" which it ponders. In passages from two other poems from the same general time period, Trakl refers to similarly "gentle" cognitive states of metanoia:

> Auch zeigt sich sanftem Wahnsinn oft das Goldne, Wahre.
>
> Also the Golden and True appear to gentle madness.
> [I, 38]

> Stirne Gottes Farben träumt,
> Spürt des Wahnsinns sanfte Flügel.
>
> Brow dreams god's colors,
> Feels the gentle wings of madness.
> [I, 54]

The altered structure of the grandson's mind contrasts distinctly with the final lightless chaos of Helian's psychic interior depicted in lines 85–89. His end seems, in fact, to be the "darker end" pondered by the grandson in the poem's final lines.

With the lowering of the "quiet" god's eyelids over him, the grandson is absorbed into a dimension even further removed from individual consciousness than the "gentle derangement" of his senses. Among the variants of the final line, two reveal an unrealized impetus to continue:

> Der heitere Gott die goldenen Lider aufschlägt
>
> The serene god opens his golden lids
> [II, 132]

> Der stille Gott die blauen Lider über ihn hebt;
>
> The quiet god raises his blue lids over him;
> [II, 132]

For these open endings, Trakl finally substituted the tranquil enclosure of the grandson in the god's field of vision, a choice that closes around unspoken images rather than explicitly ending the poem. Rilke's characterization of "Helian" as "a few enclosures around the boundless inarticulate" rings with a special truth for the poem's final image.[17]

The manifoldly determined images in "Helian," meeting points of various referential dimensions—psychical and physical as well as metaphysical, mythological and literary as well as autobiographical—suggest a graphic realization of the grandson's metanoia. The image "shattered eyes in black mouths" describes well the fragmented, nonunified speaker of "Helian" whose broken visions intermingle and whose pluralized voices overlap. The embracing metaself of the speaker evident in earlier poems can no longer be traced. Multiple eyes have become shattered eyes and "Helian" became, at least perhaps in Trakl's judgment, the realization of that poem "bursting full of movement and visions" that he had attempted to write with his "Klagelied."

The richest sources which Trakl exploited for his poem were doubtless the fluctuations and tremors of his own personality structure. The phenomenon of multifocality is, for example, a frequent hallmark of what psychiatrists call schizophrenic thought: "Schizophrenic thought often bristles with different planes of meaning and is, as I call it, *multifocal,* because it has to focus at the same time on different meanings with their different objective situations."[18] The poet turned the compulsion of this phenomenon to aesthetic advantage and into a distinguishing characteristic of his poem.

Poems of Controlled Crisis—"Untergang" and "Abendlied"

Trakl's instability was a painful physical and mental reality at the time he was composing "Helian," as well as a source of

[17] *Erinnerung an Georg Trakl,* p. 10.
[18] Arieti, *Interpretation of Schizophrenia,* p. 263.

poetry. On February 19, 1913, little more than a month after the completion of the poem, he wrote to Karl Borromäus Heinrich about the alienation and suffering which he was experiencing at his home in Salzburg: "My days at home are not easy ones and I exist between feverish and unconscious states in these sunny rooms where it is unspeakably cold. Strange spasms of metamorphosis, physically experienced to the point of being intolerable; visions of darkness to the point of being certain that I've died; ecstasies to the point of stony solidification; and further dreaming of sad dreams" (I, 503). In a letter written four days later to Ficker, Trakl expressed his frightened uncertainty at the "unspeakable emotions which are intent either on destroying or perfecting me" (I, 504). His remark to Buschbeck—cited at the beginning of the chapter—that he could have let the "crisis" come to a head in Vienna, suggests, however, that he had at least tenuous control over his precarious mental situation. His poetry illustrates this control.

Nowhere is the sense of flux and metamorphosis more directly stated in his poetry than in the last line of an unpublished version of "Untergang" ("Demise"—I, 387), a poem belonging to the large complex of poems out of which "Helian" finally emerged:

> O mein Bruder, verwandelt sich dunkel die Landschaft der Seele.
>
> O my brother, the soul's landscape alters darkly.

In dedicating the final version of "Untergang" to Heinrich, with whom he exchanged "brotherly" salutations in letters as well, Trakl recognized a kinship of mental disposition rather than literary talent. This "extremely labile personality," whom Trakl had known only since December 1912, returned the recognition with an adulatory essay for Trakl that was published in the first March issue of *Der Brenner*.[19] It was the same issue in which the fifth and final version of "Untergang" (I, 116) appeared:

[19]Gerald Stieg, *Der Brenner und die Fackel: Ein Beitrag zur Wirkungsgeschichte von Karl Kraus* (Salzburg: Otto Müller, 1976), p. 285.

On the Soul's Landscape

Über den weißen Weiher
Sind die wilden Vögel fortgezogen.
Am Abend weht von unseren Sternen ein eisiger Wind.

Über unsere Gräber
Beugt sich die zerbrochene Stirne der Nacht.
Unter Eichen schaukeln wir auf einem silbernen Kahn.

Immer klingen die weißen Mauern der Stadt.
Unter Dornenbogen
O mein Bruder klimmen wir blinde Zeiger gen Mitternacht.

Over the white pond
The wild birds have migrated.
In the evening an icy wind wafts from our stars.

Over our graves
The night's shattered brow bends low.
Under oaks we pitch on a silver skiff.

Ceaselessly the white walls of the city chime.
Under boughs of thorns
O my brother we climb blind hands toward midnight.

In each of the poem's successive versions, Trakl undertook changes which give the appearance of being fresh starts rather than revisions. From the fourth version—which Heinrich received on February 19 and which became the immediate impetus for his essay on Trakl (II, 704)—to the form of the published poem, the poet retained the essence of only four lines. They became the final poem's beginning and ending. If the poet is to be believed, however, the appearance of fresh starts and different poems is deceiving. To Ficker, he explained that the final changes in the poem came about because the earlier versions contained too much that was "only intimation" (I, 504). While this remark does nothing to clarify the content of Trakl's intimation, it does indicate the poet's control of his language and, more important, that he held the signifying element of his language to be self-evident.

Even without knowledge of the poem's drawn-out origins, its tightly knit structure betrays a painstaking formative process.[20] Shorter than any of its predecessors, the final version has three strophes, each consisting of two sentences, one two lines long and the other a single line long. Their sequence remains the same in the first two strophes, but is reversed in the third one. The length in syllables of corresponding lines of the first two strophes is nearly identical, and all strophes have precisely the same total number of syllables. The coloration of the landscape is slight but consistent. Time and place designations are, on the other hand, more prominent and centrally important—every sentence begins by marking either one or the other. The poem progresses, moreover, from evening into night and toward midnight within the span of its three strophes.

Directed motion—first away from the speaker and then toward him—characterizes the three images in the poem's opening five lines. The birds have earlier flown away while, in contrast, the wind and bending "brow" of the night move from a distant point closer to the speaker and his companion. The pitching to-and-fro motion of the "silver skiff" in line 6 embodies both the going and coming, yet is distinguishable as neither. It is an image of synthesis that bridges the spatial opposition of the directed motions. Something similar with regard to temporal dimensions occurs in the following line. Past, present, and future are all caught up in the word "ceaselessly," their distinctions lost in a single concept, just as the image of the pitching skiff assimilates the opposition between going and coming. The poem's structure underscores the pivotal nature of these images—one follows the other in the only two contiguous short lines of the poem.

Although the hour of midnight appears to be a straightforward terminus to a poem entitled "Untergang," the final lines pointedly create an ambiguity in an image that intertwines spatial and

[20]My interpretation of "Untergang" owes a large debt to Detlev Lüders, "Abendmuse. Untergang. Anif.: Drei Gedichte von Georg Trakl," *Wirkendes Wort,* 11 (1961), 89–102.

temporal elements. This last image merges these dimensions in a way that suspends their separate unequivocalness. While the poetic figures move toward midnight, their "climb" is likened to that of the upward swing of a clock's hands, an unambiguous motion of ascent. The paradox of the climb up toward demise is, moreover, intensified by the blindness of the clock's hands—*Zeiger* is literally "pointers" in German. As these hands, the figures move on a fixed path that leads toward the nadir of the poem's progression in time, yet blindness prevents them from seeing its nature. The poem presages a demise, yet for the poetic figures as well as the reader, it is wrapped in ambiguity. Its consequences are uncomprehended.

"Abendlied" ("Evening Song"—I, 65) is another of the poems that took separate shape in Trakl's mind alongside "Helian," and, like "Untergang," it is highly structured:

Am Abend, wenn wir auf dunklen Pfaden gehn,
Erscheinen unsere bleichen Gestalten vor uns.

Wenn uns dürstet,
Trinken wir die weißen Wasser des Teichs,
Die Süße unserer traurigen Kindheit.

Erstorbene ruhen wir unterm Hollundergebüsch,
Schaun den grauen Möven zu.

Frühlingsgewölke steigen über die finstere Stadt,
Die der Mönche edlere Zeiten schweigt.

Da ich deine schmalen Hände nahm
Schlugst du leise die runden Augen auf,
Dieses ist lange her.

Doch wenn dunkler Wohllaut die Seele heimsucht,
Erscheinst du Weiße in des Freundes herbstlicher Landschaft.

In the evening when we walk on dark paths
Our pale forms appear before us.

When thirst overtakes us,
We drink the pond's white waters,
The sweetness of our sad childhood.

Expired, we rest under the elder bush,
Watch the grey gulls.

Spring's clouds climb over the dark city
Which is silent of the monks' nobler times.

As I took your slender hands
You gently opened your round eyes;
This is long since past.

Yet when dark harmony haunts the soul,
You appear, white one, in the friend's autumnal landscape.

The poem's nearly symmetrical proportions rest on the twice-repeated pattern of a three-line strophe enclosed by two two-line strophes. The corresponding first two strophes of each repetition have exactly the same syllable length, and the last strophe is only slightly longer than its counterpart.

As so often in Trakl's poems, "Abendlied" begins with a walk. Yet while to the reader the poem's form is reassuringly symmetrical and the opening image familiar, the identity of the walkers is as enigmatically "dark" as their paths. Their identity, however, matters less to the poem than the changing contours of their relationship. In the poem's first half the speaker employs a bridging perspective from which he speaks for himself as well as the other. After the third strophe the *We*-form retreats from the reader's direct view, but the relationship between two figures remains the center of the poem. Split into an *I* and the familiar form of German *You,* it takes the shape of a dialogue of gesture in the fifth strophe. The final lines pose the most concrete identities in the poem: a feminine figure addressed in the second-person form appears alongside a "friend."

The poem's first three strophes depict a jointly experienced landscape, a world loosely bound to the empirically real one where the figures walk, drink, and rest. The "pale forms" that appear before them in the second line, a kind of double experience of doubles, introduce a hallucinatory or preternatural element onto their experiential landscape. Depicted literally as "expired ones" in line 6, the figures are nevertheless conscious and in a state of intoxicated awareness that follows suggestively close upon their drink in the preceding strophe. At the midpoint in the poem, they lose their function as conjoined actors on the poem's landscape and become spectators along with the reader.

From the simple watching of the "grey gulls" in line 7, the poem passes onto an altered plane of vision, a transition less abrupt because it takes place against the fixed background of the sky. But the sky has broadened from its concretely real dimension to the arena of a cultural-historical vision. The "spring clouds" vaguely promise rejuvenation or threaten destruction to the "dark city" unreflective of its ties to a "nobler" past. This elegaic scene of a present time in which the echoes of a more ideally conceived past are silent, yields in turn to a miniature scene—actually no more than a gesture and response—played in yet another set of visionary coordinates. As the site of the poem's only past tenses and, as the plaintive tone of its last line reveals, this fifth strophe too is elegaic in nature. The poem has again easily shifted its visionary plane, this time from a brief excursion onto a cultural-historical level back to the poem's dominant individual-historical dimension. The scene of childlike innocence, its actors bound in trust through reciprocal gestures, parallels on a miniature scale the "monks' nobler times." It points back, moreover, to the reciprocity of ties between the figures of the poem's first half, a reciprocity expressed in those lines through shared perspective and shared experience.

But while the poem emphasizes that the scene in lines 10–12 is "long since past," its opening three strophes seem unquestionably to belong to the present. The key to the paradox lies in the poem's final strophe. Here, although the identity of the "friend" is finally indeterminate, the speaker comments on the recovery of the past and its transposition into terms of the present. Turning on its countering "Yet . . . ," the final strophe answers the plaintive, elegaic tone of the preceding lines. At harmonious moments, the *You,* that lost figure of the past, takes tangible shape on the "friend's autumnal landscape," a variation of the "soul's landscape" quoted earlier from a version of "Untergang." Both images are poetic shorthand for metanoiac states, but neither is as direct as the image of "pious derangement" (II, 121) that depicted the "friend's" condition in a variant of "Abendlied." It is in this deranged state that the past becomes present and that the speaker can speak in the plural voice of the poem's first three strophes. The last strophe then, besides answering the preceding strophe's elegaic tone and concluding the poem, is also an introduction of sorts to the poem as a whole. This circular motion, by which the end also becomes the beginning, is further suggested by the poem's structure. The "if . . . then" clause characteristic of the opening strophes is repeated as well as two key words from the first strophe—"dark" and "appear." "Abendlied" exemplifies a circular type of composition which one critic has found to be a structural law recurrent throughout Trakl's work.[21]

During the first quarter of 1913, all of the single poems from the so-called "Helian"-complex were published for the first time in *Der Brenner.* Seeing his works appear so regularly must have allayed some of the misery the poet endured in Salzburg, where he remained until the end of March. Early in the month, however, he was deeply shaken by an event, which, as he wrote to Ficker, left him with a "feeling of wild despair and horror" (I, 505). K. B. Heinrich had attempted to take his own life. Trakl's strong reaction probably included a measure of self-recrimination since Heinrich had a few days earlier requested sleeping drugs from his brotherly friend (II, 769). And Heinrich's letter clearly implies that Trakl had fulfilled earlier requests of the same nature. What-

[21]Kemper, *Georg Trakls Entwürfe,* pp. 92–105.

ever Trakl's role in the episode, Ficker came to the aid of both men. *Der Brenner* appears to have paid Heinrich's hospital expenses while Ficker's brother provided the beleagured Trakl with a few weeks of emotional recuperation.

4

Poetic Figures of Altered Consciousness

"An den Knaben Elis"

Despite the year's bleak beginnings, the events of the first six months in 1913 seemed to promise brighter prospects, at least externally in Trakl's life. During all of April and parts of May and June, he was a guest of Ficker's brother at Hohenburg, a mountain retreat outside of Igls near Innsbruck. His poetry, initially rejected by one publisher, even after covert promotion by Heinrich and the unflagging assistance of Buschbeck, was solicited by the Kurt Wolff publishing house and published in July. Added to Trakl's growing list of admirers during these months was Franz Werfel, who with the publication of *Der Weltfreund* (*The World's Friend*) and *Wir sind* (*We Are*), had begun to acquire a reputation which for many years far outstripped Trakl's own. Writing to Trakl on behalf of Kurt Wolff, Werfel expressed "great admiration" for his poetry, an accolade that surely fell upon grateful ears (II, 790).

Once more, during April and May 1913, Trakl placed in the title of two of his finest poems a proper name that has since been the subject of extensive speculation.[1] The Elis poems were originally parts of a larger whole which, however, was never published, and

[1]For a concise summary of this speculation, see Clemens Heselhaus, "Die Elis-Gedichte von Georg Trakl," *Deutsche Vierteljahrsschrift*, 28 (1954), p. 387, n. 7. See also Lindenberger, *Georg Trakl*, p. 84.

after Trakl's customary rewriting, finally separated into two distinct poems: "An den Knaben Elis" ("To the Boy Elis"—I, 84) and "Elis" (I, 85–86). Their publishing history attests to the self-sufficiency of each poem in the poet's mind. "An den Knaben Elis" appeared in the May 1 edition of *Der Brenner* while "Elis" did not appear there until July 1. Moreover, Trakl chose to include only the former in the volume published by Kurt Wolff, and at a recitation of his poetry in December, he read "Elis" without its counterpart. They appeared together for the first time in the posthumously published *Sebastian im Traum.* Neither poem has the sweep or multidimensionality of "Helian," although the figure of Elis appeared again in 1914 in a poem of comparable breadth, the second version of "Abendland" ("The Occident"—I, 403–408):

> Oder es läuten die Schritte
> Elis' durch den Hain,
> Den hyazinthenen,
> Wieder verhallend unter Eichen.
> O des Knaben Gestalt
> Geformt aus kristallenen Tränen
> Und nächtigen Schatten.
>
> Or the steps of Elis
> Resound through the grove,
> The hyacinthlike,
> Fading away again under oaks.
> O the boy's figure
> Formed from crystalline tears
> And gloomy shadows.

Trakl took over these lines almost intact into the drastically shortened final version of "Abendland" (I, 139–140), a poem whose image of "dying peoples" matches the scale of the cataclysm in "Helian."

"An den Knaben Elis," however, makes no attempt at such broad poetic statement. Its origins, moreover, are clearly traceable to legend and subsequent literary manifestations of the Elis figure in numerous works of various genres from the nineteenth and early twentieth centuries.[2] The legend itself had grown up around reports of an actual series of events in seventeenth- and eighteenth-century Sweden. In 1719 at the copper mines of Falun, the body of a miner was unearthed, his remains perfectly preserved for almost fifty years in the mine's fortuitous mixture of chemical elements. While this circumstance alone would probably have sufficed to ensure the survival of the story in legend, another aspect lent it added fascination. The youthful-appearing corpse could only be identified by the man's former fiancée, now an ancient spinster. The story had a strong appeal for the Romantics, who freely commandeered its nucleus while expanding and emphasizing various aspects. Achim von Arnim's poem personified the demonic allure of the mine's depths in the figure of a mountain queen. This figure also plays a role in E. T. A. Hoffmann's narrative masterpiece "The Mines at Falun." The main character, Elis Fröbom, at first a sailor, is lured from the sea to the mines by the mysteriously sinister miner Torbern. In Falun he soon loses his heart to the beautiful Ulla, the daughter of the mine's owner. Yet the demonic mountain queen claims Elis, when on the day of his wedding to Ulla, he descends the mineshaft to retrieve a precious jewel as his gift to his bride and is buried by an earthslide. The discovery of his corpse years later by Ulla is only a minor epilogue in Hoffmann's version.

The most nearly contemporary version of the legend for Trakl was Hugo von Hofmannsthal's drama "The Mine at Falun." In the first act, possibly the only part of the play which Trakl knew, the sailor Elis returns home after a long sea voyage and finds that his mother had died during his absence.[3] Despondent about this

[2]Wunberg summarizes the figure's repeated appearance in *Der frühe Hofmannsthal,* pp. 72–73.

[3]Because of the erratic course of the play's publication, the most Trakl could have known of Hofmannsthal's work was Acts I, IV, and V. The first act, published in 1900, was followed by Act V (1908), Act IV (1911), Act II (1918), and finally Act III (1932). I once more use the translations of Hofmannsthal in *Poems and Verse Plays.* All further references to this translation appear in the text.

turn of events as well as the earlier death of his father, Elis feels powerfully drawn to the depths where his "father and mother lie asleep" (315). With the mysterious aid of the old miner Torbern, Elis descends into the interior of a mountain and simultaneously into a timeless realm of the mind, belonging to neither life nor death, nor to dream consciousness. His first words to the radiant mountain queen he meets there are: "I dream, / And only dream that I'm awake." She answers: "No, Elis, / Now you have ceased to dream" (331). Elis' first stay in the subterranean realm is of short duration. While it strengthens and gives substance to the yearnings he had felt on earth, his attachment "to those up above" (353) remains too strong. He must return to earth, follow Torbern to the mines at Falun where he is to become a miner, and gradually approach a permanent union with the mountain queen.

The internal split in Hofmannsthal's Elis, developed and intensified in the rest of play by his growing attraction to an earthly sweetheart, comes to a crisis only at the end, but exists even in the first act. Two selves, one drawing him back to the mountain queen and one finally impelling him toward ordinary wedded bliss, conflict in Elis' character. Yet the maintenance of the split is precisely the condition upon which his further existence depends.[4] As long as he opts for neither self over the other and maintains the tension in his personality, he is able to survive. He brings about his own final end by destroying the equilibrium between the two forces. The dualism in Elis' character expresses the recurring tension in Hofmannsthal's early poetry and verse dramas—repeatedly dealing with the artist—between a life primarily grounded in aesthetic pleasures and a life determined by ethical responsibilities. An 1894 note in his diary describes the "split of the ego" as "the form of existence of the reproductive genius," and he later characterized the "Mine at Falun" as an "analysis of poetic existence."[5] For Hofmannsthal, the legend of Elis became a means for reflecting his notion of the poet's problematic existence.

[4]Wunberg, p. 80.
[5]As cited by Wunberg, p. 90.

In his typically abbreviated lyrical style, Trakl dismembers the legend and selectively borrows from it.[6] Yet while the borrowings are fragmentary and idiosyncratic to a greater degree than any of the previous versions, a primary element of the legend other than the name of the title figure is clearly evident. Trakl's poems are built around the dualism which is essential to the source as well as its adaptations. The dualism exists in Trakl's version between Elis, who in the opening lines of "An den Knaben Elis" falls downward toward another plateau of reality or level of existence, and the poem's speaker who remains behind, acting as commentator on this transition and a mediating eye into Elis' altered state.[7] Trakl captures a sense of immediacy and familiarity in this relationship by using second-person forms of address. The speaker addresses his words to Elis rather than to the reader who is thus put into the position of overhearing the poem. The relationship remains perceptibly intact until the poem's final line:

> Elis, wenn die Amsel im schwarzen Wald ruft,
> Dieses ist dein Untergang.
> Deine Lippen trinken die Kühle des blauen Felsenquells.
>
> Laß, wenn deine Stirne leise blutet
> Uralte Legenden
> Und dunkle Deutung des Vogelflugs.
>
> Du aber gehst mit weichen Schritten in die Nacht,
> Die voll purpurner Trauben hängt,
> Und du regst die Arme schöner im Blau.
>
> Ein Dornenbusch tönt,
> Wo deine mondenen Augen sind.
> O, wie lange bist, Elis, du verstorben.
>
> Dein Leib ist eine Hyazinthe,

[6]Cf. Heselhaus, p. 385.

[7]Jost Hermand comments on the existential levels in the poem: "Der Knabe Elis: Zum Problem der Existenzstufen bei Georg Trakl," *Monatshefte,* 51 (1959), 225–236.

In die ein Mönch die wächsernen Finger taucht.
Eine schwarze Höhle ist unser Schweigen,

Daraus bisweilen ein sanftes Tier tritt
Und langsam die schweren Lider senkt.
Auf deine Schläfen tropft schwarzer Tau,

Das letzte Gold verfallener Sterne.

Elis, when the black thrush in the black forest calls,
This is your downfall.
Your lips drink the coolness of the blue rock spring.

Endure, when your forehead quietly bleeds
Age-old legends
And dark interpretation of the birds' flight.

You however go with soft steps into the night,
Which hangs full of purple grapes,
And you move your arms more beautifully in the blue.

A thorn bush sounds,
Where your lunar eyes are.
O, how long have, Elis, you been dead.

Your body is a hyacinth,
Into which a monk dips his waxen fingers.
Our silence is a black cave,

Out of which occasionally steps a gentle animal
And slowly lowers its heavy lids.
Black dew drips upon your temples,

The last gold of expired stars.

Elis' downfall at the poem's inception suggests a beginning as well as an end—the gesture of drinking from the blue rock spring counterbalances the call of the black thrush. The bird's traditionally sinister color is not only offset by the water's propitious blue, but the German word for "spring" contains an even stronger suggestion than the English of source and origin. Trakl's poem "Geburt" ("Birth"—I, 115) envelops its title event in similar imagery:

> O, die Geburt des Menschen. Nächtlich rauscht
> Blaues Wasser im Felsengrund;
>
> O, the birth of man. Nightly
> Blue water murmurs in the rocky deep.

The second and third strophes of "An den Knaben Elis" function as signposts marking the direction from which Elis comes and the direction toward which he moves. Lines 4–6 depict Elis during the transition from one state of consciousness into another. From the time of the poem's publication, the apparent grammatical irregularities of the passage have caused confusion about its interpretation with the quandary centering around what appears to be a missing comma after "bleeds" (blutet) in line 4. Without this punctuation, the verb assumes an unusual transitive role. That is, it takes as objects the nouns in both lines 5 and 6, and the verb "Laß," here translated as "endure," becomes intransitive. One critic chose to supply the comma as if it were inadvertently omitted and translated the lines:

> When your forehead softly bleeds, refrain from
> Primeval legends
> And [the] dark interpretation of bird flight.

In a footnote, reference is made to an additional interpretive possibility in which "Laß" might be translated as "No more."[8]

Neither of these translations corresponds to Trakl's own idea about the lines, and both overlook the metanoia that is the essence of the poem. This passage is one of the very few for which

[8]Lindenberger, *Georg Trakl,* pp. 83 and 151.

the poet offered some valuable help. In a letter of May or June 1913 which was sent as an answer to his publisher concerning these very lines, Trakl's comments reveal an awareness and control of even the smallest details in his poetry: "My reply to your inquiry is that the passage of the sentence in question is entirely correct. The 'Laß' has here the meaning 'dulden' (endure); therefore no comma after 'bluten'" (I, 518). The conscious liberties Trakl takes with language are mild compared to the radical assault on grammatical structures by his contemporary in Berlin, August Stramm, the leading poet and theoretician of the circle of poets around the Expressionist periodical *Der Sturm*. Yet Trakl's slight grammatical improprieties rend new and previously unnoticed meanings from language. The forehead bleeding "age-old legends and dark interpretation of the birds' flight" is literally being emptied of structures and interpretations of reality inherent to the stage of existence from which Elis has fallen.

Hofmannsthal's Elis, in his first vision of the underworld for which he longs and where his parents already reside, expresses his longings in terms of blood imagery:

> House, open up! Yield up your threshold to me:
> It is a son who knocks! Open, deep vault
> Where hand in hand and hair entwined in hair
> Father and mother lie asleep. I'm here!
> Strip yourself bare, all you mysterious veins!
> Silently mine already shed their blood!
> [315]

Later, after his descent, he says to the mountain queen:

> A radiance, like a bloom, your hands emit.
> I feel as though my blood flowed out from me,
> Released, when I look there.
> [335]

In both cases, as a death wish in the first passage and as an irresistible attraction to the mountain queen in the second one, the loss of blood signifies for Hofmannsthal's Elis a release from mortal life. The process marks the transition to an underworld, whether it is death or a realm of unearthly pleasures or a purposefully ambiguous mixture of both.

The speaker in Trakl's poem gently enjoins Elis to let the process of destructuralization of consciousness, the rite of passage to the psychical underworld, take its course. The "quietly" bleeding forehead points to the gentle, nonviolent transition upon which Elis embarks. In the single other usage in Trakl's poetry of an intransitive "Laß," the speaker gives similar encouragement to surrender passively to a state of intoxication: "Endure, when drunk with wine your head sinks into the gutter" (I, 81–82). "Unterwegs" ("On the Way"), the poem which this line closes, was written in June 1913, shortly after the "Elis" poems were written. In the lines from "An den Knaben Elis," the youth is also "on the way" to an altered state of consciousness.

In the final lines of yet another poem from the same time period, Trakl again uses the term "legend" in a way not tied exclusively to meaning or content:

> Leise klirrt ein offenes Fenster; zu Tränen
> Rührt der Anblick des verfallenen Friedhofs am Hügel,
> Erinnerung an erzählte Legenden; doch manchmal erhellt sich die
> Seele,
> Wenn sie frohe Menschen denkt, dunkelgoldene Frühlingstage.
> [I, 79]

> Quietly an open window clanks; moved to
> Tears by the view of the decayed cemetery on the hill,
> Remembrance of legends told; yet sometimes the soul is illumined,
> When it thinks of happy people, dark golden spring days.

Parallel to the turn in the poem from darker to brighter thoughts, there is a contrast of modality of thought between memories channeled through "legends told" and those of the enlightened soul. In "An den Knaben Elis," the formal significance of both the "legend" and "interpretation" is primary. Elis' fall signifies a passage out of the perceptual state of seeing through, or by means of these structures of mind, into a realm which line 7 begins to depict.

Consistent with the atmosphere of the lightly bleeding forehead in line 4, Elis enters the night with "soft steps." Night is synonymous in this context with what has been called Trakl's blue world, a world juxtaposed to an ominous black world more fully explored in "Elis."[9] Physical movement is more beautiful in the blue medium—the body's freedom parallels the mind's liberation from its perceptual filters. To convey the loss of individuality in the world of both Elis poems, Trakl repeatedly singles out parts of the body seemingly isolated one from the other. By doing so, he creates a figure that exists less as a coherent individual than as a collection of components which lacks the binding sense of wholeness inherent to normal egoic consciousness, a figure "dead" (12) to the world he has left. The arms in line 9 seem oddly detached, not moving in obedience to some governing center, but rather in a free and more beautiful manner under their own volition.

Hofmannsthal's mountain queen, in a long passage directed at Elis, remarks about the paradox of the earth's interior which encloses and sustains her while it decomposes the remains of mortals:

> I know you never sleep for long, but when
> You do lie down to seek unbroken sleep
> You are no longer you: the depth of earth,
> That like a resonant shell encloses me,
> Dissolves your limbs, estranged from one another,
> And from your breast great trees rise up, and corn
> Strikes roots within the hollows of your eyes.
> [337]

Where the mountain queen is at home, mortal man decays. Trakl's imagery plays on a similar paradox between sustenance

[9]Lindenberger, *Georg Trakl,* p. 83.

and dissolution, but by combining the paradoxical elements in Elis' underworld existence rather than separating them. He is both dissolved and sustained in this blue world. The queen's baroque vision of the corn drawing nourishment from the corpse's eyes seems, moreover, to be a starkly realistic prefiguration of Trakl's imagery in lines 10–11:

> A thorn bush sounds,
> Where your lunar eyes are.

While both plants reach a common underground source and both extend from this source above the surface of the earth, the image of the bush is richer in connotation since it draws on the biblical account of God's message to Moses through the burning bush. The thorn bush of the poem has no religious message, however, but brings echoes of Elis' preternatural state into the world of the speaker.

The relationship between the bush and Elis' "lunar eyes" may be adequately interpreted in a concrete or figurative sense, each corroborating rather than contradicting the other. Concretely, the imagery evokes a surrealistic configuration in which the thorn bush is spatially superimposed on the eyes, the sound coming from the organ of visual perception. A variation of synesthesia and, as such, appropriate to Elis' altered state, the image reverses the elements of the "gentle insanity" in "Helian": "shattered eyes in black mouths." Here, vision seemed somehow embedded in the site of vocal articulation, while in "An den Knaben Elis," sound issues from the organs of vision. When "where" in line 11 is read figuratively, the relationship between the images changes from spatial congruence to equal significance. Elis' eyes share in the symbolism of the biblical bush as a natural link to a preternatural existence. They communicate with the speaker from Elis' blue world.

Further religious overtones resonate in lines 13–14, and the identification of Elis' body with the hyacinth, a flower commonly found on graves, places him in death's proximity.[10] Yet while conventional notions of religion and death are obliquely woven into the poem's imagery, their conventional significations are subordinate to their function in further delineating Elis' preternatural state. Elis is a Christ-figure only in the sense that he exists beyond mortality. He is dead only in the sense that he has characteristics in common with the dead of mortal man—his physical absence, the bodily dismemberment and permeability associated with a corpse's decaying state. The lines contain the outline of a quasi-religious ritual in which a monk penetrates Elis' body—echoes of the crucified Christ pierced by the soldier's lance are discernible here—in order to enter into and to share his existence. It is a form of secular communion between the monk and Elis, an image illustrating the bond between the speaker and Elis.

With the word "our" in line 15, the presence of the bond is explicitly articulated for the first and only time in the poem. But even though this happens only once, the reader is aware from the beginning of a dualism, a dualism between mediated figure and mediating consciousness. The mediating consciousness or the unspoken *I* of the speaker is as essential to Trakl's version of the Elis legend as the figure which it addresses as its counterpart *You*.

By using second-person forms, Trakl created a unique perspective on the Elis figure and a unique variant of the legendary material. Had the poetic text carried through the third-person perspective of the title, it would have had expressly to verbalize and objectify both elements of the figure's split character. That is, the earthbound Elis as well as the one attracted to a subterranean realm would have had to be realized in the written text. Trakl probably sensed that this solution could slip from poetry into narrative prose. Instead, he used a situation of direct address,

[10]E. L. Marson compares Trakl's Elis with the mythological figure Hyakinthos, "a youth [who was] beloved of a divinity, and as a result died and was transformed, positively as it were, into a flower" ("Whom the Gods Love: A New Look at Trakl's Elis," *German Life and Letters*, NS 29 [1976], 372).

letting the *You* of the poem embody that one self of Elis pulled downward and letting the speaker embody the earthbound self. While Elis goes "down," the eyes which watch him remain above. Together the *I*, implied by the speaker's voice and visual perspective, and the *You* called Elis comprise both parts of that split character which legend and literature depict physically as one figure.

Trakl's Elis remains throughout the poem an apparently unresponsive partner in what is in essence a situation of dialogue. It is, however, a unique silence that binds him to the speaker:

> Our silence is a black cave,
>
> Out of which occasionally steps a gentle animal
> And slowly lowers its heavy lids.

Normal communicational modes between Elis and the speaker are closed. Silence and blackness are negative measurements, pure absences of sound and sight; a cave is a void, defined by its very emptiness. Although they are bound by an image that indicates the absence and lack of communicational signals, the bond between Elis and the speaker "occasionally" becomes fertile. A "gentle animal" emerges from the womblike cavern of their silence.

To interpret this fragile offspring as a poem is perhaps to overstep the bounds of justified speculation. Trakl at least remained characteristically unhelpful. Yet Hofmannsthal's allusion to his own Elis-drama as an "analysis of poetic existence" lends a kind of tenuous evidence for this interpretation. The most that can be said with any degree of certainty about Trakl's poem is that the silence between the *You* and the speaker—a single split figure in the poem's predecessors—is creative. The "gentle animal" is the fruition of their bond. Moreover, when at the end of the poem, Elis begins to fade, the speaker's voice also quickly ceases. His mediating consciousness makes no shift in the last lines to comment on Elis' absence from a third-person perspective. As Hofmannsthal's split character can exist only in a state of tension, so too can Trakl's speaker exist only in a relationship of direct address to its "Elis."

"Kaspar Hauser Lied"

Innsbruck had not always been a haven for Trakl. In April 1912, about a month prior to his first meeting with Ficker, he began a probationary military service in the garrison hospital there. A letter to Buschbeck at the time expressed his attitude toward the city in no uncertain terms:

> I would never have imagined that I would have to live through this already difficult time in the most brutal and vulgar city that exists on the face of this burdened and accursed earth. And when I think, moreover, that an alien will will perhaps cause me to suffer here for a decade, I can fall into a convulsion of tears of the most desperate hopelessness.
>
> Why the vexation? I will, in any case, always be a poor Kaspar Hauser.
>
> [I, 487]

Kaspar Hauser was probably as familiar to Buschbeck as his friend's overwrought state. This historical figure had through public controversy and literary treatment grown to nearly mythical proportions since his mysterious appearance and death in the early nineteenth century. Particularly in a novel by Jakob Wassermann (1908), the fictionalized version most nearly contemporary to Trakl, Hauser had come to stand for the innocent brought to ruin in the city by its inhabitants' "indolent hearts."[11] In November 1913, more than a year and a half after its mention in the letter, Trakl cast the figure in his own "Kaspar Hauser Lied" ("Kaspar Hauser Song"—I, 95).

[11] *Caspar Hauser oder die Trägheit des Herzens* (Stuttgart and Leipzig: Deutsche Verlagsanstalt, 1908). The subtitle of Wassermann's novel translates: "The Indolence of the Heart." Page references to the novel appear in the text and refer to the translation: *Caspar Hauser: The Enigma of a Century,* trans. Caroline Newton (New York: Liveright, 1928).

Wassermann's novel, a "literary narration" of the "actual facts as they occurred," was the primary source for Trakl's imagery (p. ix).[12] Yet Trakl's borrowings from history and fiction were every bit as idiosyncratic as they were in "An den Knaben Elis." The real Kaspar Hauser, oddly enough, spent most of his early life where Elis Fröbom ended his days—under the earth separated from almost all human contact. When in 1828, at the age of sixteen or seventeen, Hauser mysteriously appeared on the streets of Nuremberg, he could scarcely walk or talk and would take only bread and water as nourishment. According to a letter which he carried with him, ostensibly from a foster parent, the boy had originally been a foundling and had been raised in total isolation. No longer able to afford his keep, the writer continued, he had set the boy loose upon the mercy of the world. The boy's later recollections, however, were of long years spent in a dark hole with almost total human neglect.

Wassermann's novel begins with Hauser's appearance in Nuremberg and centers on his painfully belated process of maturation in the hands of partly misguided, partly ill-willed guardians. Controversy surrounded the boy almost from the beginning. Some, including his most powerful protector, a high-ranking magistrate, believed that he was the rightful heir to the throne of

[12]Critical opinions about influence vary in the placement of their emphasis. Gottfried Stix and Regine Blass recognize a primary influence by Wassermann (Gottfried Stix, *Trakl und Wassermann* [Rome: Edizioni di Storia e Letteratura, 1968]; Regine Blass, "Kaspar Hauser Lied," *Die Dichtung Georg Trakls: Von der Trivialsprache zum Kunstwerk* [Berlin: Erich Schmidt, 1968], pp. 223–235). Hans-Georg Kemper gives more weight to Trakl's originality: "Just as some verses . . . are reminiscent of Wassermann's novel, others cannot be understood on the basis of this source" ("Trakl-Forschung der sechziger Jahre," p. 556). For Walther Killy, "When Georg Trakl wrote his 'Kaspar Hauser Lied,' he probably had in mind the verses of Verlaine which bear the title 'Gaspard Hauser chante' " ("Der Tränen nächtige Bilder: Trakl und Benn," *Wandlungen des lyrischen Bildes*, 5th expanded ed. [Göttingen: Vandenhoeck & Ruprecht, 1967], p. 116). See also Herbert Thiele, "Das Bild des Menschen in den Kaspar-Hauser-Gedichten von Paul Verlaine und Georg Trakl," *Wirkendes Wort*, 14 (1964), 351–356, and Ernst Erich Metzner, "Die dunkle Klage des Gerechten—Poésie pure?: Rationalität und Intentionalität in Georg Trakls Spätwerk, dargestellt am Beispiel 'Kaspar Hauser Lied,' " *Germanisch-romanische Monatsschrift*, 24 (1974), 446–472.

Baden who had been the victim of court machinations. Partisans of this view found persuasive evidence for their case in the several attempts on the boy's life. He finally did fall victim to the knife of an unknown murderer in 1833. Others, even some of his various tutors, became convinced that his innocence and naïveté were the mask of a lazy swindler. Wassermann was convinced of Hauser's royal heritage, but his interest in the material was on a more general human level. The focal point of his novel was, as he wrote, "the representation of the development of a human being and the responsibility of the uncomprehending world for the destruction of a human soul" (p. xxv). For Wassermann, as one of his characters declares near the end of the book, all of the "indolent hearts" held final responsibility for Kaspar's death.

Trakl's "Kaspar Hauser Lied" is perhaps the most transparent of his poems with regard to its roots in fact and fiction. The real Kaspar Hauser's story left its unmistakable imprint on the poem. Yet it has also been thoroughly appropriated into a lyrical idiom just as unmistakably of Trakl's own stamp:

Er wahrlich liebte die Sonne, die purpurn den Hügel hinabstieg,
Die Wege des Walds, den singenden Schwarzvogel
Und die Freude des Grüns.

Ernsthaft war sein Wohnen im Schatten des Baums
Und rein sein Antlitz.
Gott sprach eine sanfte Flamme zu seinem Herzen:
O Mensch!

Stille fand sein Schritt die Stadt am Abend;
Die dunkle Klage seines Munds:
Ich will ein Reiter werden.

Ihm aber folgte Busch und Tier,
Haus und Dämmergarten weißer Menschen
Und sein Mörder suchte nach ihm.

Frühling und Sommer und schön der Herbst
Des Gerechten, sein leiser Schritt

The Poet's Madness

An den dunklen Zimmern Träumender hin.
Nachts blieb er mit seinem Stern allein;

Sah, daß Schnee fiel in kahles Gezweig
Und im dämmernden Hausflur den Schatten des Mörders.

Silbern sank des Ungebornen Haupt hin.

He verily loved the sun which, purple, descended the hill,
The paths of the wood, the singing blackbird
And the joy of the green.

Earnestly he lived in the shadow of the tree
And his countenance was pure.
God spoke a soft flame to his heart:
O Man!

Silently, his step found the city in the evening.
The dark lament of his mouth:
I want to become a rider.

But bush and animal followed him,
House and dusky garden of white men
And his murderer sought him out.

Spring and summer and beautiful the fall
Of the just one, his quiet step
Past the dark rooms of dreaming ones.
Nights he remained with his star alone;

Saw, that snow fell into bare branches
And in the hall's half-light, the shadow of the murderer.

Silver, the head of the unborn one sank away.

Pared to a minimum of language and void of the novel's melodrama, the skeletal frame of the legend is, however, still visible behind Trakl's taciturn lines. In only one aspect does the poem make an apparent departure from the frame. Kaspar Hauser initially appears in the imagery of the poem on an Arcadian landscape, a background seemingly far removed from the subterranean cell of history. Yet from the time soon after he appeared in Nuremberg, chroniclers of his story viewed these early years of isolation through the roseate glasses of a Rousseauistic primitivism. As early as 1832, G. F. Daumer, Hauser's first tutor, described him as "the living proof that man is created noble but corrupted by society."[13] The privation and neglect of the early years assumed an entirely different hue when they were seen in terms of preconceived notions of a Natural Man, a theoretical species of which Kaspar Hauser became a living example. The first two strophes of Trakl's poem are not so much a departure from history as they are an adaptation to this interpretation of it.

The structure of the first strophe—its adherence to empirical reality, its uncomplicated syntax, its simple enumeration—matches the straightforward, uncomplicated relationship of Kaspar Hauser to his environment. The essence of the sun image in the opening line can be traced to a particular scene in Wassermann's novel.[14] Late in the afternoon of an excursion into the country with his guardians, Kaspar wakes up from a short nap in time to observe a magnificent sunset: "It was a beautiful sight. The purple disk was descending as though it were cutting its way into the earth along the border of the sky" (p. 69). Kaspar, whose eyes for many years had been accustomed to the darkness of his cell, is understandably moved by this sight, to which Wassermann devotes a full paragraph. Watching his reactions, Daumer reflects: "So may Adam . . . have trembled as his first night broke in Paradise" (p. 69). In response to his questioning, Daumer links the sun to a concept of God which he had a few days earlier begun to inscribe on the spiritual *tabula rasa* of this latter-day Adam. Kaspar, still skeptical of anything beyond his

[13]A. F. Bance, "The Kaspar Hauser Legend and Its Literary Survival," *German Life and Letters,* NS 28 (1974/75), 203.

[14]Stix, pp. 34–35.

perceptual grasp, replies nevertheless with total artlessness: "Caspar loves the sun" (p. 70).

The images of the blackbird and the tree and the vocative "O Man!" in line 7 have counterparts in the novel, each, however, less convincing as models than the sunset scene.[15] Even though the same legendary watermark has been impressed into the fabric of both works, the poem is not a miniature of the novel or a kind of lyrical script whose every sign can be deciphered by referring to the more expansive version. The poem is, as the title states, a "Kaspar Hauser Song," not "Kaspar Hauser's Song."[16] Especially in the first two strophes, the images are as straightforward as the mode of existence of the figure in their midst.

Trakl is as much concerned here as he was in "An den Knaben Elis" with capturing a quality or mode of existence. The qualifying words of these lines, the adverbs and adjectives, "verily," "earnestly," and "pure," have special prominence and stress Kaspar's total openness and ingenuousness toward his surroundings. In two letters written on consecutive days to Ficker, Trakl singles out the first two of these modifiers as matters of last-minute concern to him before the poem's publication (I, 526–527). His vacillations about the use and placement of these qualifying words indicate their importance to the poem's final shape. The manner of Kaspar's "living" is as artless as that of Wassermann's Kaspar. His openness, moreover, is directed toward metaphysical realities as well as physical ones. God's words of recognition find their way directly to the "heart." Trakl combines in this image the legendary Kaspar's initial ignorance of language with his purported hyperacute sensitivity, here a sort of sixth sense for the supernatural.

In the third strophe, Kaspar literally steps out of Arcadia into the city. He passes from a stationary condition of "living" into one filled with movement and progression. His time in the world which he has entered, measured out by the flow of its seasons,

[15] Stix, pp. 50, 55, 68–71.

[16] Cf. Killy, *Über Georg Trakl,* pp. 5–6, and Metzner, 452–455.

expires in a wintry scene that recalls the December death of the real Kaspar. "Death" however is an imprecise term for the end of Trakl's Kaspar: "Silver, the head of the unborn one sank away." Kaspar, the "unborn one"—a "stranger" in a variant line (II, 163)—exits from an alien world into which he was never really born.

Earlier in the poem, as the twice-repeated image of his "step" in lines 8 and 15 indicates, Kaspar seems to be in transit through this world whose inhabitants' dreamlike state (16) contrasts with his own hyperconsciousness. He moves past their "dark rooms" and remains essentially alone (17). In Wassermann's novel, Kaspar's heightened sensitivities supply his detractors with concrete grounds for their suspicions. Trakl's Kaspar too brings into the city evidence of such sensitivities in the form of an animal magnetism. And in close conjunction with the images of "bush and animal" that follow him are images of those that pursue and hunt him (11–13).

The letter which the historical Kaspar Hauser carried with him was addressed to a cavalry captain and urged that the boy be allowed to become a soldier. Apparently in order that this wish might appear to be the boy's own, his keeper had taught him the single rote phrase: "I should like to become a horseman like my father." While Wassermann capitalizes on the irony of the boy's repeated use of these words in every situation, there is no internal evidence of this irony in Trakl's poem:

> The dark lament of his mouth:
> I want to become a rider.

Still, the irony of the words in the legend clings to them in the poetic text almost as if it had become intrinsic to the passage. And in terms of Trakl's own situation when he alluded to himself as a "poor Kaspar Hauser," an ironic interpretation becomes a distinct possibility. The words in Kaspar's mouth can mean everything and thus mean nothing. They are spoken by him but were not conceived by him nor do they stem from his own volition. "I want" is in Kaspar's case really "He wants." And Trakl's identification with Kaspar Hauser in his letter seems to some extent to rest on his fear that an "alien will" (meaning the military authorities) may be the cause of an extended stay in Innsbruck.

Read without irony, a reading that matches the poetic figure's own artlessness, the words must be taken at their face value. They are the lamentful wish of the youth who has just embarked upon a painful transit through an alien world. In words of total candor, Kaspar longs for the means to shorten this passage. The murderer in Trakl's poem brings the wish to fulfillment and hastens Kaspar's departure from a world whose terms of existence were not his own. As he came into it in the evening, so he departs from it in the darkness as well. As if illuminated by the moon, another transient in the evening sky, Kaspar's "silver" head sinks "down" (or "away"—*hin*) in the poem's final line.

Trakl's remark to Buschbeck that he would "always" be a Kaspar Hauser suggests a sense of identification that was not tied to passing circumstances. To a Swiss patron of *Der Brenner,* he once reportedly asserted, "I was only just half born," a remark that recalls his reaction to Kraus's parable of seven-month children.[17] For Kaspar Hauser, the "unborn one" in Trakl's poem, birth meant only the physical entry into the world. Lacking was the simultaneous entry into a network of human relationships in which self-identity could be realized and developed. Because he was never fully born in this double sense, others remained "dreamers" to him as if their lives crossed his without intermingling. And in the absence of mutual assertion, recognition, and response, his own sense of identity remained equally nebulous. This appears to have been the heart of Trakl's affinity for Kaspar Hauser. Yet for Trakl, the sense of not being fully born reflected an undoing of self-identity as much as a lack of its development. Hauser lived from the beginning outside the rudimentary network

[17]Reference to the remark is found in: Hans Limbach, "Begegnung mit Georg Trakl," *Erinnerung an Georg Trakl,* p. 115.

of human relationships that establish and stabilize identity. For the poet, as the prose poems more tellingly reveal, a self-identity too heavily dependent on this network became a false self, an imposed structure of personality which nurtured the seeds of its own destruction.

"An einen Frühverstorbenen"

Late in December 1913, Trakl apostrophized yet another figure in one of his poems, a figure with no apparent roots in legend which he simply called the "Frühverstorbene" (I, 117). The title of the poem in German is as simple as the translation, "To One Who Died Early," is awkward:

O, der schwarze Engel, der leise aus dem Innern des Baums trat,
Da wir sanfte Gespielen am Abend waren,
Am Rand des bläulichen Brunnens.
Ruhig war unser Schritt, die runden Augen in der braunen Kühle
des Herbstes,
O, die purpurne Süße der Sterne.

Jener aber ging die steinernen Stufen des Mönchsbergs hinab,
Ein blaues Lächeln im Antlitz und seltsam verpuppt
In seine stillere Kindheit und starb;
Und im Garten blieb das silberne Antlitz des Freundes zurück,
Lauschend im Laub oder im alten Gestein.

Seele sang den Tod, die grüne Verwesung des Fleisches
Und es war das Rauschen des Walds,
Die inbrünstige Klage des Wildes.
Immer klangen von dämmernden Türmen die blauen Glocken des
Abends.

Stunde kam, da jener die Schatten in purpurner Sonne sah,
Die Schatten der Fäulnis in kahlem Geäst;
Abend, da an dämmernder Mauer die Amsel sang,
Der Geist des Frühverstorbenen stille im Zimmer erschien.

O, das Blut, das aus der Kehle des Tönenden rinnt,

Blaue Blume; o die feurige Träne
Geweint in die Nacht.

Goldene Wolke und Zeit. In einsamer Kammer
Lädst du öfter den Toten zu Gast,
Wandelst in trautem Gespräch unter Ulmen den grünen Fluß hinab.

O, the black angel which quietly stepped from inside the tree,
When we were gentle playmates in the evening,
On the edge of the bluish well.
Tranquil was our step, the round eyes in the brown coolness of
autumn,
O, the purple sweetness of the stars.

But that one went down the stone stairs of the Mönchsberg,
A blue smile on his face and strangely pupated
Into his quieter childhood and died;
And in the garden the silvery face of the friend stayed behind.
Eavesdropping in the foliage or in the old stone.

Soul sang the death, the green decay of the flesh
And there was the murmuring of the woods,
The ardent lament of the wild animal.
Ceaselessly from the darkening towers rang the blue bells of
evening.

Hour came, when that one saw the shadows in the purple sun,
The shadows of putrefaction in bare branches;
Evening, when on the darkening wall the black thrush sang,
The spirit of the one who died early silently appeared in the room.

O, the blood which flows from the throat of the intoning one,
Blue flower; o the fiery tear
Wept into the night.

Golden cloud and time. In lonely chamber
You often invite the dead one,
Amble in intimate talk, under the elms, down the green river.

Elements of structure and imagery recur with such regularity in

Trakl's poetry that more than one critic has commented on the "one poem" underlying his entire production.[18] Yet attempts to distill consistent meaning from similar or even identical structures and images over the entire spectrum of this production have been largely futile. Each poem presents a pattern and arrangement of elements that are familiar, but unique. It is within this tension between the familiar and the unique that a poem like "An einen Frühverstorbenen" is situated.

The fundamental signature of the poem is that of departure and return. Death, as the exit from mortality, appears initially in the unusually straightforward guise of an allegorical "black angel." Its effect is apparent only in the second strophe, however, where it removes the mortal presence of one of the poem's two main figures from the poetic landscape. The physical bond between the playmates is severed, the tranquil unity of their "step" interrupted. Echoing Trakl's "An den Knaben Elis," the departing figure descends while the "friend" remains behind (9). Later in the poem, he returns in "spirit" (18) to the song of the same bird—the black thrush—that called Elis to his demise. The poetic formulation of this "death" and of the friend's perception of it differ, however, from those aspects of the Elis poem.

In "An einen Frühverstorbenen," the path of death's descent begins on the "Mönchsberg," a hill in Salzburg which Trakl used in the title of a poem written a few months earlier (I, 94). Although there may be autobiographical significance hidden in the poet's choice of sites, the name "Monk's Hill" is in itself appropriate as a departure point for "a withdrawal from the world."[19] The death that the figure undergoes is represented by a combination of images of descent and regression. The movement is existential as well as spatial as the figure climbs down and into a chrysalid state. In this latter image, death acquires the semblance of

[18]See especially Martin Heidegger, "Georg Trakl: Eine Erörterung seines Gedichts," *Merkur,* 7 (1953), 226–258, and Killy, *Über Georg Trakl,* p. 52.

[19]Lindenberger, *Georg Trakl,* p. 97.

transformation—pupation is both death and life, a departure as well as an anticipated return.

With death's removal of the one figure's physical presence, the poem turns to the friend left behind. In contrast to the speaker of the Elis poem whose mediation of Elis' preternatural state was primarily visual, the friend perceives the phenomenon of his companion's death by listening. What he hears when he eavesdrops "in the foliage or in the old stone" is the song of death that all of nature sings in the third strophe. Precisely at the midpoint of the poem, these four lines mark a midpoint between departure and return. The word "Soul," without the limits imposed by either definite or indefinite article, hovers like an embracing principle over all the single sounds in nature's chorus, those of the forest and the wild animal as well as those of man's bells.

Up to this point the poem has left little room for ambiguity about the separate identities of its two main figures. They exist intimately but distinctly in the shared activity and in the perspective of the first strophe. They are closely attached but, at the same time, a plural identity, conjoined and separated as an *I* and a *You* by the pronoun *We*. The second strophe shifts the perspectives on both figures. They appear on the poetic landscape in a third-person perspective, one which strengthens the sense of alienation and distance which the departure of the one figure creates. This figure has become merely "that one" to the speaker, barely recognizable and identifiable by an impersonal pronoun that indicates nothing more than gender and location. It is little more than a nod to the reader by the speaker in the general direction of the figure. On the other hand, the implied *I* of the first strophe becomes simply the "friend" in the second strophe. It is as if without the *You,* the *I* can no longer be an *I*—the speaker is estranged not only from his counterpart *You,* but from himself as an *I* as well.

While both figures recede from the poem in the third strophe, either one or perhaps both reappear in the following lines. The reference to "the one who died early" (18) is clear enough—his return as a "spirit" has been anticipated by the image of pupation earlier in the poem. With the figure in line 15, however, an ambiguity enters the poem and begins to erode this certainty with which the reader can distinguish one figure from the other. An uncertainty arises as to whether lines 15 and 16 allude to the friend left behind who, upon perceiving mysterious omens in nature, is confronted by the reappearance of "the one who died early." Or does "that one" again refer to the figure in the poem's title as it did in line 6? Such consistency is suspect in a poem of changing names and perspectives. The "intoning one" in line 19 blurs even further the distinction between the two figures. It appears, in fact, that dualism has been abandoned. The poem first shifts its cast from the two separate but unified figures of the first strophe to the estranged figures of the second strophe. On the other side of the pivotal third strophe—that is, after the "death" of one figure—a unity without separation begins to emerge, first in the ambiguous "that one" and then in the equally ambiguous "intoning one." The final strophe appears to redefine a dualism: "You often invite the dead one." For the moment of this line, there are again two figures on the poetic landscape, figures which with another twist of perspective can be traced to the original two. But the dualism is short-lived. The subject of the final line—an unspoken *You* apparent only in the inflected form of the German verb *Wandelst*—is singular: "Amble in intimate talk, under the elms, down the green river." The walk that had begun as a "step" in unison of two figures is continued at the poem's end by a singular *You* that has absorbed both poles of the poem's dualism. The one remaining sign of this dualism is the "talk" or dialogue (*Gespräch*) in which the solitary figure is engaged.

The poem registers the effect of the reappearance of "the one who died early" by an abrupt shift of tense in line 19, an effect that lasts for the rest of the poem. To this point, the past tense had acted as a buffer between the poem's imagery and the reader, a kind of time barrier which eased the resistance to this hallucinatory world. As it does in legend and fairy tale, the past tense here allows Trakl's poem to manipulate and overcome the reader's normative structures of consciousness. When the shift to the present tense does occur, the effect is jarring. Yet the aim of this jolt is not to alienate the reader and thus reaffirm normative structures of consciousness that the past tense had helped to suspend. It is rather to authenticate with all possible immediacy and presentness the truth of the poem's imagery that merges one identity with another. The shift in tense is part of what one critic has named Trakl's "poetics of truth-telling," a facet readily verified by Trakl's letters.[20] It asserts the physical and temporal presence of the singular *You* as the final heir to the poem's merging identities.

[20]James Rolleston, "The Expressionist Moment: Heym, Trakl and the Problem of the Modern," *Studies in Twentieth Century Literature*, 1 (Fall 1976), 70.

5

Conflict and the Imperative of Transformation: The Prose Poems

In Salzburg during the month from mid-June to mid-July 1913, Trakl's usual depressed mood at home became all the worse when Grete failed to arrive from Berlin for an expected visit. By July 15 he was in Vienna, again working at a minor civil service post which, to no one's surprise, he held for only a few days. His own distaste for the menial tasks of the job were undoubtedly strengthened by renewed contacts with Karl Kraus, whom he had met a year earlier.[1] In the latter half of August, Trakl joined Kraus and some friends—the Fickers among them—on a holiday trip to Venice. The extent of Kraus's influence on Trakl at the time can be gauged from an acrimonious letter written by Robert Müller, a member of the *Brenner* circle, to Buschbeck in early September complaining about Trakl's withdrawal of his poems from a planned anthology. The anthology had been meant originally only for young Viennese poets and Müller had had to exert pressure to have Trakl included. It no doubt added to Müller's vexation that he had in the spring of 1912 recommended the unknown Trakl to Ludwig von Ficker and had been the first to place

[1]A card dated July 18 and sent to Ludwig von Ficker's son Florian was jointly signed by Trakl and Kraus. In a letter to Ficker written on one of the immediately following days, Trakl describes his unpaid position as "intensely loathsome" (I, 521).

a Trakl poem in Ficker's hands. Suspecting Kraus's role in Trakl's withdrawal from the anthology, the doubly betrayed Müller harshly condemned this more powerful patron as "a cripple in body and soul" (II, 706–707).

Whatever the truth of the matter may have been, Kraus was himself known for his sharply critical journalistic style. One of his favorite targets was the writer who compromised his art by subordinating it to nonartistic purposes. To those who found themselves on his side, he was a master at detecting and attacking a split in a writer between his life and art. It may have been the perceived absence of this split that attracted him to Trakl. Trakl, whose inability to compromise extended at times even to relationships with his friends, counted among the few contemporary poets Kraus admired.[2] His *Fackel* carried an invitation to subscribe to a volume of Trakl's poetry several months before the first collection, *Gedichte,* had even found a publisher (II, 683).

Many years later, in 1928, Kraus published in *Die Fackel* several poems whose author he initially believed was a mental patient in a Rumanian asylum. Public attention had first been directed at these poems by an asylum psychiatrist who, as Kraus reported, believed that insanity sometimes heightened artistic ability in previously uncreative people to the point that they only became "poets and artists in the asylum."[3] This particular patient turned out to be a poor illustration of his theory, however. It was discovered that the "poet" possessed only an astonishing memory for lines of verse which he had memorized many years before

[2]Heinrich noted that Trakl's essential character (*Wesen*) was entirely one with appearances and that he had little talent for what he termed the "mimicry which we call our capability of adaptation" (*Erinnerung an Georg Trakl,* p. 106). An exchange of letters during the summer of 1913 between Trakl and Ficker plainly indicates that the poet could at times treat even his benefactor harshly.

[3]Kraus, "Aus Redaktion und Irrenhaus," *Die Fackel,* Nos. 781–786 (June, 1928), p. 95. This idea has recurred regularly in psychiatry. For example: "Quite a few poets, writers and scientists worked better after going through a schizophrenia. In some of them their talent was manifested only after the disease" (Eugeniusz Brzezicki, "Über Schizophrenien, die zu einem sozialen Aufstieg führen—I. Mitteilung: Positive Wandlung der ganzen Persönlichkeit," *Confinia psychiatrica,* 5 [1962], 187).

and whose author was unknown. Kraus's enthusiasm remained undiminished, however, and he compared the poems favorably with the poetry of Claudius, Hölderlin, Mörike, Trakl, and Else Lasker-Schüler, or as he put it, "the highest peaks of German lyric poetry."[4] What drew Kraus to these particular poets was undoubtedly his concern for language, an aggressive concern described by one commentator as the "battle against the false facade of language, against every pattern, because in them the truth of the word suffocates in the lie of cliché."[5]

Trakl, for his part, knew Kraus's essays and had dedicated the major poem "Psalm" to him, and in June 1913 his short poem "Karl Kraus" (I, 123) had appeared in *Der Brenner:*

> Weißer Hohepriester der Wahrheit,
> Kristallne Stimme, in der Gottes eisiger Odem wohnt,
> Zürnender Magier,
> Dem unter flammendem Mantel der blaue Panzer des Kriegers
> klirrt.
>
> White high priest of truth,
> Crystalline voice, in which God's icy breath lives,
> Angry magician,
> Whose blue-warrior armament clatters under the flaming coat.[6]

Trakl wrote a short poem "An Novalis" (I, 324–326), but Kraus is the only other literary figure directly addressed in the title of one of his poems. For Trakl, as for many others, Kraus's aggressive journalism uncovered the hypocrisies of Austrian culture, exposing its sham to the light of truth. Through the medium of language,

[4]Kraus, p. 97.

[5]Adalbert Schmidt, *Dichtung und Dichter Österreichs im 19. und 20. Jahrhundert* (Salzburg: Bergland-Buch, 1964), p. 253.

[6]In June and July 1913, *Der Brenner* published three issues with comments on Karl Kraus by a large number of writers. Besides Trakl, these included Else Lasker-Schüler, Richard Dehmel, Frank Wedekind, Thomas Mann, Peter Altenberg, Adolf Loos, Carl Dallago, Arnold Schönberg, K. B. Heinrich, Karl Hauer, Hermann Broch, Stefan Zweig, Alfred Mombert, Franz Werfel, Oskar Kokoschka, and others.

this "angry magician" whom Trakl esteemed so highly attempted to transform by reforming.

Trakl's own poetry continued to return to variations on the process of inner transformation. The first of his four prose poems, all written during the nine-month period from September 1913 to May 1914, is entitled "Verwandlung des Bösen" ("Transformation of Evil"—I, 97–98). Its technique of character portrayal and theme relate it more closely to the long, difficult prose poems of 1914, "Traum und Umnachtung" ("Dream and Derangement"—I, 147–150) and "Offenbarung und Untergang" ("Revelation and Demise"—I, 168–170) than to "Winternacht" ("Winter Night"—I, 128), which follows it chronologically (December 1913).

"Winternacht" has by far the clearest outline of a traditional prose plot: at midnight on a snowy evening, a drunken figure leaves the companionship of his fellow drinkers and stumbles out alone into the wintry landscape. Under the "evil signs" (5) of his stars, the wanderer charges like a soldier through the bitter cold. Juxtaposed to the torment of the freezing weather is an inner burning and laceration: "Frost and smoke. A white starry shirt burns the shoulders wearing it and God's vultures mangle your metal heart" (14–15). Crushed between the exterior and interior sources of torment, the wanderer surrenders to exhaustion and falls asleep in the snow. He awakens unharmed, however, the next morning to the sound of the village bells and watches the sun rise in the east. Although all of the prose poems have a strongly autobiographical cast, "Winternacht," so claimed one critic, arose from a specific incident in Trakl's life.[7] The others are most conspicuously related by a common thematic center, the family.

In "Winternacht" the poem's speaker addresses a single character in the familiar second-person form and places it within a stable frame of reference. In the second, fourth and fifth paragraphs of "Verwandlung des Bösen," a figure addressed as *You*

[7] "It is a poem from Trakl's life in the literal sense" (Eduard Lachmann, *Kreuz und Abend,* p. 56).

also appears, but the disjointed landscape resembles Trakl's lyric poetry more than conventional prose. The various figures and scenes of the first paragraph appear to be the hallucinatory reveries of a "leper" in the poem's opening lines as he "listens attentively" to the tumultuous display of imagery in his own mind. The third paragraph more explicitly depicts a dream sequence, a sequence that apparently takes place in the psyche of the figure addressed in the second-person form. Lending an element of cohesion to the disparate array of imagery are varied statements of a juxtaposition of psychic forces with an ultimate source and gathering point in the speaker. "Verwandlung des Bösen" is both monologue and dialogue in a manner similar to, yet more complex than that of "An den Knaben Elis"; it is the dialogue of the unspoken *I* with multiple facets of itself. While the first-person pronoun remains unspoken in the prose poems until "Offenbarung und Untergang," it is not unheard.

It poses the central question in the second paragraph of "Verwandlung des Bösen": "What compels you to stop on the decayed steps in the house of your fathers?" (19–20). The question stems from a preliminary draft of the prose poem entitled "Erinnerung" ("Remembrance"—I, 382), a fragmentary memory of childhood which places its central character in a disturbed familial context of mother, father, and sister: "What compels this stopping on decayed winding stairs in the house of the fathers. . . ." The deletions and alterations which this question undergoes from the fragment to the finished prose poem reflect an increased assertiveness on the part of the speaker who poses it. The question in the original, apart from having no grammatical designation as a question, is embedded within a compound sentence, the challenge to the "house of the fathers" almost unheard. Its force of inquiry lacks conviction and a sense of direction. Without aiming at a specific figure, the unquestioning question falls into empty space. The question is pointed squarely at the *You* in the prose poem. The challenge is direct and the tenor of the interrogating voice has stiffened, taking on a censorious edge, all the more reproachful since it is essentially self-accusation.

The short reply to the question—"Leaden blackness" (20)—manifests one pole of the juxtaposition of forces acting on the figures and through the images in the entire prose poem. A preceding scene at the end of the first paragraph foreshadows the oppressive atmosphere in the paternal home and ties it to the concept of evil in the title:

> The barberrys have disappeared; one dreams for years in the leaden air under the pines. Fear, green darkness, the gurgling of a drowning man: out from the starry pond a fisherman pulls a large, black fish, face full of cruelty and madness. The voices of the reed, of quarreling men at his back, that one pitches over freezing autumn waters in the red canoe, living in dark sagas of his race and his eyes stonily opened over nights and virginal terrors. Evil. [12–18]

A "leaden" force, a smothering heaviness weighs down upon each of the figures in the scene. Both the drowning man and the fish are trapped in suffocating elements foreign to their nature, imagery reminiscent of the marble-encased "son of Pan" in "Helian." The figure designated as "that one"—the demonstrative pronoun *jener* points to a figure which has preceded in a sequence—apparently points back to the source of all the images in the first paragraph, the hallucinating "leper." From the "evil" constraint at work in his life issues the deadly force acting on the other figures. Living "in" a set of lineal "sagas" or traditions, he is limited in his perceptions of the world to the calcified patterns of his ancestry. Through his "stonily" seeing eyes, the world is terrifying and evil.

Counter to this implosive, inwardly destructive force is the destruction by dismemberment and dissolution in other images: the hunter who disembowels his prey (5), for example, and the imagery with allusions to fire and murder (9–12). The juxtaposition of these contrary forces comes clearly to view in the *You* of the second paragraph. Immediately following its depiction in the "leaden" blackness of the home, it experiences a narcotic dissolution of consciousness: "What do you raise with silver hand to the eyes; and the lids sink as drunken from the poppy?" (20–21). This intoxication opens an inner clairvoyant eye whose gaze penetrates the "stone wall," an image in contrast to the "stonily" seeing eyes in the previous paragraph: "But through the stone wall you see the starry heaven, the Milky Way, Saturn; red" (21–22).

Repetitions and variations of the same words, images and motifs wander from poem to poem in Trakl's works, yet few recur as often as those associated with the stars.[8] In a poem ambiguously entitled "Geistliche Dämmerung" ("Spiritual Dawn" or "Spiritual Twilight"—I, 118) which originated at the same time as "Verwandlung des Bösen," Trakl invokes a similar constellation of imagery:

> Auf schwarzer Wolke
> Befährst du trunken von Mohn
> Den nächtigen Weiher,
>
> Den Sternenhimmel.

> On a black cloud
> You navigate drunken from the poppy
> The gloomy pond,
>
> The starry heaven.

While more perceptibly grounded in a concrete landscape, the imagery of these lines makes a metaphorical statement as well by linking drug intoxication to a vision of the "starry heaven," a statement related to that in the prose poem. In a poem from the

[8]In his relatively small vocabulary, "Stern" (star) stands in thirty-eighth place among the most frequent words and fifth among nouns. See Wetzel, *Konkordanz zu den Dichtungen Georg Trakls,* p. 813.

previous year (I, 53), Trakl used the planet Saturn—the only planet he mentions by name in his poetry—in a manner typifying the connection between celestial bodies and fate often found in his verse:[9]

> Am Abend wieder über meinem Haupt
> Saturn lenkt stumm ein elendes Geschick.
>
> Again in the evening over my head
> Saturn mutely directs a wretched fate.

Stars are used in apposition to "drops of blood" in "Erinnerung," a highly condensed metaphor for the transmission of the family's fate through the blood line to the boy who is born in the poem's first lines. In the first and second versions of "Passion" (I, 392–397), written a few months afterward, a transgression against this blood tie brings down the "stars" of the race on the wrongdoers:

> Zwei Wölfe im finsteren Wald
> Mischten wir unser Blut in steinerner Umarmung
> Und die Sterne unseres Geschlechts fielen auf uns.
>
> Two wolves in the dark forest
> We mingled our blood in stony embrace
> And the stars of our race fell on us.

The stars upon which the clairvoyant eye gazes in "Verwandlung des Bösen" are those destinies other than the oppressive one passed down through the familial lineage. The glimpse through the "stone wall," the momentary dissolution of the rigid vision portends a "transformation" of evil through a change of mind. Several lines later in the second paragraph, the speaker repeats the crucial question in yet another modified form: "What compelled

[9]Lucia Getsi commented: "The image of the stars is pervasive in Trakl's work. Stars function in the poetry as a symbol of destiny, as the object of the process of becoming" (*Poems*, p. 10).

you to stop on decayed steps in the house of your fathers?" (28–29). In the past tense, it has lost its immediacy and, without the article "the" before "decayed," it has lost a degree of specificity. If the changes tend to remove the question from the here and now, the following and last sentence ends the paragraph on an upsurge: "Underneath at the gate an angel knocks with crystalline finger" (29). The angel's appearance following the question and its translucent finger suggest it to be another portent of the transcendence of the "leaden blackness." Its emergence from below recalls the spatial inversion in "An den Knaben Elis" and his descent into an altered consciousness of creativity. In an exuberant postcard to Buschbeck just prior to his trip to Venice, Trakl plays on a similar inversion: "The world is round. On Saturday I'm falling down to Venice. Further and further—to the stars" (I, 523). The postcard clarifies what is clear in the poetry only after close reading: that is, that the falling motion reflected in Trakl's writing cannot be used as unambiguous evidence of an inexorable downward curve in his life.

The visions of evil's transformation" are unsustained. The momentary escape from the mind's inherited structures are the poem's only resolution and the contrary forces continue to act on the poem's central figure. These reach a peak at the end of the fourth paragraph: "You, a green metal and inside a fiery vision which wants to go and from the hill of bones sing dark times and the flaming plunge of the angel. O! Despair which breaks down to its knee with mute cry" (42–45). Outwardly restrained and rigid, the figure is inwardly a seething cauldron of destructive visions. Its existence resembles that quiet at the eye of a hurricane, a deceptive inactivity masking the proximity of murderous forces. The "mute cry" unintentionally parodies the exaggerated pathos cultivated by many of Trakl's Expressionist contemporaries.[10] An emotion frozen at the moment of its greatest intensity, it ex-

[10]In his anthology of Expressionist poetry first published in 1920, Kurt Pinthus entitled the first section "Sturz und Schrei"—Fall and Cry (*Menschheitsdämmerung: Ein Dokument des Expressionismus* [Berlin: Rowohlt, 1920]).

presses the paralysis of the figure caught at the point of greatest stress between opposed forces of eruption and restraint.

The tormented dreamer in the third paragraph—his dream apparently motivated by guilt feelings toward the figure of an unnamed woman he has destroyed—is torn by conflicting emotions toward her: "Worship, purple flame of desire" (33). In "Erinnerung," the sister plays a similar double role of temptress and victim, while in the first published version of "Verwandlung des Bösen," Trakl had called the woman "Sonja," an identity he borrowed from Dostoyevsky's sympathetic prostitute in *Crime and Punishment*. His final choice of the unnamed female figure is symptomatic of a tendency in the latter parts of the work to generalize and even mythologize. The images in the following lines, the glowing fruit in the apple trees and the molting snake in the grass, suggest an interpretation of the dreamer's relationship to the woman in terms of original rather than particular sin and archetypal rather than individual guilt. A semblance of religious myth casts its shadow back on these lines, further divesting the figures of individual identities.

The two closely related figures in the final two paragraphs acquire an element of religio-mythic stature by virtue of the imagery surrounding their appearances. The first of these figures—"Someone" (35)—leaves the *You* at a "crossroads." The German word can also be translated as "Way of the Cross" (*Kreuzweg*). It is of course an inversion of Christian belief that the poetic Christ figure abandons the *You* to suffer its guilt and mental torment alone. The rhythm of departure and return, familiar from such poems as "An einen Frühverstorbenen," is completed in the prose poem by the meeting with a "dead man" (46) in the final paragraph. Once more, imagery suggesting a Christ figure—the "self-spilt blood," the meeting by the olive tree, and the ensuing "Immortal night"—adds to the impression of a religio-mythic superstructure.[11]

[11]Lachmann simply equates the figure with Christ (p. 219).

Unlike the nearly seamless integration of the religious stratum of connotation and meaning in "Helian," the religio-mythic level of "Verwandlung des Bösen" enters late in the prose poem, striking the reader as being superimposed on the familial level, rather than blending in with it or providing it with a broader base of resonance. The distress of the central figure in the second paragraph and the intensified statement of this distress in lines 42–45 of the fourth paragraph remain the center of the work. The prose poem's origins in "Erinnerung" and the explicit family setting retain a greater determinative power than the attempt to mythologize.

Distinct echoes of this fragment sound again in the two long prose poems from 1914. In "Traum und Umnachtung," the series of scenes strongly colored by autobiographical details begins: "Sometimes he remembered his childhood" (3). The child, still unborn in the first lines of "Erinnerung," exists in the "nightlike cavern" of his mother's womb. In "Traum und Umnachtung," the speaker depicts the boy's childhood days spent in the "dark cavern" (25) of his home. Many of the poem's details, quite apart from the sister figure—a figure in which Trakl's childhood memories mingle with the real crisis involving Grete during the fall of 1913 and March 1914—clearly have roots in Trakl's past. One critic recognized scenes from the Salzburg landscape of his youth, while Ficker, probably a reliable witness, considered "Offenbarung und Untergang" to be autobiographical.[12] Other Trakl poems, however, underscore the obvious—that is, that the prose poems are more than poetic confessions. One example can suffice for many. In "Kindheit" ("Childhood"—I, 79), Trakl wrote the lines: "Childhood lived peacefully in the blue cavern." Apart from valuing too lightly the artistic, constructed nature of the poems, to ask which expression of childhood is closest to au-

[12]Lindenberger, the single critic who has commented on "Traum und Umnachtung" at any length, describes its landscape as "the Salzburg world of Trakl's childhood" (*Georg Trakl*, p. 112). Saas refers to Ficker's opinion of "Offenbarung und Untergang" as autobiographical on page 56.

tobiographical truth looks past the fact that only in combination do they parallel the poet's own waverings and ambivalence about his childhood.

Moreover, both prose poems again show at points an effort to overlay the autobiographical level with a general significance. Even though "Offenbarung und Untergang" is primarily narrated by an *I* limited to its own perspective, it begins with a remark from an overview: "The nightlike paths of men are strange." In the middle of "Traum und Umnachtung," following a temporary shift from narrative past to present tense, the narrator remarks: "O the accursed race. When in defiled rooms each such destiny is accomplished, death enters with mouldering steps into the house" (68–69). The speaker's remark appears to generalize the narrative at this point although the events narrated in the present tense in the next few lines differ little from those previously narrated in the past. The tense shift effaces the distinct line between past and present, departicularizes the narrative and elevates it beyond a specific sequence of events in the past to a timeless sequence.

All three of the central figures in the prose poems—the *You* in "Verwandlung des Bösen," the boy in "Traum und Umnachtung," and the *I* in "Offenbarung und Untergang"—are figures being torn apart, their very existence threatened. In "Winternacht" too, the main character stands at the intersection of contrary forces bent on destroying him. In "Verwandlung des Bösen," the result of these forces is a stalemate, a schizoid balance that neutralizes the action of the figure and intensifies his agony. In both "Traum und Umnachtung" and "Offenbarung und Untergang," the force tearing the protagonist is the unspoken incest taboo and the associated guilt in conflict with his desire for the sister. The crisis of identity and self-consciousness arising from the conflict—a crisis psychiatry could only label schizophrenic—resembles a plot playing against the background of the poems' rhythmical movement. However foreign the conventional notion of plot may be, there is a line of discernible development in the relationship of the main figure to the sister and to himself.[13] The repetition of the path motif and the frequent directed motion of the central figures or their metaphorical forms strengthen the impression of movement cutting across the poem's more obvious oscillating motions.

These characteristic rhythms occur on the broadest as well as the narrowest structural levels of the prose poems and are not always limited to a formal significance. "Traum und Umnachtung," for example, begins with the burden of the "degenerated race" bearing down upon the boy. The work ends with the "accursed race" being "devoured" by the night. Oppression and release are the antipodal positions of this broad rhythmical curve, a curve repeated in reverse sequence and on a smaller scale by the boy's repeated departures from the family home and his returns. Visions of renewal directly follow deadening visions of guilt:

> Death is bitter, the fare of the guilt-laden. . . . But that one sang softly in the green shadow of the elder, as he awoke from evil dreams. Sweet playmate, a rosy angel drew near to him so that he, a gentle wild animal, dozed off into the night; and he saw the starry face of purity. [98–103]

In "Offenbarung und Untergang," sinking and rising motions in short succession, especially well defined in lines 36, 37; 44, 47, 48; and 62, 63, 66 indicate a number of curves with smaller spans. "Crystalline" images regularly alternate with "dark" phenomena in both prose poems, although with more consistent juxtaposition in "Offenbarung und Untergang." The "crystalline tears" shed at two separate points (7, 32) appear in both instances in contrast to dark images: the "black shadow" (4) and the "blackish cloud" (31–32). Later in the poem, madness and night (44–45) contrast to the enlightened "crystalline eyes" (48). Two final examples: the onset of darkness implied by the "sinking sun" brings in its wake

[13]Lindenberger sees the movement of "Traum und Umnachtung" determined by "the alternation of contrary states of the mind" (*Georg Trakl,* p. 116).

the image of the "crystalline meadow" (51–52); darkness and "crystalline crags" contrast in lines 62–65.

Isolation characterizes the position of the boy within the family at the beginning of "Traum und Umnachtung." The father has grown old, the mother's face is petrified. In an earlier variant as well as in "Offenbarung und Untergang" (8), events begin with an allusion to the father's death. Against this background of alienation from the parental figures, the sister's image steps from the surface of a mirror (5–6). The momentary realization of a mirror-identity with her stands in sharp contrast to the absence of other human ties within the family. Much of the prose poem deals with keeping this insistent realization silent, and just prior to the sister's reappearance as a mirror image at the end, a family gathering is depicted at which the family members silently observe one another from behind "crimson masks" (118), mutually incomprehensible and unapproachable. Trakl left aside overt sexual overtones in the early lines, but a discarded variant strongly suggests their presence: "he longed for the red flesh of fruits" (II, 265). The boy's reaction to the reflected image—"he plunged as if dead into the darkness" (6)—tacitly acknowledges the profound conflict in which the truth of the mirror stands with society's most powerful taboo and makes his isolation total.

The double and, more specifically, the mirror motif have a long history of literary expression.[14] Since Freud the interpretations of these phenomena have found a base of agreement in his concept of narcissism.[15] Oscar Wilde's *Picture of Dorian Gray,* the fateful tale of a man who falls in love with a painting of himself, is perhaps the most famous literary exemplification of this morbid self-love. It is a book, moreover, which belonged to Trakl's small

[14]See Otto Rank, *The Double: A Psychoanalytic Study,* trans. and ed. with an introduction by Harry Tucker, Jr. (Chapel Hill: University of North Carolina Press, 1971); Robert Rogers, *A Psychoanalytic Study of the Double in Literature* (Detroit: Wayne State University Press, 1970); Ralph Tymms, *Doubles in Literary Psychology* (Cambridge: Bowes & Bowes, 1949).

[15]Sigmund Freud, "On Narcissism: An Introduction," *Collected Papers,* ed. Ernest Jones (London: Hogarth Press, 1949), IV, pp. 30–59.

private library. Freud's disciple Otto Rank, in his book on the double, reports a late version of the original myth of Narcissus in which the boy finds not his own, but his beloved twin sister's reflection in the water, a version he labels "plainly narcissistic."[16] In Trakl's prose poems, however, there is no suggestion of the enraptured self-observation of the myth or its variant. Here, the sister signifies that counterpart *You* in Buber's sense upon which the existence of the main figure depends. For Trakl's protagonist, the mirror is a source of existential confirmation rather than narcissistic titillation. Rudolf Kassner, a contemporary of Trakl's and a fleeting acquaintance, argued several years later against the pejorative, narcissistic significance of the mirror: "The self needs the mirror, namely for its existence and the discovery of its dimension."[17] Latter-day existential psychiatry has expressed the need of Trakl's protagonist for the sister in terms of complementarity: "All 'identities' require an other: some other in and through a relationship with whom self-identify is actualized. . . . By complementarity I denote that function of personal relations whereby the other fulfills or completes self."[18]

From the dark, enshrouded atmosphere in the home, the boy in "Traum und Umnachtung" turns to dreams (8), cemeteries (9) and a "forgotten" past (24). He enters a world of lower forms in nature, both animate and inanimate (18–21), whose responsiveness contrasts to the void of his family life. In this state of openness or clairvoyancy (15), the boy opens up as well toward a kind of religious experience against which he is armored in the family circle: "An organ chorale filled him with God's shudders. But in the dark cavern . . . God's anger chastised his metal shoulders" (24–30). The oceanic feeling of religious experience occurs out-

[16]Rank, p. 70.

[17]Kassner, *Narciss oder Mythos und Einbildungskraft* (Leipzig: Insel, 1928), p. 31. In a letter written to Wolfgang Schneditz in 1950, Kassner recalled his brief meeting with Trakl in 1913. His most lasting impression was what he vaguely called the poet's "schizophrenic" bearing or presence (*Georg Trakl in Zeugnissen der Freunde,* ed. Wolfgang Schneditz [Salzburg: Pallas, 1951], p. 105).

[18]R. D. Laing, *Self and Others* (Harmondsworth: Penguin, 1971), p. 82.

side the family framework—within that framework, God is the ultimate agent of retribution.

The apparently regressive search of the self beyond the network of human relationships is a compensatory act which seeks an experience of mutuality, of being with some "other" since it cannot find this "other" in human terms nor can it accept the incestuous "other" in the mirror. This search for life paradoxically leads to death later in the work: "He loved the stately works of stone more deeply; the tower which storms the blue starry sky at night with hellish grimaces; the cool grave in which man's fiery heart is preserved" (61–64). The act of compensation by which a tenuous grasp on life is preserved has grown more radical, but remains a form of self-preservation. It attempts to preserve that self which knows of its profound affinity for the sister, but which must remain hidden to the family. In the "dark cavern" of his home, the boy must lie, steal, and dissimulate in order to conceal the unpermitted realities of his own experience: "But in the dark cavern he spent his days, lied and stole and hid himself, a flaming wolf, from the white face of his mother" (25–27).

In both prose poems, allusions are made to the presence of the mother figure combined with an arousal of guilt. In "Traum und Umnachtung," she seems to suddenly discover the children at the very moment of the incestuous act: "The blue rustling of a woman's garment hardened him into a pillar and in the door stood the gloomy figure of his mother. At his head rose up the shadow of evil" (37–39). In a more ethereal manner in the later poem, the "mother's dark lament" arrived on the night wind and the youth "saw the black hell" in his heart (9, 10). The inducement to experience the incestuous relationship as evil and the implantation of guilt originates from the mother figure in "Erinnerung" as well. The main figure in the long prose poems is checkmated between his experience and the demand for its denial by the social taboo. The contradiction between experience and obligatory behavior grows destructive.

The actions of the boy whose experience is thus violated in "Traum und Umnachtung" become themselves violent as "the shadow of the murderer" (28) falls over him: "Hate scorched his heart, lust, as in the greening summer garden he ravished the mute child [and] recognized in the radiant face his deranged visage" (31–33). While the explicitly sexual nature of the violence brings the incestuous act into more vivid relief, the recognition of identity between the figures as if in mirrored opposition relates the scene to the earlier one between brother and sister. Yet the sister is not the sole victim of the violence. Since the mirror has established their oneness, the boy violates himself as well by violating her.

The two faces represent not merely the two separate figures, but a split in the boy between violator and victim. In "Verwandlung des Bösen," the *You* simultaneously appears at one point as sacrificial animal and as the priest who performs the sacrifice: "You, a blue animal which trembles slightly; you, the pale priest who butchers it at the black altar" (24–25). The violator in "Traum und Umnachtung" is associated with the boy's "deranged" face—benighted, shrouded in darkness, more concretely convey the sense of the German *umnachtet*—and is that part of him which presents the lie of his existence to the family. It is that internal guardian of family rules which oversees and shapes the boy's experience and his actions. Since it contradicts the truth of his experience of the sister, it is a false self. The victim's face is radiant, light-emitting, but belongs to the mute child—it is the true self brought to silence by the violence practiced on it.

Analogous pairs of figures appear throughout the second section as the cat, the cripple, the dove, and the Jewess suffer at the hands of the boy (44–56). At a later point, the boy discovers "the white figure of the child, bleeding for the coat of its bridegroom" (82–83). There is in this imagery both duality and a propensity to unite as if the figures were elements of a split whole, a higher marriage transcending their separation. The boy, however, stands immobile and unable to respond: "He, however, stood buried in his steely hair, mute and suffering before her" (83–84).

Violence against an innocent creature also provokes a crisis of self-identity in "Offenbarung und Untergang." Just prior to the sister's emergence from "decaying blueness" (18)—a variation of the mirror motif—"a dead lamb" (18) lies at the feet of the speaker, a guise in which the sister had appeared in "Erinnerung." A few lines later as a "wild hunter" chasing "snowy" game (28–29), he again unleashes destructive impulses on an innocent target. The sister gives voice to his guilt and lust: "Prick black thorn" (20). He experiences himself as a "beaming corpse" (17), a metaphor which incorporates into one image both the beaming and benighted faced of the boy in "Traum und Umnachtung." Light, life, the experiential truth of the self stand juxtaposed in both prose poems to darkness and a state of death in life under which this truth is submerged.

The "red shadow with flaming sword" (23), an explicitly sexual image recalling the rivalry for the "sisters" in both "Helian" (47–52) and "Traum und Umnachtung" (91–92), adds a further complication to the protagonist's split existence.[19] The lament "O bitter death" follows directly upon the forcible intrusion. In the image of the frenzied horse, the elemental dimensions of the self's conflict become clear—the horse's eyes threaten madness, his frenzy can only be violently suppressed:

> And a dark voice spoke from within me: in the nightlike forest I broke the neck of my black horse as madness sprang from his crimson eyes. The shadows of the elms fell upon me, the blue laughing of the spring and the black coolness of the night as I, a wild hunter, raised a snowy wild animal; my face died in stony hell. [25–29]

The series of metaphors used for the poem's speaker in lines 35–43 traces the growing dissolution of his existence down to the insanity which can no longer be contained and a despairing suicidal urge. From the assertive *I* (I want . . . -35), he becomes a

[19]Heinrich Goldmann exemplifies the "phallic" implications of the color red with this passage from "Offenbarung und Untergang" (*Katabasis: Eine tiefenpsychologische Studie zur Symbolik der Dichtungen Georg Trakls,* Trakl-Studien 4 [Salzburg: Otto Müller, 1957], p. 38).

"silent one" (35), a stranger (36), a wild animal (37), and a "twilight-filled head" (38). The metaphors become increasingly insubstantial as the concrete designations for the speaker yield further to an indistinct perception of his movement ("hesitating strides"-39) and finally to indirect allusions to his presence in the landscape (40–41). His figure fades out of the poem's imagery as it blends into the surroundings. The autonomous subject is absorbed into the world of objects. He not only disappears from the reader's view, but as the poem's speaker in the first-person form, he loses sight of himself. The reduction of his presence is matched by the silent withdrawal of the villagers into their huts (41–42), a poetic suggestion of the reciprocity of madness. That is, the lines suggest that madness is not simply an interior process whereby self-consciousness grows extinct, but perhaps even more crucially, a rupture of relationships within a network of people, a process primarily carried out between people rather than in a person.

Madness appears to come from outside rather than from within in the next lines when it takes on an almost concrete existence, "seizing" its victim:

> But as I climbed down the rocky path, madness seized me and I cried loudly in the night; and as I bent down on silvery fingers over the silent waters, I saw that my face had left me. And the white voice spoke to me: Kill yourself! Sighing, the boy's shadow in me rebelled [rose up] and looked at me beaming from crystalline eyes, so that I sank down weeping under the trees, the vast vault of the stars. [44–49]

The sequence of images involving madness and the loss of the facial reflection repeats a similar sequence in earlier lines—the madness of the wild horse followed by the face which "died" (29). With the departure of the reflected image from the silent waters, nature too withdraws her confirmation of the speaker's existence. His presence has ceased to find resonance in his own eyes, in the eyes of the villagers, and finally on the surface of the waters. Losing the assurance from each of these sources that he is seen, he loses the assurance that he exists.

Throughout "Offenbarung und Untergang," the main figure appears in motion along a path in the poetic landscape. In these lines, he reaches a low point on the path, literally as well as figuratively in his own sense of self—the clash of its split elements has become self-annihilating. The "white voice" demands self-destruction, but the rebelling shadow of the true self with its propitiously beaming and crystalline eyes asserts a counter-thrust.[20] It challenges the suicidal voice and reverses death's momentum at its very peak, a force which had been gathering strength since the early scenes of the work.

The path in the next two paragraphs leads the main figure away from that final act which would have ended an existence already experienced as death. The appearance of the indeterminate *You* (53), although amid further imagery of destruction, begins to fill this void. It enters that vacuum of alienation which had separated the figure from others as well as from its mirror image. It prefigures the benign reappearance of the sister in the following lines:

> As I went into the twilight-filled garden and the black figure of evil had withdrawn from me, the hyacinth quietness of the night embraced me. And I went in crescent-shaped canoe over the calm pond and sweet peace touched my petrified brow. Speechless I lay under the old willows and the blue sky was high above me and full of stars. And as contemplating I expired, fear and pain died most deeply in me. And there rose the blue shadow of the boy, beaming in the dark, gentle song; there rose on lunar wings over the greening treetops, crystalline crags, the white face of the sister. [57–65]

More explicitly than in the prose poem of the same name, Trakl depicts in this paragraph a transformation of evil. In directing the protagonist on his wanderings into a garden and then by boat over the pond, he mingles into the lines overtones of myth which strike

[20]Goldmann describes white as having, among other implications, "the quality of that which Freud describes as the superego" (p. 36).

familiar chords in the reader's mind. As if out of place in this prototypical garden of innocence, evil withdraws from the central figure in tangible form and a death of sorts follows the ride across the quasi-Stygian waters. Yet each occurrence affects the protagonist only partially. Part of him leaves in the "black figure of evil" and part of him—"fear and pain"—dies.

That which remains of the self after this partial death, the "shadow of the boy," rises up in the accompaniment of an image of the sister's face. The same boy's shadow had risen to defy the suicidal urge and had represented the last traces of vitality in the self already near exhaustion through madness. Here, however, the image rises not in defiance of total extinction, but in a state of rebirth after a partial death. What remains is an innocent self no longer torn by pain and fear. In terms of the earlier image of the "beaming corpse" (17), the half of the protagonist's split existence connoted as the "corpse" is cast out, dispossessed and dissolves like "fluffy snow" (70). That part of the split self experienced from the very beginning as a lie, as the "dead" exterior to a very much alive experiential truth, undergoes the downfall of the title in the final lines of the prose poem.

The sister's appearance no longer arouses desire and guilt. On the contrary, her face rising simultaneously with that of the innocent self—another variation of the mirror motif—replaces the reflected face of the protagonist which had earlier departed from the water's surface. His new guiltless self, now without pain and fear, openly recognizes the sister as a kind of reflected or complementary being. Although forbidden by taboo, she is now part of a self-identity which the protagonist can accept. Beyond this, however, in regaining a reflected image, he regains what he had lost in lines 44–49, that is, the assurance of his own existence brought by his reflection in the eyes of an "other." In "Offenbarung und Untergang," the opposition of forces acting on the main figure is brought to a resolution. The taboo against incest and the guilt surrounding its transgression fall away, leaving him able to affirm the long and painfully suppressed truth of the tie to his sister.

And, in finding his way back to her, he finds his way back to himself.

A related epiphany is embedded in the ambiguity of the final lines of "Traum und Umnachtung":

> A crimson cloud clouded his head so that he fell silently upon his own blood and likeness, a lunar face; stonily he sank down into the emptiness, when in the broken mirror, a dying youth, the sister appeared; the night devoured the accursed race. [125–129]

The downward motion in these lines is unequivocal, but the effect that the sister's mirror image has on the boy is ambiguous. A cursory reading indicates that her reflection is but the final, completing aspect of his fall, a sort of last vision of the reality of the incestuous tie that pushes him into the oblivion to which the "race" is consigned in the poem's closing words. Yet along with this reading is another one whose presence and implications cannot be overlooked. The sister's sudden appearance can be read as a brake to the precipitous motion, a saving vision for the boy which halts his plunge and supplies the grounds for the disaster that befalls the "race." The first reading may in isolation be the most evident one; the second one gains plausibility from a consideration of the prose poem as a whole.

In a variation of the boy's encounter with his sister as a mirror reflection at the prose poem's beginning, he sees her again, this time in the "broken mirror" of his shattering psyche. Only a few lines earlier, her unseeing eyes and "madness" (114) had apparently relegated her to the circle of the silent family. Her image in the final lines counters and reverses this alienation and is noticeably free of the guilt and violence which mark her appearance at all other points. By identifying with his own sister by means of a mirror image, the boy identifies with the self which he was forced to suppress and cripple earlier in the poem.

Even the punctuation suggests a change rather than a continuation of the boy's falling motion. The pause at the last semicolon and after the sister's appearance separates the boy's fall from the cataclysm of the family line. The semicolon replaces a comma from an earlier variant and can be read as a break in his precipitous movement. According to the reading that imputes salvation, not damnation to the sister's image, the boy is not swept up in the demise of the fathers, but saved by a vision which implies the certainty of this demise. The guiltless recognition of the tie between siblings undermines the incest taboo and anticipates the destruction of the family. Although the transcendence of the incest taboo has a preservative function for the boy as an individual—it enables him to affirm his identity with his sister and thus his true self—it bodes calamity for the social order built on the taboo. Somewhere between the contending readings of this last passage in "Traum und Umnachtung" lies the poet's ambivalent attitude toward an ever-present personal dilemma.

In a generation of poets and writers in impassioned revolt against the fathers, Trakl's prose seems fragile, its aim ineffectually ambiguous compared to the numerous and blatant literary patricides committed by his contemporaries. Yet no revolt against the fathers reaches a more elemental base than the oedipal revolt, even in the secondary form of sibling incest.[21] And what Trakl's revolt lacked in explicit defiance, it made up for by being grounded in a personal dilemma that for most other writers had to be entirely fictionalized.

[21]For Freud, the original erotic love between siblings, without modification into an asexual tie of affection, comes into opposition to the expanding momentum of civilization which seeks to bind people together in cultural units larger than the family. Incestuous love gratifies itself within the boundaries of the family and is essentially nonprocreative (*Civilization and Its Discontents*, trans. and ed. James Strachey [New York: Norton, 1961], pp. 49–52). Herbert Marcuse has remarked on the insurrection against the fathers inherent in sexual perversions: "Psychoanalytic theory sees in the practices that exclude or prevent procreation an opposition against continuing the chain of reproduction and thereby of paternal domination—an attempt to prevent the 'reappearance of the father' " (*Eros and Civilization: A Philosophical Inquiry into Freud* [New York: Vintage, 1962], p. 45).

6

The Thwarted Imperative

The Enduring Passion

Ficker's *Brenner* was but one of many periodicals in Austria and Germany around which intellectual and literary life flourished during the first decades of the twentieth century. These ranged from Herwarth Walden's influential *Sturm* and Kurt Hiller's *Aktion,* whose issues were eagerly awaited, read, and discussed in the cafés over a period of years, to the numerous smaller ones, some ceasing publication after only a few issues.[1] A main function of these journals was to promote young talent. Besides providing an outlet in print, the publishers organized literary evenings at which the public, for a small fee, could hear the authors read from their own works. Trakl shared center stage at such an event in early December 1913 with Robert Michel, a minor writer and contributor to *Der Brenner.* Not surprisingly, the generally positive reactions from local critics to his poetry—including "Helian"—were mixed with perplexity. Although he was most certainly a poet, Trakl's time—so claimed one critic—was yet to come (II, 718–721).

At the beginning of March 1914, Trakl sent Kurt Wolff a second

[1]Paul Raabe lists a hundred of these journals more or less specifically associated with Expressionism in *Die Zeitschriften und Sammlungen des literarischen Expressionismus: Repertorium der Zeitschriften, Jahrbücher, Anthologien, Sammelwerke, Schriftenreihen und Almanache 1910–1921* (Stuttgart: Metzler, 1964). For a fascinating study of the literary circles in Berlin grouped around these journals, see Roy F. Allen, *Literary Life in German Expressionism and the Berlin Circles* (Göppingen: Alfred Kümmerle, 1974).

collection of poems entitled *Sebastian im Traum.* It was accepted a month later, but the chaotic war situation during the summer of 1914 delayed publication until early 1915, several months after Trakl's death. His anxious letters to the publisher reflect the same attention to detail and nuance that is evident from the multiple variants. He added and deleted several poems, meticulously corrected the printer's proofs and was concerned about the typeface to be used. At one point he requested confirmation that one particular misspelled word had been corrected and that two superfluous hyphens had been removed, errors which he insisted falsified the poems' meanings (I, 540).

Trakl was equally intent at times on much more radical revisions. "Passion" and "Abendland" ("The Occident"), poems that appeared in condensed forms in *Sebastian im Traum,* were originally published during the first six months of 1914 in much longer versions in *Der Brenner.* Each of these works was reduced by almost two-thirds of its original length before it found its way into the collection. The *Brenner* version of "Passion" (I, 392–394) became the subject of a controversy and exchange of scholarly articles concerning Trakl's poetry in the 1950s. Countering a narrowly Christian reading, Walther Killy pointed to the equally insistent mythological and personal levels of the poem. According to Killy, for the reader either to ignore or to make absolute any of its multiple perspectives was to limit the poem's polyvalence, its capability of simultaneously radiating various meanings.[2]

Killy's notion of overlapping perspectives, each drawing the reader toward one interpretation while he is restrained by two other perspectives with equal claims, is a theoretically attractive way of dealing with much of Trakl's imagery. But it is questionable whether all three of these perspectives do in fact make equal claims in "Passion." A recent critic, although he alludes to the

[2]See Walther Killy: "Strukturen des Gedichts: Über die Passion," *Über Georg Trakl,* pp. 21–37, and "Nochmals über Trakls 'Passion', mit Rücksicht auf die handschriftliche Überlieferung," *Euphorion,* 52 (1958), 400–413. See also Eduard Lachmann, "Georg Trakls herbstliche 'Passion'," *Euphorion,* 52 (1958), 397–399.

poem's shorter version, terms it "a late poem . . . concerned with incest."[3] The revisions which Trakl undertook from the longer version, through a slightly shortened second stage published only in 1958, and finally to the version in *Sebastian im Traum* clearly demonstrate a progressive weakening of the Christian perspective. Another critic calls this last version "a contraction to the passion of man." With reference to the end of the *Brenner* version, the same critic also notes that "the 'divine' Passion only supplies images for the 'human' passion: the angel does not step from Christ's grave . . . but *from the grave of the lovers.*"[4] The gradual reduction of the Christian allusions in the stages of "Passion" undercuts Killy's notion of equality among contending perspectives. Instead of suspending images in a kind of open semantic field between poles that exert equally powerful attractive forces, Trakl employed familiar religious and mythological structures to enrich his poem with resonance and to supply "transfiguring motifs"[5] for the theme around which poem after poem revolves: the theme of incest.

Killy not only relativizes, but in a sense, trivializes this perspective of "Passion" by making it representative of a metaphysical dilemma.[6] In becoming a mere sign for a higher meaning, incest loses its force as a physical and psychological reality that found its way from Trakl's life into his work. Not without justification, this reality of the "fundamental experience around which his poems constantly revolve . . . the incestuous relationship to his sister," has been termed a traumatic reality.[7]

The *Brenner* version of "Passion" falls into three main divisions, each a series of scenes linked together by the three perspectives as well as various recurring structures and motifs. The mythological perspective, introduced immediately onto the

[3]Lindenberger, *Georg Trakl,* p. 38.

[4]Ludwig Dietz, *Die lyrische Form Georg Trakls,* p. 158.

[5]Ibid.

[6]Killy, *Über Georg Trakl,* p. 26.

[7]Gunilla Bergsten, "Georg Trakls traumatischer Kode," *Studia Neophilologica,* 43 (1971), 336.

poetic landscape in the figure of Orpheus, rapidly loses its dominance in the course of the poem's first main division:

When Orpheus' silvery touch stirs the lute,
Lamenting something dead in the evening garden–
Who are you resting one under tall trees?
The autumnal reed murmurs the lament,
The blue pond.

Alas, the boy's slender form
Which glows crimson,
Grievous mother, in blue mantle
Veiling her holy outrage.

Alas, the one born, that he might die
Before he has tasted the glowing fruit,
The one bitter with guilt.

For whom do you weep under darkening trees?
The sister, dark love
Of a wild race,
From which the day thunders away on golden wheels.

O, that more piously the night might come,
Crist.

What do you keep silent under black trees?
The starry frost of winter,
God's birth
And the shepherds at the straw manger.

Blue moons,
The blind one's eyes sank in hairy cavern.

A corpse, you seek under greening trees
Your betrothed,
The silver rose
Hovering over the nocturnal hill.

The poem's opening line casts Orpheus immediately onto its landscape. At the end of this first section, an Orphic search has begun for a "betrothed," a search extended in the poem's second section "along the black shores of death" (29–30). Yet the relationship of Trakl's poem to the myth is askew from the beginning. Orpheus' musical lament is not directed toward a dead lover, but "ein Totes," a figure whose asexuality strikes an alien chord in this story of tragic love. In line 25, it is the one who searches who is dead—the "corpse"—not the object of the search, the betrothed. Eurydice, for whose love the mythological Orpheus descended to the realm of the dead, fails to appear at all by name in the poem. The searcher, moreover, is never identified by name as Orpheus, but rather as *You*. The figure from the myth plays only a cameo role in the poem. His name prompts certain expectations in the reader's mind, but when they are met, they are met by the figure addressed as *You*.

Three times before the poem's speaker begins the narration of this latter figure's quest in lines 25–26, he questions him:

> Who are you resting one under tall trees? [3]
>
> For whom do you weep under darkening trees? [13]
>
> What do you keep silent under black tres? [19]

The first of these questions stands precisely at the structural midpoint of the first strophe. Without it, the other four lines yield a conventional portrait of the Orphic musical lament and its resonance in nature. The question stands between the condition—When Orpheus plays—and the result—Nature echoes his song (4–5). In the midst of constructing the poetic landscape, the speaker interrupts himself to ask about the identity of a resting figure, perhaps the same figure which Orpheus laments in line 2. This first question, however, remains unanswered until later in the poem. The speaker shifts to a new landscape in the next two scenes, leaving the Orpheus of mythology behind. This new landscape, where the poem's concern with incest begins, contains an immediately recognizable constellation of images: the boy aglow with lust, the outraged mother and the guilt that grows to self-destructive proportions. The only figure missing in this constellation appears in answer to the second question in line 13:

> The sister, dark love
> Of a wild race.

In answer to the final question of the section, the third perspective of the poem comes into view. The *You* remains silent about the incarnation of God on earth (20–22), the specifically Christian hope for its deliverance from the guilt associated with this "dark love." Its muteness is a kind of nonrecognition, a repudiation of the key figure and event in the Christian pattern of expiation and absolution. Its silence is an absence of a verbal confirmation of faith and thus a denial. By not confirming the structural pattern which Christianity offers for the absolution from guilt, the guilty do penance without reason or hope. The image in lines 23–24 suggests such a blind penance, a penance unencompassed by a larger pattern that allows the guilty one to foresee his absolution. Thus, the poem's first main section appears to establish by question and answer an incestuous guilt that cannot be erased by resorting to the traditional Christian path of atonement. The search that begins in the last four lines of this section and continues into the next one, is, in one sense, a search for an alternate penitential path.

With line 25, the speaker goes from interrogator of the poem's *You* to the narrator of its Orphic journey. The second section finds him in the realm of the dead:

> Wandering along the black shores
> Of death,
> The hellish flower blossoms crimson at heart.
>
> Inclined over sighing waters
> See your mate: Face rigid with leprosy
> And her hair flutters wildly in the night.

Two wolves in the dark forest
We mingled our blood in stony embrace
And the stars of our race fell on us.

O, the spur of death.
Expired, we behold one another at the crossroad
And in silver eyes
The black shadows of our savagery are reflected,
Ghastly laughing which shattered our mouths.

Thorny steps sink into the darkness,
So that more redly from cool feet
The blood might pour out onto the stony field.

On crimson flood
The silver sleeper tosses wakefully.

The questioning attitude of the speaker has given way to a narrative stance in the opening lines of the section, a shift which implies a sense of recognition of the central figure. This shift toward recognition and familiarity is carried still further by the imperative in line 33. Here the speaker directs the *You* to look at his "mate" or consort in the waters, where, in a variation of the mirror images at the beginnings of the prose poems, a terrifying female figure gazes back at him. It is yet another realization of the forbidden unity underlying the incestuous bond.

In the two scenes that follow, the speaker directly involves himself in this unity via the pronoun *We*. It is a consistent extension of his growing familiarity with his protagonist by which he implicitly answers the poem's initial question, "Who are you?" with the reply: I, the speaker am the tormented *You* of the poem. In contrast to the detached depiction of incest earlier in the poem (6–16), the speaker shares directly in the nightmarish memory of blood guilt in lines 35–42. He himself now feels the "spur of death" (38)—the *You* who undertakes the Orphic voyage in line 25 is a "corpse"—and is one of the "expired" (39) in the Orphic realm. In other words, the speaker's initial questioning of the

You, the switch to a narrative and then to an imperative stance, and finally the use of the pronoun *We,* depict stages in a gradual process of his identification with this *You.* The speaker's interrogation turns out to have been self-interrogation and the poem, a process of self-recognition.

The incestuous lovers meet in a realm of the dead, but "shadows of... savagery" (41) hang like damning clouds over their reunion. It is not the mythological figures of Orpheus and Eurydice who joyously meet here, but ones whose further course is a path of sinking "thorny steps" (43). The mythological Orpheus descended to the realm of the dead to retrieve his bride. Trakl's poem depicts a path of descent that leads still further down from this realm, a metaphorical descent which brings continued suffering after the scene of reunion. It is that alternate way of penance created by the poet as a substitute for the way of Christianity rendered "silent" in the poem's first section.[8]

In the middle section's final two lines, a female figure appears alone, her metaphorical disguise as a "silver sleeper" linking her to the "betrothed" (26), the "silver rose" (27) who was the object of the Orphic search at the end of the previous section. In the opening line of the third section, reference is made to a single male figure:

> But that one became a snowy tree
> At the hill of bones,
> An animal looking round out of festering wound,
> Again a silent stone.
>
> O, the gentle starry hour
> Of this crystalline repose,
> As in thorny chamber
> The leprous face fell from you.

[8]Late in his life, Trakl expressed the thought to Ficker that his poetry represented an "atonement" for his "unabsolved guilt," albeit an "incomplete atonement" (I, 463). According to Basil, Trakl immediately retracted even this ambivalent statement with the words: "But, of course—no poem can be atonement for guilt" (Basil, p. 146).

Nocturnal sounds issue from the soul's lonely lyre,
Full of dark rapture
At the silvery feet of the penitentress
In the lost garden;
And on the thorny hedge the blue spring buds.

Under dark olive trees
Steps the rosy angel
Of morning from the grave of the lovers.

The male figure of the opening lines goes through a series of transformations as if in reverse evolutionary transit through nature's forms. This regressive metamorphosis from tree to animal to stone has, moreover, apparently run through repeated cycles—in line 51, he "again" becomes a stone.

The silence of the stone in line 51 underscores this state as the lowest rung in the regressive process. It is a state of pure autism appropriate to the "crystalline repose" of the next lines (53). The figure seems to have withdrawn into the very interior of the stone's crystal structure. Immediately following this point of deepest descent and withdrawal stand the lines:

As in thorny chamber
The leprous face fell from you.

At the nadir of the regressive movement, the diseased face drops away from the figure which the speaker again confronts as the *You*. It is his own absolution—he *is* the poem's *You*—as well as that of his "mate" in line 33: "See your mate: Face rigid with leprosy." Their fates and identities are joined in a mirror relationship like the brother and sister in the prose poems. The absolution occurs—so to speak—underneath the Orphic realm of the second section, in a state of "crystalline repose" in the interior of "silent stone." Mythological imagery gives way to natural imagery at this crucial point of absolution in the poem. In the final two strophes, spring emerges from among the thorns and an angel from the lovers' grave under the olive trees. The biblical overtones of these images support the suggestion of regeneration after penitential suffering.

"Passion" begins with a single direct allusion to mythology—the musical lament of Orpheus' lute—and ends with an image of the musical rapture of the "soul's lonely lyre." The tie between beginning and end is as obvious as its precise nature is difficult to explain. One thing is certain however: mythology imposed no rigid structural frame on the poem—"Passion" seems rather to have resisted this kind of patronage. Trakl manipulated the familiar story of the myth to encompass a variation of a story repeatedly told in his late poems. The solid base of "Passion" is an incestuous experience so heavily burdened with self-reproach and guilt as to be self-alienating. The speaker initially addresses this guilty self as *You*. In the latter two sections, however, he identifies with it and creates a poetic path that leads to absolution and regeneration. The negative experience of incest is thus only a prelude in the poem, its initial source of guilt and alienation which is, in turn, superseded by a transfigured experience of the self.

Trakl's enduring passion not only continued to assert itself in poetry, but around the middle of March 1914, it exerted itself directly in the poet's life once more. With unusual decisiveness, Trakl hastily traveled from Innsbruck to Berlin where his sister Grete lay in critical condition following a miscarriage. During the crisis-ridden days of her recovery, Trakl wrote the long, five-part *Brenner* version of "Abendland" (I, 403–408). He also made the acquaintance of the poetess Else Lasker-Schüler, one of the most familiar and eccentric figures of Berlin's literary café society. It was to Lasker-Schüler—who had the habit of addressing her friends with whimsical private names or titles—that Trakl dedicated this complex poem of interlocking allusions and ponderous gravity. From her letters to Ludwig von Ficker, it appears that for a short time after Trakl's death the following autumn, Lasker-Schüler attempted to befriend and console the poet's sister. But she soon saw her generous efforts badly repaid by Grete's overt anti-semitism. She became increasingly bitter toward Grete, whom she called a "bad copy" of her dead friend and blamed for her own inability to commemorate Trakl in verse.[9] She overcame this block in time, however, and wrote three poems—one only two lines long—that recall their brief acquaintance.[10]

By reason of its title, "Abendland" belongs among the countless visions of cultural pessimism coming from all quarters shortly before, during, and after World War I. Oswald Spengler published the first volume of *The Decline of the West* in 1918.[11] Yet very little of Trakl's poem is on the grand scale of historical vision. The majority of scenes focus on single figures or on pairs, many of these designated as beings without gender. The use of neuter noun forms derived from adjectives, a common occurrence in Trakl's mature poetry, can be only very clumsily duplicated in English. What in German is a true synthesis—"ein Krankes"—must be broken down in English into a quality and the being to which this quality is attached—"a sick thing." This kind of intermediate existence between genders which combines, moreover, the abstraction of an adjective with the concretion of a noun, is related to certain images in dreams which may also be partially abstract and partially concrete. Such images fit better on the microstage of psychic drama than on the broader arena of historical vision. Only in the last stanza of the poem's later version (I, 139–140) did Trakl construct a sustained series of images representing the collapse of Western civilization, a vision of a world being destroyed by nature's forces:

[9]Else Lasker-Schüler, *Lieber gestreifter Tiger: Briefe von Else Lasker-Schüler*, ed. Margarete Kupper (Munich: Kösel, 1969), I, 112.

[10]Else Lasker-Schüler, *Gedichte: 1902–1943*, Vol. I of *Gesammelte Werke in drei Bänden*, ed. Friedhelm Kemp, 2d ed. (Munich: Kösel, 1961), pp. 225, 256, 284.

[11]Theodore Fiedler terms Trakl's long version of "Abendland" "a subdued expression of cultural despair related to any number of contemporary visions of 'Untergang' from Spengler to Eliot's 'Wasteland' " ("Georg Trakl's 'Abendland': Life as Tragedy," *Wahrheit und Sprache: Festschrift für Bert Nagel zum 65. Geburtstag am 27. August 1972*, eds. Wilm Pelters, Paul Schimmelpfennig, and Karl Menges (Göppingen: Alfred Kümmerle, 1972), p. 208.

You large cities
Erected of stone
On the plain!
So the homeless one
Follows speechless
The wind with dark brow,
The barren trees on the hill.
You far-off dimming streams!
The horrid sunset
In the storm clouds
Frightens mightily.
You dying peoples!
Pallid wave
Crashing on the shore of the night,
Falling stars.

For the most part, the images of the *Brenner* version are on a much smaller scale. Closest in magnitude is the extinction of the "fathers' race" in the poem's first section, a vision reminiscent of those in "Helian" and "Traum und Umnachtung":

Decayed hamlets foundered
In brown November,
The dark paths of the villagers
Under stunted
Apple trees, the laments
Of the women in silver florescence.

The fathers' race dies away.
The evening wind is filled
With sighs,
The spirit of the forests.

Quietly the footpath leads
To roses in clouds
A pious creature on the hill.
And there resound
The blue springs in the dark,
That something gentle,
A child might be born.

Quietly at the crossroads,
The shadow left the stranger
And stony blind
Grow his gazing eyes,
So that from the lip
The song might flow more sweetly.

For it is night,
The home of the loving one.
The blue face is speechless,
Above a dead thing
The temple open;
Crystalline view.

Pursuing him on dark paths,
Along walls
Is something which perished.

Juxtaposed to the extinction of the "fathers' race" (7) is the tentative birth in the next lines (14–17), a dialectical succession of poetic visions typical of Trakl. The last four lines of the poem's second section recapitulate the repeated evidence of a vital undercurrent in this poetry whose images refuse to issue into oblivion:

Differently the brow senses perfection,
The cool, childlike one,
When over the greening hill
The spring storm resounds.

These lines also illustrate another of Trakl's methods for designating characters. Besides locating the particular mode of his figures' existences between genders and between abstraction and concretion, he often points only to a bodily part. It is as if the entire being of the represented figure were for the moment concentrated in this part alone.

Such figures appear with regularity in the bewildering and often familiar display of the poem's imagery. Graphic scenes mingling the real with the surreal arise and pass by as if on a moving band before the reader's eyes. The poem resembles a discontinuous film spliced together of these disparate scenes. The refrain of related motifs and similar movement, however, counters the impression of the poem's discontinuity. The first section, moreover, anticipates all of these and thus seems to set the linguistic limits of the entire poem. The motif of the poet and his song, for example, is here associated with a stranger who loses his shadow and sight (18–23). A song that flows "more sweetly" appears to be recompense for the blindness, a Homeric compensation for the poet's physical impairment. Early in the next section, on the other hand, "sorrows" seem to prevent the song from being sung at all:

> The petrified mouth keeps silent
> The dark song of sorrows.

Central to the allusions to the song in the third section is a series of Trakl's unique genderless figures:

> A waking one is many things
> In the starry night
> And beautiful the bluishness,
> Striding, a pale one, a breathing one,
> A lyre.

The identity of the "waking one" is fluid. As the figure moves across the scene, its existence too is in motion until it is finally metamorphosed into an instrument of song or—another possibility in the German *Saitenspiel*—into the music itself. The poem's final image of the poet and his song stands at the beginning of the fourth section:

> A boy with shattered breast,
> The song dies away in the night.

These lines associate once more suffering and song, while

through the apposition of their grammatical subjects, they clearly identify the singer and the song.

The latter two scenes are temporally located at "night," another motif that regularly recurs throughout the poem. It first appears immediately after the blinding of the poet/stranger in the first section (24) and in close proximity (33) to the silenced "song of sorrows" (41) in the second section. Yet, on the other three occasions of the poem's nocturnal scenes—lines 107, 124 and 134—there is no allusion to the poet. That is, there is no consistent connection between the motifs in a larger design that would suggest more than an echo of Hölderlin's myth of the poet and his task of commemorating the gods during the "night" of history.

The most persistent of the various motifs in "Abendland" are the paths and the accompanying figures which are often in motion along them. The first section plays off the "dark paths of the villagers" (3) against the "footpath" (11) that leads upward and toward the birth tentatively envisioned in line 17. In this juxtaposition lie the seeds of the sweeping vision of destruction which finds expression in the last stanza of the shorter version already quoted. While the cities and "dying peoples" on the plain succumb to the annihilating storm, "So the homeless one / Follows speechless / The wind" to an elevated point above the destruction. This vision of poetic megalomania which opposes images of civilization's destruction to a single surviving figure, is a relatively unequivocal statement for Trakl. In the greater part of the *Brenner* version of "Abendland," the individual figures, their identities fluid, travel along paths whose ends are unforeseen and equivocal.

The poem's second section begins:

> When it has become night
> Our stars appear in the sky
> Under old olive trees;
> Or along dark cypresses
> We wander white ways.
> Sword-bearing angel:

My brother.
The petrified mouth keeps silent
The dark song of sorrows.

Here and at the beginning of the third section, the speaker shifts from the singular third-person to the plural first-person perspective. At the same time that he conjoins two figures on the poetic landscape with the plural pronoun, he narrows the distance between poem and reader as well. While the speaker maintains a third-person narrative perspective, he displays his imagery in a graphic but detached manner. When he says *We,* however, the reader is implicitly asked to share a more intimate moment in the poem's flow of scenes. It represents a close-up technique of poetic language which draws the reader nearer to what the speaker has to say about himself. In a variant of these lines, the speaker asks his reader to overhear by directly addressing the *You* of the poem:

When it has become night
Your star appears in the sky.
At the black wall
You, a bowed beggar, stand
And the wound in your breast
Sings the dark song of sorrows
My sister.

[II, 248]

The words overheard in these discarded lines touch on the one subject that never became inaudible for long in Trakl's life and poetry.

Among the figures that populate the remaining lines of the second section is an Elis-figure who strides across the landscape, the only figure in all of "Abendland" which claims the explicit identity of a proper name. Yet this claim is not assertive, but fully as tentative and as probing as the names that locate identities between genders. The scene in which Elis appears begins with

"Or," an indicator of the irresolution with which the speaker motivates his step onto the landscape.

The speaker again places himself, along with a companion, in the opening scene of the third section:

So quiet are the green forests
Of our homeland;
The sun sets at the hill
And we have wept in our sleep.
Wander with white steps
Along thorny hedge,
Singing ones in the ripe-grain summer
And ones born to pain.

From the miniature scale of this scene, with its concrete figures, the poem broadens onto an abstract plain, focusing on "man" (69) and imagery which conveys the promise of the Eucharistic sacrament. The final four lines of this scene return an individual, the "good man" (73), to the landscape, perhaps in illustration of the religious ceremony's conciliatory power. Scenes focused on individual figures mingle with statements of general purport throughout this long middle section. It closes by proclaiming the approaching end of "man's journey," but not, however, without a hint of palingenesis:

Lunar white, the path grows silent
Along those poplars
And soon
Man's journey will end,
Righteous endurance.
The nearness of angels
On crystalline meadow
Also gladdens the children's repose.

The poem's fourth section returns the path motif to prominence and uses it to construct a crossroads of poetic vision:

A boy with shattered breast,
The song dies away in the night.
Only grant going on the hill,
Under the trees,
Followed by the shadow of the creature.
The violets are sweetly fragrant in the meadowland.

Or grant walking into the stony house,
In the sorrowful shadow of the mother,
Bowing the head.
In blue dampness the lamp glows
Through the night.
For the pain rests no longer.

The lines that sketch out these options on the poetic landscape lack a central figure. The figure of the boy that becomes "song" in the introductory lines suggests itself as a possible object of the imperatives in the following lines. But, lacking a clear object, the imperative repeated in lines 99 and 103 seems to be an entreaty of the speaker to his own muse to allow the poem to continue on either of the two paths that emerge in these lines. One recalls the footpath (11) to the hill in the poem's first section while the other leads into the "stony" home and the rigid confinement of maternal surveillance.

With images that are plainly the precursors of the shorter version's last stanza, the fifth and final section of the *Brenner* "Abendland" recapitulates the linguistic limits that the first section had set:

When on the street it grows dark
And in blue linen is met
A long departed one,
O, how the resounding steps sway
And the greening head grows silent.

Built up large are cities
And stony on the plain.
But the homeless one follows

The wind with open brow,
The trees on the hill.
Oftentimes, the sunset too is frightening.

Soon the waters will murmur
Loudly in the night.
The angel touches the crystalline cheeks
Of a girl,
Her blond hair
Burdened by the sister's tears.

This is often love: a flowering
Brier touches
The cold fingers of the stranger
In passing.
And the villagers' huts
Vanish in the blue night.

In childlike repose,
In the grain where a cross towers mutely,
Appear to the gazing one,
Sighing, his shadow and departure.

In a variation of the poem's method of exhibiting its images, the figure in the first scene comes toward the reader rather than moving across his field of vision. The reader is displaced from a position of observation and "is met" by the "long departed one." By confronting the reader with a poetic figure in this way—in effect placing him on the path—the speaker involves him more closely with the text, as he did earlier by switching pronouns.

The recurring path in the poem has become by the beginning of the final section a "street," an apt shift in the poem's imagery for the approach to the cities whose outline becomes visible in the following lines (117–122). These lines, in a variant of "crossroads"-imagery, contain the nucleus of the final cataclysm in the later version of "Abendland." When the cities come into view on the plain, the "homeless one" turns away from them toward the hill. His state of existence—circumscribed by the image of an "open brow" guided by the wind—clashes with the rigid, "stony" profile that the cities cast on the horizon. The lightly condemnatory note here toward the site of urban civilization magnifies into destructive proportions in the final version of "Abendland": the "frightening" sunset (122) of the *Brenner* version becomes the stormy backdrop—"The horrid sunset / In the storm clouds"—against which the Occident finally goes under.

Poetic thoughts of such monumental scale were, however, not foremost in Trakl's mind in Berlin. The murmuring waters in the long version's final section (123) may prefigure the later version of "Abendland" and its image of threatening streams, but they point back to the first section of this version as well, where resounding springs (14–15) presage new life. The rapidly growing Berlin of 1914 doubtless confronted the poet, already antagonistic toward the city, with an urban civilization that exceeded his previous experience in every way. But the allusions to birth, the sister's tears, and the resigned statement about love that follows, locate the origin of these lines once more in Trakl's enduring passion. Moreover, this version of "Abendland" does not yet envision "dying peoples," but rather, the vanishing of the "villagers' huts," a kind of counterimage to the sober acceptance of the love described in these lines (129–134).

The final lines of the poem, in apparent answer to the loss of sight and shadow in line 19, effect a sense of narrative denouement. When one looks back over the poem from this vantage point, the impression of moving toward a goal gains strength from the filmlike succession of scenes, the moving figures in these scenes, and the path motif. The poem appears to have been on a return course to the original crossroads: sight is restored, the shadow is found. The epiphanies concerning complementary identity at the end of the prose poems echo in these lines. The final word—*Hingang*—parallels, moreover, their ambiguity and ambivalence, since it can mean "decease" as well as going away or departure. Yet "Abendland," to a greater degree than the prose poems, is a lyrical narrative without a central figure or fixed identity. The very substance of the poem is, in fact, the instability of identity and the search in poetic language for linguistic equivalents to its transitory configurations.

Invoking the Storm

The storm set loose on the world in July 1914 answered in harshest terms Trakl's longings for a resolution to the anguish which plagued him. It was a desire that found expression in his poetry—for example, lines 57–60 of the *Brenner* version of "Abendland"—as well as his correspondence. In January 1914 he wrote to Karl Borromäus Heinrich: "My condition is far from the best. Lost in intoxication and dejection, I lack the strength and desire to change a situation which daily becomes more disastrous. Only one wish remains—that a storm would break, either purifying or destroying me. O God, what guilt and darkness we have to go through. O that we might not succumb in the end" (I, 532). In a tragically ironic way, the war forced Trakl's reentry into the military, that change he mentions in the letter which he felt powerless to effect, but which he had pursued since the previous November. The war was too real and destructive a storm, however, to fill the role of cathartic force either for Trakl or for the many other poets who welcomed it in verse as a release from a civilization they perceived as stagnant, its structures calcified.

Trakl celebrated such a purgative effect in "Das Gewitter" ("The Thunderstorm"—I, 157–158), a poem published shortly before the war began. Its images follow the rhythmic pattern of the natural phenomenon, the tension in the atmosphere rising to a peak and subsiding with the passing of the critical point. The swelling buildup lasts through the first three stanzas:

> Ihr wilden Gebirge, der Adler
> Erhabene Trauer.
> Goldnes Gewölk
> Raucht über steinerner Öde.
> Geduldige Stille odmen die Föhren,
> Die schwarzen Lämmer am Abgrund,

Wo plötzlich die Bläue
Seltsam verstummt,
Das sanfte Summen der Hummeln.
O grüne Blume—
O Schweigen.

Traumhaft erschüttern des Wildbachs
Dunkle Geister das Herz,
Finsternis,
Die über die Schluchten hereinbricht!
Weiße Stimmen
Irrend durch schaurige Vorhöfe,
Zerrißne Terrassen,
Der Väter gewaltiger Groll, die Klage
Der Mütter,
Des Knaben goldener Kriegsschrei
Und Ungebornes
Seufzend aus blinden Augen.

O Schmerz, du flammendes Anschaun
Der großen Seele!
Schon zuckt im schwarzen Gewühl
Der Rosse und Wagen
Ein rosenschauriger Blitz
In die tönende Fichte.
Magnetische Kühle
Umschwebt dies stolze Haupt,
Glühende Schwermut
Eines zürnenden Gottes.

You wild mountains, the eagles'
Lofty sorrow.
Golden clouds
Smoke over stony desolation.
The pines, the black lambs at the precipice
Breathe patient tranquillity,
When suddenly the blueness,
The soft buzzing of the bumblebees
Becomes strangely silent.
O green flower—
O silence.

Dreamlike, dark spirits of the mountain torrent
Convulse the heart,
Darkness,
Which breaks in over the ravines!
White voices
Astray through ghastly vestibules,
Mutilated terraces,
The fathers' powerful rancor, the lament
Of the mothers,
The boy's golden war cry
And the unborn
Sighing from blind eyes.

O pain, you flaming contemplation
Of the great soul!
Already in the black throng
Of horses and wagons
A ghastly-rosaceous lightning bolt flashes
Into the resounding pines.
Magnetic coolness
Hovers round this proud head,
Glowing melancholy
Of an angry god.

The opening lines reflect the calm before the tempest, a serene yet desolate landscape in which activity and an air of expectancy begin to unfold. In the second stanza, the unrest of nature's gathering forces provokes an agitation of the "heart," and the cries which eerily pervade the mountain wilderness seem to stem from its aroused anguish. The tension in the anthropomorphized imagery builds to the electric level of the charged atmosphere just before the onset of a storm. The lightning flash in the third stanza heralds the critical point in the storm's development in the last stanza when the mounting tension peaks in a torrential downpour of tears and rain:

Angst, du giftige Schlange,
Schwarze, stirb im Gestein!
Da stürzen der Tränen

Wilde Ströme herab,
Sturm-Erbarmen,
Hallen in drohenden Donnern
Die schneeigen Gipfel rings.
Feuer
Läutert zerrissene Nacht.

Fear, you poisonous serpent,
Black one, perish in stone!
Then wild torrents of tears
Plunge downward,
Storm-Compassion,
The snowy peaks all round
Echo in menacing thunder.
Fire
Purifies the torn night.

The storm imagery as a phenomenon in nature remains coalesced with elements of human emotion until the cathartic torrent begins to fall. After the poem's speaker has cast the eye of Medusa on the serpent of fear, the climactic peak is reached and the landscape's anthropomorphic overlay dissolves. The thunder and lightning of the last lines reverberate in an empty mountainous landscape similar to the scene at the poem's beginning.

The sounds and rhythm alone of the German in the last stanza reflect the crescendo building to the line "Storm-Compassion" and the ensuing diminuendo. The staccato tempo and the repeated *st-*, *sch-*, and *t-* sounds in the preceding lines imitate the particularly rapid pelting beat of a rain just beginning to fall. The unusual hyphenated noun in the climactic line not only forms a bridge in the poem's pattern from intensification to catharsis, but also binds the release in nature to its emotional, human counterpart. It marks the poem's change of direction as well as the converging point for its two levels of imagery. The elongated, falling meter of the thunder which follows contrasts to the rushed beat in the preceding lines.

Catharsis, not destruction is the central message of "Das

Gewitter," a message which again counters the notion of Trakl's increasingly precipitous fall into a terminal madness. The late poetry eloquently testifies to the resilience of a creative mind destined to its dark end by the overwhelming odds of external circumstance rather than internal momentum. Trakl's allusion in the letter to the guilt and darkness which must be gone "through" reflect in autobiographical terms the preoccupation of the poetry since "Helian" with psychic transformation, not disintegration.

The Poet and the Great War

At the end of the poem "Die Schwermut" ("Melancholy"—I, 161), written before the war's outbreak, yet focused on a bloody battle, an abbess—literally a female monk—appears among the bones of mutilated soldiers:

> Herbstesnacht so kühle kommt,
> Erglänzt mit Sternen
> Über zerbrochenem Männergebein
> Die stille Mönchin.
>
> Autumn evening comes so cooly—
> Glistening with stars
> Over shattered human bones
> The quiet abbess.

After Trakl's experience of war's real misery at the battle of Grodek and in the poem commemorating the battle, he places the sister's shade on the battlefield as a similar figure who greets the fallen heroes' spirits:

> Unter goldnem Gezweig der Nacht und Sternen
> Es schwankt der Schwester Schatten durch den schweigenden
> Hain,
> Zu grüßen die Geister der Helden, die blutenden Häupter;
>
> Under golden branches of the night and stars

> The sister's shade sways through the silent grove,
> To greet the spirits of the heroes, the bleeding heads;
> [I, 167, 11–13]

The tone of this poem in its entirety, Trakl's last work, strikes a stark contrast with the ebullient mood of his countrymen left behind on the homefront. In his autobiography, *The World of Yesterday,* Stefan Zweig gave a fascinating account of the summer days in 1914 leading up to the outbreak of the war. The event which finally ignited the conflagration, the assassination in Sarajevo of the successor to the crown, at first seemed destined to pass without great consequences. It was believed that after Vienna had conveyed a suitable degree of indignation to the provincial government, the assassination would take its place among a string of political crises that had been peacefully settled in the recent past. Austria-Hungary had not known war since 1866, and its prospect seemed remote. This view proved myopic, however, as four weeks later war was declared on Serbia.

The pace of events accelerated, and soon throughout most of Europe the battle lines had been drawn. In Austria the declaration of war was greeted with widespread enthusiasm by a populace whose memories of national conflict consisted almost entirely of patriotism, heroism, and manly deeds, memories polished anew by the government and press. Modern technology had yet to rid combat of the last shreds of heroics and glory in the popular imagination. Trakl was only one among many who initially greeted the prospect of war as the approaching "storm" that could bring release from an infinite variety of private problems.[12] For others it provided the symbolic occasion for the subordination of individuality to the communal effort and a sense of cohesiveness with a national whole.

Even Sigmund Freud, the foremost champion of culture's tight reins on the destructiveness of the instincts, could not at first

[12]Wolfgang Rothe, "Der grosse Krieg: Geschichtssoziologische Marginalien," *Schriftsteller und totalitäre Welt* (Bern: Francke, 1966), p. 29.

resist the infectious enthusiasm for war. Ernest Jones wrote that "his first response [to the declaration of war] was rather one of youthful enthusiasm, apparently a re-awakening of the military ardors of his boyhood."[13] On July 26, 1914, Freud wrote to Karl Abraham that Austria's ultimatum to Serbia was a "deliverance through a bold-spirited deed" and that he felt himself to be an Austrian for the first time in thirty years. Hugo von Hofmannsthal contrasted the "desolate, faltering years" of the recent past with the "beautiful intoxication" of those days in August 1914.[14] Stefan Zweig wrote:

> And to be truthful, I must acknowledge that there was a majestic, rapturous, and even seductive something in this first outbreak of the people from which one could escape only with difficulty. And in spite of all my hatred and aversion for war, I should not like to have missed the memory of those first days. As never before, thousands and hundreds of thousands felt what they should have felt in peace time, that they belonged together.[15]

Rilke too was initially caught up in the general excitation and worked for a time—as did Hofmannsthal, Zweig, and Werfel—in the "literary group" at the War Archives in Vienna. A number of less notable writers also belonged to this group, whose function was to lend literary style to the Austrian propaganda effort. Karl Kraus was almost alone in the silence with which he at first countered the general hysteria. And later, although many like Rilke rapidly lost their enthusiasm, Kraus waged a solitary public campaign against the war without leaving Austria and despite the censorship.[16]

The high pitch of emotionalism quite naturally subsided much

[13]Jones, *The Life and Work of Sigmund Freud: Years of Maturity, 1901–1919* (New York: Basic, 1957), II, 171.

[14]Hofmannsthal, "Appell an die oberen Stände," *Prosa III* (Frankfurt: S. Fischer, 1952), p. 176.

[15]Zweig, *The World of Yesterday*, p. 223.

[16]C. E. Williams, *The Broken Eagle: The Politics of Austrian Literature from Empire to Anschluss* (London: Paul Elek, 1974), p. 206.

more quickly at the front lines than it did in the streets of Vienna. At Grodek, where Trakl's unit first saw action, one of the bloodiest battles of the Eastern campaign took place. The *Frankfurter Zeitung* printed the following report from the front on October 7, 1914:

> As the Austrians were just evacuating their positions near Lemberg, a fellow-soldier crossed the woods northeast of Grodek, woods which recur in all of the descriptions of the battle as the object of the bitterest conflict. "On a space no larger than this little room" he reported, "there lay four or five bodies everywhere. . . . I saw Russian corpses in Wereszycabach and the picture will long torment me in my dreams. They were stacked upon one another in what appeared to be ten layers. Here and there a hand still moved, a pale mouth groaned."[17]

Trakl's poem "Grodek" (I, 167) is a reflection of the sobriety which rapidly set in among those unfortunate enough to witness the beginnings of the first modern war:

> Am Abend tönen die herbstlichen Wälder
> Von tödlichen Waffen, die goldnen Ebenen
> Und blauen Seen, darüber die Sonne
> Düstrer hinrollt; umfängt die Nacht
> Sterbende Krieger, die wilde Klage
> Ihrer zerbrochenen Münder.
> Doch stille sammelt im Weidengrund
> Rotes Gewölk, darin ein zürnender Gott wohnt
> Das vergoßne Blut sich, mondne Kühle;
> Alle Straßen münden in schwarze Verwesung.
> Unter goldnem Gezweig der Nacht und Sternen
> Es schwankt der Schwester Schatten durch den schweigenden
> Hain,
> Zu grüßen die Geister der Helden, die blutenden Häupter;
> Und leise tönen im Rohr die dunkeln Flöten des Herbstes.
> O stolzere Trauer! ihr ehernen Altäre

[17]As quoted in Stupp, "Georg Trakl der Dichter und seine südostdeutsche Abkunft," p. 22.

Die heiße Flamme des Geistes nährt heute ein gewaltiger Schmerz,
Die ungebornen Enkel.

In the evening the autumn woods resound
With deadly weapons, the golden plains
And blue lakes; the sun rolls
More gloomily over them; the night embraces
Dying warriors, the wild lament
Of their shattered mouths.
Yet quietly in the pasture's hollow,
Red clouds, the spent blood gathers—
There a wrathful god lives, lunar coolness;
All roads empty into black decay.
Under golden branches of the night and stars
The sister's shade sways through the silent grove,
To greet the spirits of the heroes, the bleeding heads;
And softly the dark flutes of autumn resound in the reed.
O prouder grief! You bronze altars,
A powerful pain nourishes today the hot flame of the spirit,
The unborn grandsons.

Few poets of any nationality or language have come to such serenely poetic terms with the holocaust of twentieth-century warfare. The battle and its aftermath at Grodek presented Trakl with experiences for which there existed no commensurate language. Prior to 1914, no one could foresee the entirely novel forms of atrocities that modern technology was capable of delivering. Hofmannsthal, always finely attuned to the limits of language, recognized the enormous task in overcoming the "speechless emotion" in the face of this war's unique horrors.[18] "It is impossible to express the reality of it," he wrote about a campaign in the following year.[19] War had become impersonal, the enemy faceless and remote, and death an absurdly gratuitous event. Trakl's "Grodek" is to World War I what Paul Celan's "Todesfuge" ("Fugue of Death") later became to the concentration camps of World War II. Refusing to be struck dumb by

[18]Hofmannsthal, "Die Taten und der Ruhm," *Prosa III*, p. 243.
[19]Hofmannsthal, "Geist der Karpathen," *Prosa III*, p. 263.

events which never before had been thrust upon human sensibilities, each poet found within his language the means of poetic response.

Underlying and supporting this subdued, almost epic understatement of war's pathos are the poem's even rhythms and long lines, which, with the exception of line 10, are elements of even longer complex sentences. While the lines flow into one another, Trakl's style remains essentially paratactical, since each of the complex sentences comprises a distinct entity. The detached overview of the speaker's perspective also acts to filter away the war's immediate presence. In the poem's first four lines, his view encompasses both the localized scene of battle where it is evening and a distant landscape still under the sun's light. Although the places are separated in space and time, a common verb joins them: the woods, plains, and lake all echo with war's sounds.

The following scene, essentially a close-up of the first one, begins at the middle of line 4. At its center lie the battle's casualties, the "embrace" of their cries by the night paralleling the containment of war's emotionalism by the entire poem. The next scene, its first word (yet) indicative of its countering function, introduces an angry god. In the complex imagery of these lines, the god not only "lives" in the red clouds and spilt blood, but his very existence appears to come about in their gathering. The key word "yet" suggests that the basis of his anger is the sight of the human sacrifice rather than the irrationality of a conventional, demonic wargod. Its effect is to oppose the entire scene to the preceding six lines of the poem. The god's anger is the response to the war's carnage in these lines, not its propelling force.

The aphoristic statement in line 10 which makes claim to a general truth falls out of the sequence of graphic vignettes. Its verb (münden) normally describes in German the flow of a river at its mouth into a larger body of water. And the line marks the transition into the familiar and Novalis-like realm peculiar to Trakl beyond life, but not death, a realm into which all mortal paths are said to lead in "Grodek." Here in this scene of after-death, the sister's shade moves in a masculine tempo, accentuated by the alliteration, among the fallen heroes. She "greets" them in this wider realm—that is, her function is to receive them as a sentinel, not to console them for their loss of the wartorn world left behind. The rhythm and alliteration emphasize her strength. Her image has grown from its meaning of existential reassurance on an individual level in the prose poems to messianic proportions in "Grodek." It functions similarly although less reassuringly in another one of Trakl's last poems (I, 166):

Schwester stürmischer Schwermut
Sieh ein ängstlicher Kahn versinkt
Unter Sternen,
Dem schweigenden Antlitz der Nacht.

Sister of stormy sadness
See, an anxious skiff founders
Under the stars,
The silent face of the night.

Her quasi-religious significance in the last works contrasts even more distinctly with the decadent, titillating mixture of sin and eroticism which marked her appearance in the very early poems.

The poem's final three lines are again predominantly aphoristic and have aroused critical speculation as well as poetic response. The crucial question is whether the "unborn grandsons" are the never-to-be-born progeny of those who fell in the field or if they are a yet-to-be-born generation of spiritual descendants of the fallen. A group of young Austrian poets after World War II interpreted the lines as prophetic of their own generation: "we believe that Trakl's reticent verses concern us before all others. [They concern us as] the unborn grandsons who have not yet dared to express the powerful pain which nourished them."[20] James

[20]These words appeared in 1946 in a special issue of the radical Viennese cultural journal *Plan*. They are part of an "Attestation to Georg Trakl" ("Bekenntnis zu Georg Trakl," *Plan,* 7 [1946], p. 554).

Wright, an American poet, wrote many years after Trakl's death an "Echo for the Promise of Georg Trakl's Life":

> Quiet voice,
> In the midst of those blazing
> Howitzers in blossom.
> Their fire
> Is a vacancy.
>
> What do those stuttering machines
> Have to do
> With the solitude?
>
> Guns make no sound.
> Only the quiet voice
> Speaks from the body of the deer
> To the body of the woman.
>
> My own body swims in a silent pool,
> And I make silence.
>
> They both hear me.
> Hear me,
> Father of my sound,
> My poor son.[21]

Wright plays in the poem on the contrast of war's silent sounds with the audibility of the poet's "quiet voice." It is the latter which speaks to him and prompts the "echo." In the last stanza, Wright addresses Trakl in his dual role as poet and soldier, paying respect to him as a poetic progenitor, "Father of my sound," and extending him sympathy as one of war's casualties, "My poor son." The poem is Wright's way of testifying that these fallen sons—specifically Trakl himself—have not remained barren. Wright claims, in effect, to be one of the "unborn grandsons"

[21]Wright, *Collected Poems* (Middletown: Wesleyan University Press, 1971), pp. 179–180.

about whose future Trakl's poem seemed to have left for coming generations to decide.

During Ludwig von Ficker's last meeting with the poet at the hospital in October 1914, Trakl had read the poem aloud in a longer version. This version has been lost, but Ficker later recalled that the grandson's fate "was somewhat more broadly sketched and did not yet exhibit that abrupt perspective abridgment" of the extant version.[22] Unfortunately, even Ficker's recollections fail to indicate the direction which this longer version pointed. In any case, Trakl eventually discarded it in favor of the abridged version, a decision characteristic of the poet's method.

From July 1914 to October 1919, the war brought a halt to the regular publication of Ficker's *Brenner*. In spring of 1915, however, a special yearbook edition appeared, which included "Grodek" along with several other of Trakl's last poems. It was dedicated "in memoriam Georg Trakl."

The Unanswered Question

With reference to Spoerri's psychiatric study of Trakl, written long before the publication of the historical-critical edition and over twenty years before his own remarks, a literary critic wrote: "The symptoms which point to schizophrenia are so unsettling that one could ask whether an attempt to interpret Trakl was really worth the effort, whether a literary or intellectual confrontation with him was really possible, since it would naturally be hopeless to claim to interpret the products of an insane imagination."[23] My readings of Trakl's poems have sought to show that this categorical linking of schizophrenia to unintelligibility is as outdated in literary studies as it has become in psychiatric practice. I have tried to demonstrate that the poems can be read with a degree of understanding not in spite of schizophrenic "symp-

[22]Ludwig von Ficker, *Erinnerung an Georg Trakl,* p. 190.

[23]Gustav Kars, "Georg Trakl in wechselnder Deutung," *Literatur und Kritik,* 93 (1975), 133.

toms," but precisely because these traits point beyond language to possibilities of human experience. An unconscious aversion to the experience reflected in the poetry seems to sustain the predominance of the formalistic approach. Avoiding this disturbance radiating from Trakl's poetry, however, produces a type of reading that Frederick Crews, in a general critique of modernist criticism, has called "anaesthetic," an insulating wrap designed primarily to allay the reader's own "fear of psychic dissolution."[24] Finally, those aspects readily dismissable as reflections of a schizophrenic's downward course I have tried to bring into relief against the more encompassing process now considered by some to include reintegration as well as disintegration.

General theoretical claims about modernity in poetry have also tended to support a formalistic approach to Trakl's verse. The notion of the modern poet as a technician of language whose function is to assemble words into fascinating configurations offers little incentive to the articulation of what I have called the aura of human experience in Trakl's poetry. Language itself, at least in theory, has become the primary producer as well as sole end of a poetry from which the poet seems to have become all but excluded. The modern, nonrepresentational poem appears to exist in linguistic self-sufficiency, isolated from the reader as well as the poet except through the fascination of word patterns. Yet it is not this sterile language of fascination that continues to captivate readers of Trakl's poetry and once prompted K. B. Heinrich to write: "this poet totally captures one's soul, eye and ear."[25]

Underlying the enduring attraction of this poetry is an extralinguistic factor which Gottfried Benn touched upon in a discussion of theories of poetic modernity. Benn, in whose aesthetic theory "fascination" played a central role, allowed for the presence of what he called an "impurity," even in *poésie pure*. This "impur-

[24]Frederick Crews, "Anaesthetic Criticism," *Out of My System: Psychoanalysis, Ideology, and Critical Method* (New York: Oxford University Press, 1975), pp. 77 and 84.

[25]*Erinnerung an Georg Trakl*, p. 94.

ity'' is the poet himself, a concession of added significance coming from the pen of the cerebral modernist *par excellence:*

> Mallarmé's maxim is the most famous one: a poem arises not from feelings [*sic*], but from words. Eliot takes the most remarkable point of view: even *poésie pure* has to retain a certain measure of impurity. The subject [of the poem] must in a certain sense be appraised of its own value if a poem is to be experienced as poetry. I would say that the author stands unmistakably and incessantly behind every poem: his essence, his being, his inner condition. Even the subjects arise in the poem only because they were previously *his* subjects. He [the poet] remains then, in every case, that impurity in Eliot's sense. Fundamentally, then, I believe that there is no other subject for the lyric poem than the poet himself.[26]

My readings have asserted that ''that impurity in Eliot's sense''—the essence of what two different Trakl scholars have called its ''existential claim'' and its ''existential density''—steadily increased in Trakl's poetry as it gradually left its early derivative phase to explore the poet's own psychopathology.[27] Trakl belongs to that line of German poets who, without a direct confrontation with their unstable mental lives, might never have cultivated more than an imitative poetic talent.

Where psychopathology and aesthetic intention work in conjunction, however, it is difficult if not impossible to draw the line between them. As a poetry of ''exchanged senses,'' Trakl's poetry shares its synesthetic vision with many schizophrenics.[28] Ambivalence, which in its extremes can bring about mental and physical stasis, was clearly at work in the variants and final shapes of Trakl's poems. The rapid shifts of tenses, often apparently unmotivated, seem to imitate the outwardly arbitrary shifts from one level of awareness to another in a pathologically labile

[26]Benn, ''Probleme der Lyrik,'' pp. 509–510.

[27]Kemper, *Entwürfe,* p. 211. Philipp, p. 103.

[28]Erna Kritsch, ''The Synesthetic Metaphors in the Poetry of Georg Trakl,'' *Monatshefte,* 54 (1962), 69.

personality. Confronting a schizophrenic, one may sense "the presence of various fragments, or incomplete elements, of different 'personalities' in operation at one time."[29] It is not unusual for him to speak of himself in the second- and third-person forms as well as the first.

While the avoidance of the metaphor's traditional signifier—the "as if"—marks Trakl's imagery as particularly modern in Benn's sense, the very root of the schizophrenic's enigmatic "word salad" may lie in his inability to set the communicational mode of his fantasy—its "as if" mode—to the listener.[30] Trakl's neologisms and paratactical style resemble the schizophrenic's coinage of new words and his characteristically disjointed thought patterns. The first, however, is a time-honored poetic device and the latter was not only once claimed by Trakl to be a conscious part of his style (I, 478), but was a hallmark of Expressionist poetry as well.

Trakl's dark forebodings of cultural disaster in poems like "Helian" and "Abendland" resemble the schizophrenic's cataclysmic visions, visions explained as the projections of internal upheaval and disintegration onto external circumstances. The schizophrenic "experiences what has been termed a vision of the 'destruction of the world,' a chaotic mixture of terror and disaster with the presentiment of a turn towards something new, something unprecedented in grandeur, a dimly perceived Dawn of the Gods, Apocalypse, and Resurrection."[31] Similarly, "Helian" and "Abendland" have their deepest roots in psychic rather than political tremors. The implication that the term "projection"

[29]Laing, *The Divided Self,* p. 196.

[30]"... it seems that the 'word salad' of schizophrenia can be described in terms of the patient's failure to recognize the metaphoric nature of his fantasies. In what should be triadic constellations of messages, the frame-setting message (*e.g.,* the phrase 'as if') is omitted, and the metaphor or fantasy is narrated and acted upon in a manner which would be appropriate if the fantasy were a message of the more direct kind" (Gregory Bateson, *Steps to an Ecology of Mind* [New York: Ballantine, 1972], p. 190).

[31]Wolfgang Born, "The Art of the Insane," *Ciba Symposia,* 7 (January 1946), 217.

has in a psychiatrist's vocabulary, however—that the schizophrenic maps psychic onto empirical reality and loses the ability to distinguish between them—is clearly inappropriate to a poetry nourished by the very fusion of landscape and mind-scape. Furthermore, Trakl's gloomy images depicting, for example, the "demise of the race" and the "dying peoples" were not without basis in the sociopolitical realities of the Habsburg monarchy, whose structures and emperor were twentieth-century anachronisms. That is, while Trakl was not a political poet in any overt sense, such imagery had roots in historical reality. An East German critic praises Trakl most highly precisely for the clear view and unadulterated expression of his culture's despair.[32] She perceptively differentiates him from that category of poets for whom despair and nihilism were aesthetic playthings. Finally, the schizophrenic "presentiment of a turn towards something new" may indeed be just that, although not in the grandiose terms of the vision. It may reflect the benign turn in the course of the so-called schizophrenic process, the turn that points the way through the illness, if circumstances do not halt or reverse its natural momentum.

Many aspects common to Trakl's poetry and the experience of schizophrenia can be brought together under the rubric of what psychiatry calls ego loss, the loss of that focusing center of the individual which enables a person to relate to the world from a stable point and to say *I*. Beginning as a theme in the earliest poetry, the fragmented self next finds its way into the poems' structure. The speaker of these poems seems to view the poetic landscape through multiple eyes. Both theme and formal technique are at this point overtly tied to widespread contemporary intellectual currents. At least by the time he wrote "Helian," however, the fragmented perspective—the "shattered eyes" of the grandson—becomes identified with a "gentle" form of insan-

[32]Silvia Schlenstedt, "Georg Trakl," *Weimarer Beiträge*, 5 (1959), 513–526.

ity and returns to the poetry as a thematic concern. Metanoia and poetry become even more closely entwined in "An den Knaben Elis" where the demise of the figure addressed as *You* precedes the descent into an altered state and the formation with the speaker of a creative union. The split figures of the prose poems reflect the more sinister aspect of a disintegrating self. Its conflicting facets are engaged in a life-and-death battle. Yet at least for moments in these works, madness becomes transformation: the *I* of "Offenbarung und Untergang" not only resists the "white voice" that demands its suicide—a major symptom of most patients diagnosed schizophrenic is an authoritative hallucinatory voice—but also realizes a new selfhood. Intrinsic to this new selfhood are momentary visions of a changed relationship to the sister. And an affirmation of her image is simultaneously an affirmation of the self that created the image. By this affirmation, the new self—a "true self" in the Laingian sense—grants positive existence to a forbidden, but determinative facet of its own constitution.

It has long been noted that schizophrenics experience a sensation of transformation that seems to impel them toward a radical shift in the entirety of their relationships to the self and the world. The negative terms used to describe this condition—depersonalization and derealization—convey the normative attitude toward radical change inherent in psychiatry's nomenclature. Detachment from his past person and his past reality, is, however, the indispensable first step of the schizophrenic toward a future person and future reality. To change radically, he must neither return to his past nor remain suspended at this initial step. In the introduction to *The Inner World of Mental Illness,* Bert Kaplan singles out the "concern with the category of change and transcendence" as a salient, recurring feature of the psychopathologies described in his book: "The new state must... involve a genuine moving to a new solution, a movement which we can see would have been impossible without the illness.

Thus Lara Jefferson says, 'I cannot escape from the madness by the door I came in, that is certain—nor do I want to.' "[33]

At the "impure" level to which Benn and Eliot refer, that level absent perhaps only wholly in computer lyric, Trakl's poetry reflects the decisive break from a pathogenic reality and a false self. Yet intermittent glimpses of a resolution—fragmentarily constructed and ambivalently perceived—that naturally follows the course of this disintegration find expression throughout the latest poetry. That door leading out of his madness, slightly ajar to the very end, was violently slammed shut by the larger course of events which overran Europe in the summer and fall of 1914. Three years later Buschbeck sent a volume of personal recollections of the poet to Rilke. Rilke used the occasion of his letter of gratitude to remark on Trakl's poetry and to express his emotional reaction to Trakl's ability to "demonstrate the weight of [his] incessant downfall in such precise structures." Apparently dissatisfied with the partial truth of this thought, however, Rilke amended it in the next line of his letter with a remarkable simile that seems to capture the essence of self-rescue in Trakl's fall: "It occurs to me that this entire work has its simile in the dying of Li Tai Pe: here as well as there, falling is the pretext for the most inexorable ascension."[34]

[33]*The Inner World of Mental Illness: A Series of First-Person Accounts of What It Was Like,* ed. Bert Kaplan (New York: Harper & Row, 1964), pp. xi and xii.

[34]Rilke apparently wrote in response to receiving Buschbeck's book, *Georg Trakl* (Berlin: Neue Jugend, 1917). His letter is dated 22 February 1917 and is in *Briefe aus den Jahren 1914–1921,* eds. Ruth Sieber-Rilke and Carl Sieber (Leipzig: Insel, 1937), pp. 126–127. Rilke probably refers in his letter to Li Po or Li Tai Po (A.D. 701–762), one of China's greatest poets who, as legend tells it, met his end in the water after he had drunkenly reached down from a boat to grab for the moon's reflection.

Appendix:

Trakl's Longer Poems

PSALM

Es ist ein Licht, das der Wind ausgelöscht hat.
Es ist ein Heidekrug, den am Nachmittag ein Betrunkener verläßt.
Es ist ein Weinberg, verbrannt und schwarz mit Löchern voll Spinnen.
Es ist ein Raum, den sie mit Milch getüncht haben.
Der Wahnsinnige ist gestorben. Es ist eine Insel der Südsee,
Den Sonnengott zu empfangen. Man rührt die Trommeln.
Die Männer führen kriegerische Tänze auf.
Die Frauen wiegen die Hüften in Schlinggewächsen und Feuerblumen,
Wenn das Meer singt. O unser verlorenes Paradies.

Die Nymphen haben die goldenen Wälder verlassen.
Man begräbt den Fremden. Dann hebt ein Flimmerregen an.
Der Sohn des Pan erscheint in Gestalt eines Erdarbeiters,
Der den Mittag am glühenden Asphalt verschläft.
Es sind kleine Mädchen in einem Hof in Kleidchen voll herzzerreißender
Armut!
Es sind Zimmer, erfüllt von Akkorden und Sonaten.
Es sind Schatten, die sich vor einem erblindeten Spiegel umarmen.
An den Fenstern des Spitals wärmen sich Genesende.
Ein weißer Dampfer am Kanal trägt blutige Seuchen herauf.

Die fremde Schwester erscheint wieder in jemands bösen Träumen.
Ruhend im Haselgebüsch spielt sie mit seinen Sternen.
Der Student, vielleicht ein Doppelgänger, schaut ihr lange vom Fenster
nach.
Hinter ihm steht sein toter Bruder, oder er geht die alte Wendeltreppe
herab.
Im Dunkel brauner Kastanien verblaßt die Gestalt des jungen Novizen.
Der Garten ist im Abend. Im Kreuzgang flattern die Fledermäuse umher.
Die Kinder des Hausmeisters hören zu spielen auf und suchen das Gold
des Himmels.
Endakkorde eines Quartetts. Die kleine Blinde läuft zitternd durch die
Allee,
Und später tastet ihr Schatten an kalten Mauern hin, umgeben von
Märchen und heiligen Legenden.

Es ist ein leeres Boot, das am Abend den schwarzen Kanal
heruntertreibt.

PSALM

There is a light which the wind has extinguished.
There is a tavern on the heath which a drunk leaves in the afternoon.
There is a vineyard, burnt and black with holes full of spiders.
There is a room which they have whitewashed with milk.
The madman has died. There is a South Sea island
To receive the sun god. They strike the drums.
The men perform warlike dances.
The women sway their hips in liana and fire flowers
When the sea sings. O our lost paradise.

The nymphs have left the golden woods.
They bury the stranger. Then a glistening rain begins.
The son of Pan appears in the form of a laborer
Who sleeps away the noon by the glowing asphalt.
There are small girls in a court in dresses of heartrending poverty!
There are rooms filled with chords and sonatas.
There are shadows which embrace in front of a blinded mirror.
At the windows of the hospital the convalescents warm themselves.
A white steamer bears bloody pestilence up the canal.

The strange sister appears again in someone's evil dreams.
Resting in the hazelbush she plays with his stars.
The student, perhaps a double, gazes long after her from the window.
Behind him stands his dead brother or he descends the old winding stairs.
In the darkness of the brown chestnuts the figure of the young novice
grows pale.
In the garden it is evening. Bats flutter around the cloister.
The caretaker's children cease their play and seek heaven's gold.
Final chords of a quartet. The little blind girl runs trembling through the
lane,
And later her shadow gropes along the cold walls surrounded by fairy
tales and holy legends.

There is an empty boat which makes its way down the canal in the
evening.
Human ruins decay in the gloom of the old asylum.
The dead orphans lie at the garden wall.
Angels with filth-stained wings step out of grey rooms.

In der Düsternis des alten Asyls verfallen menschliche Ruinen.
Die toten Waisen liegen an der Gartenmauer.
Aus grauen Zimmern treten Engel mit kotgefleckten Flügeln.
Würmer tropfen von ihren vergilbten Lidern.
Der Platz vor der Kirche ist finster und schweigsam, wie in den Tagen
der Kindheit.
Auf silbernen Sohlen gleiten frühere Leben vorbei
Und die Schatten der Verdammten steigen zu den seufzenden Wassern
nieder.
In seinem Grab spielt der weiße Magier mit seinen Schlangen.

Schweigsam über der Schädelstätte öffnen sich Gottes goldene Augen.

HELIAN

In den einsamen Stunden des Geistes
Ist es schön, in der Sonne zu gehn
An den gelben Mauern des Sommers hin.
Leise klingen die Schritte im Gras; doch immer schläft
Der Sohn des Pan im grauen Marmor.

Abends auf der Terrasse betranken wir uns mit braunem Wein.
Rötlich glüht der Pfirsich im Laub;
Sanfte Sonate, frohes Lachen.

Schön ist die Stille der Nacht.
Auf dunklem Plan
Begegnen wir uns mit Hirten und weißen Sternen.

Wenn es Herbst geworden ist
Zeigt sich nüchterne Klarheit im Hain.
Besänftigte wandeln wir an roten Mauern hin
Und die runden Augen folgen dem Flug der Vögel.
Am Abend sinkt das weiße Wasser in Graburnen.

In kahlen Gezweigen feiert der Himmel.
In reinen Händen trägt der Landmann Brot und Wein
Und friedlich reifen die Früchte in sonniger Kammer.

Worms drip from their yellowed eyelids.
The square in front of the church is dark and silent as in the days of
childhood.
Earlier lives glide past on silver soles
And the shades of the damned descend to the sighing waters.
In his grave the white magician plays with his snakes.

Silently above Golgotha God's golden eyes open.

HELIAN

In the lonely hours of the spirit
It is beautiful to walk in the sun
Along the yellow walls of summer.
The steps sound quietly in the grass. Yet the son of Pan
Still sleeps in the grey marble.

Evenings on the terrace we got drunk on brown wine.
The peach glows reddish in the leaves.
Soft sonata, happy laughter.

The night's tranquillity is beautiful.
On the dark clearing
We encounter shepherds and white stars.

When it has become fall
Sober clarity emerges in the grove.
Calmed, we wander along red walls
And the rounded eyes follow the flight of the birds.
In the evening the white water sinks in the funeral urns.

In bare branches the heavens celebrate.
In pure hands the peasant bears bread and wine
And the fruits ripen peacefully in the sunny chamber.

O wie ernst ist das Antlitz der teueren Toten.
Doch die Seele erfreut gerechtes Anschaun.

Gewaltig ist das Schweigen des verwüsteten Gartens,
Da der junge Novize die Stirne mit braunem Laub bekränzt,
Sein Odem eisiges Gold trinkt.

Die Hände rühren das Alter bläulicher Wasser
Oder in kalter Nacht die weißen Wangen der Schwestern.

Leise und harmonisch ist ein Gang an freundlichen Zimmern hin,
Wo Einsamkeit ist und das Rauschen des Ahorns,
Wo vielleicht noch die Drossel singt.

Schön ist der Mensch und erscheinend im Dunkel,
Wenn er staunend Arme und Beine bewegt,
Und in purpurnen Höhlen stille die Augen rollen.

Zur Vesper verliert sich der Fremdling in schwarzer
Novemberzerstörung,
Unter morschem Geäst, an Mauern voll Aussatz hin,
Wo vordem der heilige Bruder gegangen,
Versunken in das sanfte Saitenspiel seines Wahnsinns,

O wie einsam endet der Abendwind.
Ersterbend neigt sich das Haupt im Dunkel des Ölbaums.

Erschütternd ist der Untergang des Geschlechts.
In dieser Stunde füllen sich die Augen des Schauenden
Mit dem Gold seiner Sterne.

Am Abend versinkt ein Glockenspiel, das nicht mehr tönt,
Verfallen die schwarzen Mauern am Platz,
Ruft der tote Soldat zum Gebet.

Ein bleicher Engel
Tritt der Sohn ins leere Haus seiner Väter.

Die Schwestern sind ferne zu weißen Greisen gegangen.

O how solemn is the face of the beloved dead one.
Yet the soul enjoys just contemplation.

The silence of the devastated garden is powerful,
As the young novice garlands his brow with brown foliage,
His breath drinks icy gold.

The hands touch the age of bluish waters
Or in cold night, the white cheeks of the sisters.

Quiet and harmonious is the walk past friendly rooms
Where there is solitude and the murmur of the maple,
Where perhaps the thrush still sings.

Man is beautiful and manifest in the darkness
When astonished he moves arms and legs
And in crimson sockets his eyes silently roll.

At vespers the stranger loses his way in the black destruction of
November,
Under decaying branches, along walls full of leprosy,
Where in former times the holy brother had gone,
Lost in the gentle string music of his madness.

O how lonely the evening wind ceases.
Dying, the head bows down in the darkness of the olive tree.

Shattering is the demise of the race.
In this hour the eyes of the beholder fill up
With the gold of his stars.

In the evening a carillon sinks that no longer rings.
The black walls on the square crumble.
The dead soldier calls to prayer.

A pale angel,
The son enters the empty house of his fathers.

The sisters have gone far away to white old men.

Nachts fand sie der Schläfer unter den Säulen im Hausflur,
Zurückgekehrt von traurigen Pilgerschaften.

O wie starrt von Kot und Würmern ihr Haar,
Da er darein mit silbernen Füßen steht,
Und jene verstorben aus kahlen Zimmern treten.

O ihr Psalmen in feurigen Mitternachtsregen,
Da die Knechte mit Nesseln die sanften Augen schlugen,
Die kindlichen Früchte des Hollunders
Sich staunend neigen über ein leeres Grab.

Leise rollen vergilbte Monde
Über die Fieberlinnen des Jünglings,
Eh dem Schweigen des Winters folgt.

Ein erhabenes Schicksal sinnt den Kidron hinab,
Wo die Zeder, ein weiches Geschöpf,
Sich unter den blauen Brauen des Vaters entfaltet,
Über die Weide nachts ein Schäfer seine Herde führt.
Oder es sind Schreie im Schlaf,
Wenn ein eherner Engel im Hain den Menschen antritt,
Das Fleisch des Heiligen auf glühendem Rost hinschmilzt.

Um die Lehmhütten rankt purpurner Wein,
Tönende Bündel vergilbten Korns,
Das Summen der Bienen, der Flug des Kranichs.
Am Abend begegnen sich Auferstandene auf Felsenpfaden.

In schwarzen Wassern spiegeln sich Aussätzige;
Oder sie öffnen die kotbefleckten Gewänder
Weinend dem balsamischen Wind, der vom rosigen Hügel weht.

Schlanke Mägde tasten durch die Gassen der Nacht,
Ob sie den liebenden Hirten fänden.
Sonnabends tönt in den Hütten sanfter Gesang.

Lasset das Lied auch des Knaben gedenken,
Seines Wahnsinns, und weißer Brauen und seines Hingangs,
Des Verwesten, der bläulich die Augen aufschlägt.
O wie traurig ist dieses Wiedersehn.

At night the sleeper found them under the pillars of the hall,
Returned from sad pilgrimages.

O how their hair stiffens from filth and worms,
As he stands in it with silver feet,
And deceased, they step out of barren rooms.

O you psalms in the fiery rains of midnight,
As the servants beat their soft eyes with nettles;
The childlike fruits of the elder
Bow down astonished over an empty grave.

Quietly, yellowed moons roll
Over the fever linens of the youth,
Before the silence of winter ensues.

A sublime destiny ponders down the Kidron
Where the cedar, a tender creation,
Evolves under the blue brows of the father.
At night a shepherd leads his herd over the meadow.
Or there are cries in sleep,
When a brazen angel in the grove approaches man.
The flesh of the holy one melts away on the glowing grate.

Around the mudhuts climb purple grapes,
Ringing bundles of gilded grain,
The bees' buzzing, the crane's flight.
In the evening those risen from the dead meet on rocky paths.

In black waters lepers mirror themselves;
Or they open their filth-stained robes
Crying to the balmy wind which blows from the rosy hill.

Slender servant girls grope through the night streets
Seeking the loving shepherd.
Saturdays, gentle singing sounds in the huts.

Let the song also remember the boy,
His madness, white brows and his departure;
The mouldering one who opens his eyes bluishly.
O how sad this reunion is.

Die Stufen des Wahnsinns in schwarzen Zimmern,
Die Schatten der Alten unter der offenen Tür,
Da Helians Seele sich im rosigen Spiegel beschaut
Und Schnee und Aussatz von seiner Stirne sinken.

An den Wänden sind die Sterne erloschen
Und die weißen Gestalten des Lichts.

Dem Teppich entsteigt Gebein der Gräber,
Das Schweigen verfallener Kreuze am Hügel,
Des Weihrauchs Süße im purpurnen Nachtwind.

O ihr zerbrochenen Augen in schwarzen Mündern,
Da der Enkel in sanfter Umnachtung
Einsam dem dunkleren Ende nachsinnt,
Der stille Gott die blauen Lider über ihn senkt.

WINTERNACHT

Es ist Schnee gefallen. Nach Mitternacht verläßt du betrunken von purpurnem Wein den dunklen Bezirk der Menschen, die rote Flamme ihres Herdes. O die Finsternis!

Schwarzer Frost. Die Erde ist hart, nach Bitterem schmeckt die Luft. Deine Sterne schließen sich zu bösen Zeichen.

Mit versteinerten Schritten stampfst du am Bahndamm hin, mit runden Augen, wie ein Soldat, der eine schwarze Schanze stürmt. Avanti!

Bitterer Schnee und Mond!

Ein roter Wolf, den ein Engel würgt. Deine Beine klirren schreitend wie blaues Eis und ein Lächeln voll Trauer und Hochmut hat dein Antlitz versteinert und die Stirne erbleicht vor der Wollust des Frostes;

oder sie neigt sich schweigend über den Schlaf eines Wächters, der in seiner hölzernen Hütte hinsank.

Frost und Rauch. Ein weißes Sternenhemd verbrennt die tragenden Schultern und Gottes Geier zerfleischen dein metallenes Herz.

O der steinerne Hügel. Stille schmilzt und vergessen der kühle Leib im silbernen Schnee hin.

Schwarz ist der Schlaf. Das Ohr folgt lange den Pfaden der Sterne im Eis.

Beim Erwachen klangen die Glocken im Dorf. Aus dem östlichen Tor trat silbern der rosige Tag.

The steps of madness in black rooms,
The shades of the old men under the open door;
Then Helian's soul looks upon itself in the rosy mirror
And snow and leprosy fall from his brow.

On the walls the stars are extinguished
And the white forms of light.

The remains of graves descend from the tapestry,
The silence of fallen crosses on the mound,
The sweetness of incense in the purple night wind.

O you shattered eyes in black mouths,
As the grandson in gentle derangement
Ponders the darker end in solitude,
The quiet god lowers his blue lids over him.

WINTER NIGHT

Snow has fallen. Drunk from purple wine, you depart after the midnight hour from man's dark domain, the red flame of their hearth. O the darkness!

Black frost. The earth is hard, the air tastes bitter. Your stars contract to evil signs.

You stamp along the track's embankment with petrified steps; with round eyes, like a soldier, who storms a black trench. Avanti!

Bitter snow and moon!

A red wolf which an angel throttles. Striding, your legs clatter like blue ice and a smile full of sorrow and arrogance has petrified your face and your brow grows pale from the frost's lasciviousness;

or it bends silently over the sleep of a watchman who collapsed in his wooden hut.

Frost and smoke. A white starry shirt burns the shoulders wearing it and God's vultures mangle your metal heart.

O the stony hill. Silently the cool body melts forgotten into the silvery snow.

Black is the sleep. The ear follows for a long time the path of the stars in the ice.

Upon awakening, the bells in the village were ringing. Out from the eastern gate stepped silvery the rosy day.

VERWANDLUNG DES BÖSEN

Herbst: schwarzes Schreiten am Waldsaum; Minute stummer Zerstörung; auflauscht die Stirne des Aussätzigen unter dem kahlen Baum. Langvergangener Abend, der nun über die Stufen von Moos sinkt; November. Eine Glocke läutet und der Hirt führt eine Herde von schwarzen und roten Pferden ins Dorf. Unter dem Haselgebüsch weidet der grüne Jäger ein Wild aus. Seine Hände rauchen von Blut und der Schatten des Tiers seufzt im Laub über den Augen des Mannes, braun und schweigsam; der Wald. Krähen, die sich zerstreuen; drei. Ihr Flug gleicht einer Sonate, voll verblichener Akkorde und männlicher Schwermut; leise löst sich eine goldene Wolke auf. Bei der Mühle zünden Knaben ein Feuer an. Flamme ist des Bleichsten Bruder und jener lacht vergraben in sein purpurnes Haar; oder es ist ein Ort des Mordes, an dem ein steiniger Weg vorbeiführt. Die Berberitzen sind verschwunden, jahrlang träumt es in bleierner Luft unter den Föhren; Angst, grünes Dunkel, das Gurgeln eines Ertrinkenden: aus dem Sternenweiher zieht der Fischer einen großen, schwarzen Fisch, Antlitz voll Grausamkeit und Irrsinn. Die Stimmen des Rohrs, hadernder Männer im Rücken schaukelt jener auf rotem Kahn über frierende Herbstwasser, lebend in dunklen Sagen seines Geschlechts und die Augen steinern über Nächte und jungfräuliche Schrecken aufgetan. Böse.

Was zwingt dich still zu stehen auf der verfallenen Stiege, im Haus deiner Väter? Bleierne Schwärze. Was hebst du mit silberner Hand an die Augen; und die Lider sinken wie trunken von Mohn? Aber durch die Mauer von Stein siehst du den Sternenhimmel, die Milchstraße, den Saturn; rot. Rasend an die Mauer von Stein klopft der kahle Baum. Du auf verfallenen Stufen: Baum, Stern, Stein! Du, ein blaues Tier, das leise zittert; du, der bleiche Priester, der es hinschlachtet am schwarzen Altar. O dein Lächeln im Dunkel, traurig und böse, daß ein Kind im Schlaf erbleicht. Eine rote Flamme sprang aus deiner Hand und ein Nachtfalter verbrannte daran. O die Flöte des Lichts; o die Flöte des Tods. Was zwang dich still zu stehen auf verfallener Stiege, im Haus deiner Väter? Drunten ans Tor klopft ein Engel mit kristallnem Finger.

O die Hölle des Schlafs; dunkle Gasse, braunes Gärtchen. Leise läutet im blauen Abend der Toten Gestalt. Grüne Blümchen umgaukeln sie und ihr Antlitz hat sie verlassen. Oder es neigt sich verblichen über die kalte Stirne des Mörders im Dunkel des Hausflurs; Anbetung, purpurne Flamme der Wollust; hinsterbend stürzte über schwarze Stufen der Schläfer ins Dunkel.

Appendix: Trakl's Longer Poems

TRANSFORMATION OF EVIL

Autumn: Black striding on the forest's edge; a minute of mute destruction; the brow of the leper listens attentively under the leafless tree. Long past evening which now descends over the steps of moss; November. A bell tolls and the shepherd leads a herd of black and red horses into the village. Under the hazelbush the green hunter disembowels a wild animal. His hands reek with blood and the animal's shade sighs in the leaves above the man's eyes, brown and silent; the forest. Crows which disperse; three. Their flight resembles a sonata full of faded chords and masculine melancholy; a golden cloud gently dissolves. Near the mill, boys ignite a fire. Flame is the brother of the most pallid one and that one laughs buried in his purple hair; or it is a place for murder past which a stony path leads. The barberrys have disappeared; one dreams for years in the leaden air under the pines. Fear, green darkness, the gurgling of a drowning man: out from the starry pond a fisherman pulls a large, black fish, face full of cruelty and madness. The voices of the reed, of quarreling men at his back, that one pitches over freezing autumn waters in the red canoe, living in dark sagas of his race and his eyes stonily opened over nights and virginal terrors. Evil.

What compels you to stop on the decayed steps in the house of your fathers? Leaden blackness. What do you raise with silver hand to the eyes; and the lids sink as drunken from the poppy? But through the stone wall you see the starry heaven, the Milky Way, Saturn; red. Raving, the leafless tree knocks at the stone wall. You on decayed steps: tree, star, stone! You, a blue animal which trembles slightly; you, the pale priest who butchers it at the black altar. O your smiling in the darkness, sad and evil, that a child grows pale in its sleeping. A red flame sprang from your hand and a moth was burnt up. O the flute of light; o the flute of death. What compelled you to stop on decayed steps in the house of your fathers? Underneath at the gate an angel knocks with crystalline finger.

O the hell of sleep; dark street, brown garden. The dead woman's form rings lightly in the blue evening. Green flowers flutter about her and her face has left her. Or it bends ashen over the cold brow of the murderer in the darkness of the hall; Worship, purple flame of desire. Perishing, the sleeper plunged over black steps into the darkness.

Someone left you at the crossroads and you look back for a long time. Silver stride in the shadow of crippled apple trees. The fruit shines crimson in the black branches and the snake molts in the grass. O! the darkness; the sweat which breaks out on the icy brow and the sad dreams

Jemand verließ dich am Kreuzweg und du schaust lange zurück. Silberner Schritt im Schatten verkrüppelter Apfelbäumchen. Purpurn leuchtet die Frucht im schwarzen Geäst und im Gras häutet sich die Schlange. O! das Dunkel; der Schweiß, der auf die eisige Stirne tritt und die traurigen Träume im Wein, in der Dorfschenke unter schwarzverrauchtem Gebälk. Du, noch Wildnis, die rosige Inseln zaubert aus dem braunen Tabaksgewölk und aus dem Innern den wilden Schrei eines Greifen holt, wenn er um schwarze Klippen jagt in Meer, Sturm und Eis. Du, ein grünes Metall und innen ein feuriges Gesicht, das hingehen will und singen vom Beinerhügel finstere Zeiten und den flammenden Sturz des Engels. O! Verzweiflung, die mit stummem Schrei ins Knie bricht.

Ein Toter besucht dich. Aus dem Herzen rinnt das selbstvergossene Blut und in schwarzer Braue nistet unsäglicher Augenblick; dunkle Begegnung. Du—ein purpurner Mond, da jener im grünen Schatten des Ölbaums erscheint. Dem folgt unvergängliche Nacht.

TRAUM UND UMNACHTUNG

Am Abend ward zum Greis der Vater; in dunklen Zimmern versteinerte das Antlitz der Mutter und auf dem Knaben lastete der Fluch des entarteten Geschlechts. Manchmal erinnerte er sich seiner Kindheit, erfüllt von Krankheit, Schrecken und Finsternis, verschwiegener Spiele im Sternengarten, oder daß er die Ratten fütterte im dämmernden Hof. Aus blauem Spiegel trat die schmale Gestalt der Schwester und er stürzte wie tot ins Dunkel. Nachts brach sein Mund gleich einer roten Frucht auf und die Sterne erglänzten über seiner sprachlosen Trauer. Seine Träume erfüllten das alte Haus der Väter. Am Abend ging er gerne über den verfallenen Friedhof, oder er besah in dämmernder Totenkammer die Leichen, die grünen Flecken der Verwesung auf ihren schönen Händen. An der Pforte des Klosters bat er um ein Stück Brot; der Schatten eines Rappen sprang aus dem Dunkel und erschreckte ihn. Wenn er in seinem kühlen Bette lag, überkamen ihn unsägliche Tränen. Aber es war niemand, der die Hand auf seine Stirne gelegt hätte. Wenn der Herbst kam, ging er, ein Hellseher, in brauner Au. O, die Stunden wilder Verzückung, die Abende am grünen Fluß, die Jagden. O, die Seele, die leise das Lied des vergilbten Rohrs sang; feurige Frömmigkeit. Stille sah er und lang in die Sternenaugen der Kröte, befühlte mit erschauernden Händen die Kühle des alten Steins und besprach die ehrwürdige Sage des blauen Quells. O, die silbernen Fische und die Früchte, die von verkrüp-

from the wine in the village tavern under beams black with smoke. You, still savage, who conjures up rosy islands from the brown tobacco clouds and dredges from the inner self the wild cry of a griffin, when it hunts in the sea, storm and ice around black crags. You, a green metal and inside a fiery vision which wants to go and from the hill of bones sing dark times and the flaming plunge of the angel. O! Despair which breaks down to its knee with mute cry.

A dead man visits you. The self-spilt blood runs from the heart and an unspeakable moment nests in black brow; dark encounter. You—a purple moon when that one appears in the green shadow of the olive tree. Immortal night comes afterward.

DREAM AND DERANGEMENT

In the evening the father became an old man. In dark rooms the face of his mother turned into stone and on the boy weighed the curse of the degenerated race. Sometimes he remembered his childhood, filled with sickness, terrors and darkness, secret games in the starry garden, or that he fed the rats in the twilight-filled court. The slim figure of the sister stepped out of blue mirror and he plunged as if dead into the darkness. By night his mouth broke open like a red fruit and the stars glistened above his speechless sorrow. His dreams filled the old house of the fathers. In the evening he liked to walk over the ruined cemetery, or he looked at the corpses in the twilight-filled mortuary, the green spots of decay on their beautiful hands. At the gate of the cloister he asked for a piece of bread. The phantom of a horse sprang out of the darkness and frightened him. When he lay in his cool bed, unutterable tears overcame him. But there was no one who might have placed a hand on his forehead. When autumn came, he walked, a clairvoyant, in brown pasture. O, the hours of wild rapture, the evenings on the green river, the hunts. O, the soul which softly sang the song of the yellowed reed; fiery piety. Quietly he looked and long into the starry eyes of the toad, felt with shivering hands the coolness of the old stone and conjured the venerable legend of the blue spring. O, the silver fish and the fruits which fell from the stunted trees. The chords of his steps filled him with pride

pelten Bäumen fielen. Die Akkorde seiner Schritte erfüllten ihn mit Stolz und Menschenverachtung. Am Heimweg traf er ein unbewohntes Schloß. Verfallene Götter standen im Garten, hintrauernd am Abend. Ihm aber schien: hier lebte ich vergessene Jahre. Ein Orgelchoral erfüllte ihn mit Gottes Schauern. Aber in dunkler Höhle verbrachte er seine Tage, log und stahl und verbarg sich, ein flammender Wolf, vor dem weißen Antlitz der Mutter. O, die Stunde, da er mit steinernem Munde im Sternengarten hinsank, der Schatten des Mörders über ihn kam. Mit purpurner Stirne ging er ins Moor und Gottes Zorn züchtigte seine metallenen Schultern; o, die Birken im Sturm, das dunkle Getier, das seine umnachteten Pfade mied. Haß verbrannte sein Herz, Wollust, da er im grünenden Sommergarten dem schweigenden Kind Gewalt tat, in dem strahlenden sein umnachtetes Antlitz erkannte. Weh, des Abends am Fenster, da aus purpurnen Blumen, ein gräulich Gerippe, der Tod trat. O, ihr Türme und Glocken; und die Schatten der Nacht fielen steinern auf ihn.

Niemand liebte ihn. Sein Haupt verbrannte Lüge und Unzucht in dämmernden Zimmern. Das blaue Rauschen eines Frauengewandes ließ ihn zur Säule erstarren und in der Tür stand die nächtige Gestalt seiner Mutter. Zu seinen Häupten erhob sich der Schatten des Bösen. O, ihr Nächte und Sterne. Am Abend ging er mit dem Krüppel am Berge hin; auf eisigem Gipfel lag der rosige Glanz der Abendröte und sein Herz läutete leise in der Dämmerung. Schwer sanken die stürmischen Tannen über sie und der rote Jäger trat aus dem Wald. Da es Nacht ward, zerbrach kristallen sein Herz und die Finsternis schlug seine Stirne. Unter kahlen Eichbäumen erwürgte er mit eisigen Händen eine wilde Katze. Klagend zur Rechten erschien die weiße Gestalt eines Engels, und es wuchs im Dunkel der Schatten des Krüppels. Er aber hob einen Stein und warf ihn nach jenem, daß er heulend floh, und seufzend verging im Schatten des Baums das sanfte Antlitz des Engels. Lange lag er auf steinigem Acker und sah staunend das goldene Zelt der Sterne. Von Fledermäusen gejagt, stürzte er fort ins Dunkel. Atemlos trat er ins verfallene Haus. Im Hof trank er, ein wildes Tier, von den blauen Wassern des Brunnens, bis ihn fror. Fiebernd saß er auf der eisigen Stiege, rasend gen Gott, daß er stürbe. O, das graue Antlitz des Schreckens, da er die runden Augen über einer Taube zerschnittener Kehle aufhob. Huschend über fremde Stiegen begegnete er einem Judenmädchen und er griff nach ihrem schwarzen Haar und er nahm ihren Mund. Feindliches folgte ihm durch finstere Gassen und sein Ohr zerriß ein eisernes Klirren. An herbstlichen Mauern folgte er, ein Mesnerknabe, stille dem schweigen-

and contempt for men. On the way home he came upon an uninhabited castle. Ravaged gods stood in the garden, mourning away in the evening. But it seemed to him: I lived here forgotten years. An organ chorale filled him with God's shudders. But in the dark cavern he spent his days, lied and stole and hid himself, a flaming wolf, from the white face of his mother. O, the hour when he sank down with stony mouth in the starry garden, the shadow of the murderer came over him. With crimson forehead he went into the bog and God's anger chastised his metal shoulders. O, the birch trees in the storm, the dark beasts which shunned his deranged paths. Hate scorched his heart, lust, as in the greening summer garden he ravished the mute child [and] recognized in the radiant face his deranged visage. Alas, in the evening at the window, when a greyish skeleton, death, stepped from purple flowers. O, you towers and bells. And the phantoms of the night fell stonily upon him.

No one loved him. His head burned lies and fornication in twilight-filled rooms. The blue rustling of a woman's garment hardened him into a pillar and in the door stood the gloomy figure of his mother. At his head rose up the shadow of evil. O, you nights and stars. In the evening he went with the cripple along the mountain. On the icy peak lay the rosy splendor of the sunset and his heart rang lightly in the twilight. The stormy firs sank heavily over them and the red hunter stepped from the forest. As it became night, his heart shattered crystallike and the darkness struck his forehead. Under barren oak trees he strangled a wild cat with icy hands. Complaining, on the right side, the white figure of an angel appeared, and the shadow of the cripple grew in the dark. He, however, lifted a stone and threw it at that one, so that he fled screaming and the gentle face of the angel vanished, sighing in the shadow of the tree. He lay for a long time on the stony field and saw in wonderment the golden vault of the stars. Pursued by bats, he rushed forth into the dark. Breathless he stepped into the ruined house. In the court he, a wild animal, drank from the blue waters of the spring until be became cold. Feverish he sat on the icy staircase, raving to God that he might die. O, the grey face of terror, when he lifted his round eyes over the slit throat of a dove. Flitting over strange steps he met a Jewess and he grasped for her black hair and he took her mouth. Something hostile followed him through dark alleys and an iron clattering rent his ear. Along autumnal walls he, a sexton's boy, quietly followed the silent priest. Under withered trees he drunkenly breathed the scarlet of that sacred garment. O, the fallen orb of the sun. Sweet agonies consumed his flesh. In a devastated gatehouse his bleeding figure appeared to him rigid with filth. He loved the stately works of

den Priester; unter verdorrten Bäumen atmete er trunken den Scharlach jenes ehrwürdigen Gewands. O, die verfallene Scheibe der Sonne. Süße Martern verzehrten sein Fleisch. In einem verödeten Durchhaus erschien ihm starrend von Unrat seine blutende Gestalt. Tiefer liebte er die erhabenen Werke des Steins; den Turm, der mit höllischen Fratzen nächtlich den blauen Sternenhimmel stürmt; das kühle Grab, darin des Menschen feuriges Herz bewahrt ist. Weh, der unsäglichen Schuld, die jenes kundtut. Aber da er Glühendes sinnend den herbstlichen Fluß hinabging unter kahlen Bäumen hin, erschien in härenem Mantel ihm, ein flammender Dämon, die Schwester. Beim Erwachen erloschen zu ihren Häuptern die Sterne.

O des verfluchten Geschlechts. Wenn in befleckten Zimmern jegliches Schicksal vollendet ist, tritt mit modernden Schritten der Tod in das Haus. O, daß draußen Frühling wäre und im blühenden Baum ein lieblicher Vogel sänge. Aber gräulich verdorrt das spärliche Grün an den Fenstern der Nächtlichen und es sinnen die blutenden Herzen noch Böses. O, die dämmernden Frühlingswege des Sinnenden. Gerechter erfreut ihn die blühende Hecke, die junge Saat des Landmanns und der singende Vogel, Gottes sanftes Geschöpf; die Abendglocke und die schöne Gemeine der Menschen. Daß er seines Schicksals vergäße und des dornigen Stachels. Frei ergrünt der Bach, wo silbern wandelt sein Fuß, und ein sagender Baum rauscht über dem umnachteten Haupt ihm. Also hebt er mit schmächtiger Hand die Schlange, und in feurigen Tränen schmolz ihm das Herz hin. Erhaben ist das Schweigen des Walds, ergrüntes Dunkel und das moosige Getier, aufflatternd, wenn es Nacht wird. O der Schauer, da jegliches seine Schuld weiß, dornige Pfade geht. Also fand er im Dornenbusch die weiße Gestalt des Kindes, blutend nach dem Mantel seines Bräutigams. Er aber stand vergraben in sein stählernes Haar stumm und leidend vor ihr. O die strahlenden Engel, die der purpurne Nachtwind zerstreute. Nachtlang wohnte er in kristallener Höhle und der Aussatz wuchs silbern auf seiner Stirne. Ein Schatten ging er den Saumpfad hinab unter herbstlichen Sternen. Schnee fiel, und blaue Finsternis erfüllte das Haus. Eines Blinden klang die harte Stimme des Vaters und beschwor das Grauen. Weh der gebeugten Erscheinung der Frauen. Unter erstarrten Händen verfielen Frucht und Gerät dem entsetzten Geschlecht. Ein Wolf zerriß das Erstgeborene und die Schwestern flohen in dunkle Gärten zu knöchernen Greisen. Ein umnachteter Seher sang jener an verfallenen Mauern und seine Stimme verschlang Gottes Wind. O die Wollust des Todes. O ihr Kinder eines dunklen Geschlechts. Silbern schimmern die bösen Blumen des Bluts an

stone more deeply; the tower which storms the blue starry sky at night with hellish grimaces; the cool grave in which man's fiery heart is preserved. Alas, the unspeakable guilt which it proclaims. But as he went down the river under barren trees, reflecting on something glowing, a flaming demon in a hair-coat appeared to him, the sister. Upon waking the stars were extinguished at their heads.

O the accursed race. When in defiled rooms each such destiny is accomplished, death enters with mouldering steps into the house. O, that it were spring outside and a delightful bird would sing in the blooming tree. But the meager green withers greyish at the windows of the nocturnal ones and the bleeding hearts still plot evil. O, the dawning spring paths of the plotting one. The blooming hedge cheers him more justly, the new crops of the farmer and the singing bird, God's gentle creature; the evening bell and the beautiful community of men. O that he might forget his fate and the thorny spur. The brook greens freely where his foot ambles silvery and a speaking tree murmurs above his deranged head. So he lifts the snake with delicate hand and in fiery tears his heart melted away. The silence of the forest is exalted, the darkness grown green and the mossy animals, fluttering up when it becomes night. O the horror when every thing that goes on thorny paths knows his guilt. Accordingly he found in the thorn bush the white figure of the child, bleeding for the coat of its bridegroom. He, however, stood buried in his steely hair, mute and suffering before her. O the beaming angels which the crimson night wind dispersed. All night he lived in the crystalline cavern and leprosy grew silvery on his forehead. A shadow, he went down the mountain track under autumnal stars. Snow fell and blue darkness filled the house. The hard voice of the father sounded like that of a blind man and it conjured horror. Alas the stooped form of the women. Under paralyzed hands, fruit and tools fell from the horrified race. A wolf tore the first born to pieces and the sisters fled into dark gardens to bony old men. That one, a deranged seer, sang at fallen walls and God's wind devoured his voice. O the voluptuousness of death. O you children of a dark race. Silvery the evil flowers of blood glisten on that one's temple, the cold moon in his shattered eyes. O the nocturnal ones; o, the accursed one.

The slumber in dark poisons is profound, filled with stars and the white face of the mother, the stony one. Death is bitter, the fare of the guilt-laden. In the brown branches of the family tree, the earthen faces decomposed grinning. But that one sang softly in the green shadow of the

jenes Schläfe, der kalte Mond in seinen zerbrochenen Augen. O, der Nächtlichen; o, der Verfluchten.

Tief ist der Schlummer in dunklen Giften, erfüllt von Sternen und dem weißen Antlitz der Mutter, dem steinernen. Bitter ist der Tod, die Kost der Schuldbeladenen; in dem braunen Geäst des Stamms zerfielen grinsend die irdenen Gesichter. Aber leise sang jener im grünen Schatten des Hollunders, da er aus bösen Träumen erwachte; süßer Gespiele nahte ihm ein rosiger Engel, daß er, ein sanftes Wild, zur Nacht hinschlummerte; und er sah das Sternenantlitz der Reinheit. Golden sanken die Sonnenblumen über den Zaun des Gartens, da es Sommer ward. O, der Fleiß der Bienen und das grüne Laub des Nußbaums; die vorüberziehenden Gewitter. Silbern blühte der Mohn auch, trug in grüner Kapsel unsere nächtigen Sternenträume. O, wie stille war das Haus, als der Vater ins Dunkel hinging. Purpurn reifte die Frucht am Baum und der Gärtner rührte die harten Hände; o die härenen Zeichen in strahlender Sonne. Aber stille trat am Abend der Schatten des Toten in den trauernden Kreis der Seinen und es klang kristallen sein Schritt über die grünende Wiese vorm Wald. Schweigende versammelten sich jene am Tisch; Sterbende brachen sie mit wächsernen Händen das Brot, das blutende. Weh der steinernen Augen der Schwester, da beim Mahle ihr Wahnsinn auf die nächtige Stirne des Bruders trat, der Mutter unter leidenden Händen das Brot zu Stein ward. O der Verwesten, da sie mit silbernen Zungen die Hölle schwiegen. Also erloschen die Lampen im kühlen Gemach und aus purpurnen Masken sahen schweigend sich die leidenden Menschen an. Die Nacht lang rauschte ein Regen und erquickte die Flur. In dorniger Wildnis folgte der Dunkle den vergilbten Pfaden im Korn, dem Lied der Lerche und der sanften Stille des grünen Gezweigs, daß er Frieden fände. O, ihr Dörfer und moosigen Stufen, glühender Anblick. Aber beinern schwanken die Schritte über schlafende Schlangen am Waldsaum und das Ohr folgt immer dem rasenden Schrei des Geiers. Steinige Öde fand er am Abend, Geleite eines Toten in das dunkle Haus des Vaters. Purpurne Wolke umwölkte sein Haupt, daß er schweigend über sein eigenes Blut und Bildnis herfiel, ein mondenes Antlitz; steinern ins Leere hinsank, da in zerbrochenem Spiegel, ein sterbender Jüngling, die Schwester erschien; die Nacht das verfluchte Geschlecht verschlang.

OFFENBARUNG UND UNTERGANG

Seltsam sind die nächtigen Pfade des Menschen. Da ich nachtwandelnd an steinernen Zimmern hinging und es brannte in jedem ein stilles

elder, as he awoke from evil dreams. Sweet playmate, a rosy angel drew near to him so that he, a gentle wild animal, dozed off into the night; and he saw the starry face of purity. The sunflowers sank golden over the fence of the garden as it became summer. O the diligence of the bees and the green foliage of the walnut tree; the passing storms. The poppy bloomed silvery too; it bore in green capsule our nightlike starry dreams. O how quiet the house was when the father went off into the darkness. The fruit ripened crimson on the tree and the gardener stirred his hard hands. O, the hairlike signs in the beaming sun. But quietly in the evening the shadow of the dead man entered into the mourning circle of his family and his step rang crystalline over the greening meadow in front of the forest. Silent ones they assembled at the table; dying ones, they broke bread with waxen hands, the bleeding loaf. Alas the stony eyes of the sister as at the meal her madness passed over to the dark forehead of the brother; [as] the bread turned into stone in the suffering hands of the mother. O the decaying ones, when they kept hell silent with silvery tongues. Thus the lamps were extinguished in the cool chamber and the suffering people looked at each other silently from crimson masks. All night long a rain murmured and revived the field. In thorny wilderness the dark one followed the gilded paths in the grain, the song of the lark and the gentle stillness of the green branches, so that he might find peace. O, you villages and mossy steps, glowing sight. But stiff as bones the steps stagger over sleeping snakes at the forest's edge and the ear always follows the raving cry of the vulture. In the evening he found stony solitude, escort of a dead man into the dark house of the father. A crimson cloud clouded his head so that he fell silently upon his own blood and likeness, a lunar face; stonily he sank down into the emptiness, when in the broken mirror, a dying youth, the sister appeared; the night devoured the accursed race.

REVELATION AND DEMISE

The nightlike paths of men are strange. As I walked along stony rooms in my sleep and there burned in each a silent little lamp, a copper

Lämpchen, ein kupferner Leuchter, und da ich frierend aufs Lager hinsank, stand zu Häupten wieder der schwarze Schatten der Fremdlingin und schweigend verbarg ich das Antlitz in den langsamen Händen. Auch war am Fenster blau die Hyazinthe aufgeblüht und es trat auf die purpurne Lippe des Odmenden das alte Gebet, sanken von den Lidern kristallne Tränen geweint um die bittere Welt. In dieser Stunde war ich im Tod meines Vaters der weiße Sohn. In blauen Schauern kam vom Hügel der Nachtwind, die dunkle Klage der Mutter, hinsterbend wieder und ich sah die schwarze Hölle in meinem Herzen; Minute schimmernder Stille. Leise trat aus kalkiger Mauer ein unsägliches Antlitz—ein sterbender Jüngling—die Schönheit eines heimkehrenden Geschlechts. Mondesweiß umfing die Kühle des Steins die wachende Schläfe, verklangen die Schritte der Schatten auf verfallenen Stufen, ein rosiger Reigen im Gärtchen.

Schweigend saß ich in verlassener Schenke unter verrauchtem Holzgebälk und einsam beim Wein; ein strahlender Leichnam über ein Dunkles geneigt und es lag ein totes Lamm zu meinen Füßen. Aus verwesender Bläue trat die bleiche Gestalt der Schwester und also sprach ihr blutender Mund: Stich schwarzer Dorn. Ach noch tönen von wilden Gewittern die silbernen Arme mir. Fließe Blut von den mondenen Füßen, blühend auf nächtigen Pfaden, darüber schreiend die Ratte huscht. Aufflackert ihr Sterne in meinen gewölbten Brauen; und es läutet leise das Herz in der Nacht. Einbrach ein roter Schatten mit flammendem Schwert in das Haus, floh mit schneeiger Stirne. O bitterer Tod.

Und es sprach eine dunkle Stimme aus mir: Meinem Rappen brach ich im nächtigen Wald das Genick, da aus seinen purpurnen Augen der Wahnsinn sprang; die Schatten der Ulmen fielen auf mich, das blaue Lachen des Quells und die schwarze Kühle der Nacht, da ich ein wilder Jäger aufjagte ein schneeiges Wild; in steinerner Hölle mein Antlitz erstarb.

Und schimmernd fiel ein Tropfen Blutes in des Einsamen Wein; und da ich davon trank, schmeckte er bitterer als Mohn; und eine schwärzliche Wolke umhüllte mein Haupt, die kristallenen Tränen verdammter Engel; und leise rann aus silberner Wunde der Schwester das Blut und fiel ein feuriger Regen auf mich.

Am Saum des Waldes will ich ein Schweigendes gehn, dem aus sprachlosen Händen die härene Sonne sank; ein Fremdling am Abendhügel, der weinend aufhebt die Lider über die steinerne Stadt; ein Wild, das stille steht im Frieden des alten Hollunders; o ruhlos lauscht das dämmernde

candlestick, and as I, freezing, sank down upon my bed, there stood at its head the black shadow of the strangress again, and keeping silent I hid my face in my slow hands. At the window the hyacinth had also blossomed bluely and there appeared on the crimson lips of the breathing one the old prayer, there fell from the eyelids crystalline tears wept for the bitter world. At this hour of my father's death I was the white son. In blue shudders the night wind came from the hill, the mother's dark lament again dying away and I saw the black hell in my heart; minute of shimmering stillness. Softly an unspeakable face emerged from the chalky wall—a dying youth—the beauty of a race returning home. White as the moon the coolness of the stone embraced the waking temple, the strides of the shadows faded away on decayed steps, a rosy dance in the little garden.

Silently I sat in the abandoned inn under the wooden beams black with smoke and lonely with my wine; a beaming corpse bent over something dark and there lay a dead lamb at my feet. From the decaying blueness appeared the pale figure of the sister and her bleeding mouth then spoke: Prick black thorn. Alas my silvery arms still ring from wild storms. Blood, flow from the lunar feet blooming on gloomy paths over which the crying rat flits. Flare up you stars in my arched brows; and my heart chimes quietly in the night. A red shadow with flaming sword broke into the house, fled with snowy forehead. O bitter death.

And a dark voice spoke from within me: in the nightlike forest I broke the neck of my black horse as madness sprang from his crimson eyes. The shadows of the elms fell upon me, the blue laughing of the spring and the black coolness of the night as I, a wild hunter, raised a snowy wild animal; my face died in stony hell.

And, shimmering, a drop of blood fell into the wine of the lonely one. And as I drank of it, it tasted more bitter than the poppy. And a blackish cloud enveloped my head, the crystalline tears of damned angels. And the blood ran lightly from the sister's silvery wound and fell, a fiery rain, upon me.

I want to walk on the edge of the woods, a silent one from whose speechless hands the hairy sun sank; a stranger on the evening hill who weeping, lifts his eyelids over the stony city; a wild animal which stands calmly in the peace of the old elder; o the twilight-filled head listens restlessly or the hesitating strides follow the blue cloud on the hill, the solemn stars as well. At one side the young crops silently go along, the roe gives shy escort on mossy forest paths. The villagers' huts have

Haupt, oder es folgen die zögernden Schritte der blauen Wolke am Hügel, ernsten Gestirnen auch. Zur Seite geleitet stille die grüne Saat, begleitet auf moosigen Waldespfaden scheu das Reh. Es haben die Hütten der Dörfler sich stumm verschlossen und es ängstigt in schwarzer Windesstille die blaue Klage des Wildbachs.

Aber da ich den Felsenpfad hinabstieg, ergriff mich der Wahnsinn und ich schrie laut in der Nacht; und da ich mit silbernen Fingern mich über die schweigenden Wasser bog, sah ich daß mich mein Antlitz verlassen. Und die weiße Stimme sprach zu mir: Töte dich! Seufzend erhob sich eines Knaben Schatten in mir und sah mich strahlend aus kristallnen Augen an, daß ich weinend unter den Bäumen hinsank, dem gewaltigen Sternengewölbe.

Friedlose Wanderschaft durch wildes Gestein ferne den Abendweilern, heimkehrenden Herden; ferne weidet die sinkende Sonne auf kristallner Wiese und es erschüttert ihr wilder Gesang, der einsame Schrei des Vogels, ersterbend in blauer Ruh. Aber leise kommst du in der Nacht, da ich wachend am Hügel lag, oder rasend im Frühlingsgewitter; und schwärzer immer umwölkt die Schwermut das abgeschiedene Haupt, erschrecken schaurige Blitze die nächtige Seele, zerreißen deine Hände die atemlose Brust mir.

Da ich in den dämmernden Garten ging, und es war die schwarze Gestalt des Bösen von mir gewichen, umfing mich die hyazinthene Stille der Nacht; und ich fuhr auf gebogenem Kahn über den ruhenden Weiher und süßer Frieden rührte die versteinerte Stirne mir. Sprachlos lag ich unter den alten Weiden und es war der blaue Himmel hoch über mir und voll von Sternen; und da ich anschauend hinstarb, starben Angst und der Schmerzen tiefster in mir; und es hob sich der blaue Schatten des Knaben strahlend im Dunkel, sanfter Gesang; hob sich auf mondenen Flügeln über die grünenden Wipfel, kristallene Klippen das weiße Antlitz der Schwester.

Mit silbernen Sohlen stieg ich die dornigen Stufen hinab und ich trat ins kalkgetünchte Gemach. Stille brannte ein Leuchter darin und ich verbarg in purpurnen Linnen schweigend das Haupt; und es warf die Erde einen kindlichen Leichnam aus, ein mondenes Gebilde, das langsam aus meinem Schatten trat, mit zerbrochenen Armen steinerne Stürze hinabsank, flockiger Schnee.

closed themselves off and the blue lament of the wild brook is alarming in the black stillness of the wind.

But as I climbed down the rocky path, madness seized me and I cried loudly in the night; and as I bent down on silvery fingers over the silent waters, I saw that my face had left me. And the white voice spoke to me: Kill yourself! Sighing, the boy's shadow in me rebelled [rose up] and looked at me beaming from crystalline eyes, so that I sank down weeping under the trees, the vast vault of the stars.

Journey without peace through the wild rocks far from the evening hamlets, herds returning home; far off, the sinking sun pastures on crystalline meadow and its wild song is deeply moving, the bird's lonely cry dying away in blue peace. But you come softly in the night as I lay waking on the hill or raving in the spring storm. And melancholy clouds over the departed head ever blacker; ghastly flashes of lightning terrify the gloomy soul, your hands tear my breathless breast to pieces.

As I went into the twilight-filled garden and the black figure of evil had withdrawn from me, the hyacinth quietness of the night embraced me. And I went in crescent-shaped canoe over the calm pond and sweet peace touched my petrified brow. Speechless I lay under the old willows and the blue sky was high above me and full of stars. And as contemplating I expired, fear and pain died most deeply in me. And there rose the blue shadow of the boy, beaming in the dark, gentle song; there rose on lunar wings over the greening treetops, crystalline crags, the white face of the sister.

With silvery soles I climbed down the thorny steps and I entered into the whitewashed chamber. A candlestick burned quietly there and I silently hid my head in the crimson linen. And the earth ejected a childlike corpse, a lunar structure which stepped slowly from my shadow, sank down stony precipices with shattered arms, fluffy snow.

PASSION

1. Fassung

Wenn silbern Orpheus die Laute rührt,
Beklagend ein Totes im Abendgarten—
Wer bist du Ruhendes unter hohen Bäumen?
Es rauscht die Klage das herbstliche Rohr,
Der blaue Teich.

Weh, der schmalen Gestalt des Knaben,
Die purpurn erglüht,
Schmerzlicher Mutter, in blauem Mantel
Verhüllend ihre heilige Schmach.

Weh, des Geborenen, daß er stürbe,
Eh er die glühende Frucht,
Die bittere der Schuld genossen.

Wen weinst du unter dämmernden Bäumen?
Die Schwester, dunkle Liebe
Eines wilden Geschlechts,
Dem auf goldenen Rädern der Tag davonrauscht.

O, daß frömmer die Nacht käme,
Kristus.

Was schweigst du unter schwarzen Bäumen?
Den Sternenfrost des Winters,
Gottes Geburt
Und die Hirten an der Krippe von Stroh.

Blaue Monde
Versanken die Augen des Blinden in härener Höhle.

Ein Leichnam suchest du unter grünenden Bäumen
Deine Braut,
Die silberne Rose
Schwebend über dem nächtlichen Hügel.

PASSION

1st Version

When Orpheus' silvery touch stirs the lute,
Lamenting something dead in the evening garden—
Who are you resting one under tall trees?
The autumnal reed murmurs the lament,
The blue pond.

Alas, the boy's slender form
Which glows crimson,
Grievous mother, in blue mantle
Veiling her holy outrage.

Alas, the one born, that he might die
Before he has tasted the glowing fruit,
The one bitter with guilt.

For whom do you weep under darkening trees?
The sister, dark love
Of a wild race,
From which the day thunders away on golden wheels.

O, that more piously the night might come,
Crist.

What do you keep silent under black trees?
The starry frost of winter,
God's birth
And the shepherds at the straw manger.

Blue moons,
The blind one's eyes sank in hairy cavern.

A corpse, you seek under greening trees
Your betrothed,
The silver rose
Hovering over the nocturnal hill.

Wandelnd an den schwarzen Ufern
Des Todes,
Purpurn erblüht im Herzen die Höllenblume.

Über seufzende Wasser geneigt
Sieh dein Gemahl: Antlitz starrend von Aussatz
Und ihr Haar flattert wild in der Nacht.

Zwei Wölfe im finsteren Wald
Mischten wir unser Blut in steinerner Umarmung
Und die Sterne unseres Geschlechts fielen auf uns.

O, der Stachel des Todes.
Verblichene schauen wir uns am Kreuzweg
Und in silbernen Augen
Spiegeln sich die schwarzen Schatten unserer Wildnis,
Gräßliches Lachen, das unsere Münder zerbrach.

Dornige Stufen sinken ins Dunkel,
Daß röter von kühlen Füßen
Das Blut hinströme auf den steinigen Acker.

Auf purpurner Flut
Schaukelt wachend die silberne Schläferin.

Jener aber ward ein schneeiger Baum
Am Beinerhügel,
Ein Wild äugend aus eiternder Wunde,
Wieder ein schweigender Stein.

O, die sanfte Sternenstunde
Dieser kristallnen Ruh,
Da in dorniger Kammer
Das aussätzige Antlitz von dir fiel.

Nächtlich tönt der Seele einsames Saitenspiel
Dunkler Verzückung
Voll zu den silbernen Füßen der Büßerin
Im verlorenen Garten;
Und an dorniger Hecke knospet der blaue Frühling.

Wandering along the black shores
Of death,
The hellish flower blossoms crimson at heart.

Inclined over sighing waters
See your mate: Face rigid with leprosy
And her hair flutters wildly in the night.

Two wolves in the dark forest
We mingled our blood in stony embrace
And the stars of our race fell on us.

O, the spur of death.
Expired, we behold one another at the crossroad
And in silver eyes
The black shadows of our savagery are reflected,
Ghastly laughing which shattered our mouths.

Thorny steps sink into the darkness,
So that more redly from cool feet
The blood might pour out onto the stony field.

On crimson flood
The silver sleeper tosses wakefully.

But that one became a snowy tree
At the hill of bones,
An animal looking round out of festering wound,
Again a silent stone.

O, the gentle starry hour
Of this crystalline repose,
As in thorny chamber
The leprous face fell from you.

Nocturnal sounds issue from the soul's lonely lyre,
Full of dark rapture
At the silvery feet of the penitentress
In the lost garden;
And on the thorny hedge the blue spring buds.

Unter dunklen Olivenbäumen
Tritt der rosige Engel
Des Morgens aus dem Grab der Liebenden.

ABENDLAND

2. Fassung

1

Verfallene Weiler versanken
Im braunen November,
Die dunklen Pfade der Dörfler
Unter verkrüppelten
Apfelbäumchen, die Klagen
Der Frauen im silbernen Flor.

Hinstirbt der Väter Geschlecht.
Es ist von Seufzern
Erfüllt der Abendwind,
Dem Geist der Wälder.

Stille führt der Steg
Zu wolkigen Rosen
Ein frommes Wild am Hügel;
Und es tönen
Die blauen Quellen im Dunkel,
Daß ein Sanftes,
Ein Kind geboren werde.

Leise verließ am Kreuzweg
Der Schatten den Fremdling
Und steinern erblinden
Dem die schauenden Augen,
Daß von der Lippe
Süßer fließe das Lied;

Denn es ist die Nacht
Die Wohnung des Liebenden,
Ist sprachlos das blaue Antlitz,

Under dark olive trees
Steps the rosy angel
Of morning from the grave of the lovers.

THE OCCIDENT

2d Version

1

Decayed hamlets foundered
In brown November,
The dark paths of the villagers
Under stunted
Apple trees, the laments
Of the women in silver florescence.

The fathers' race dies away.
The evening wind is filled
With sighs,
The spirit of the forests.

Quietly the footpath leads
To roses in clouds
A pious creature on the hill.
And there resound
The blue springs in the dark,
That something gentle,
A child might be born.

Quietly at the crossroads,
The shadow left the stranger
And stony blind
Grow his gazing eyes,
So that from the lip
The song might flow more sweetly.

For it is night,
The home of the loving one.
The blue face is speechless,

Über ein Totes
Die Schläfe aufgetan;
Kristallener Anblick;

Dem folgt auf dunklen Pfaden
An Mauern hin
Ein Abgestorbenes nach.

2

Wenn es Nacht geworden ist
Erscheinen unsre Sterne am Himmel
Unter alten Olivenbäumen,
Oder an dunklen Zypressen hin
Wandern wir weiße Wege;
Schwerttragender Engel:
Mein Bruder.
Es schweigt der versteinerte Mund
Das dunkle Lied der Schmerzen.

Wieder begegnet ein Totes
Im weißen Linnen
Und es fallen der Blüten
Viele über den Felsenpfad.

Silbern weinet ein Krankes,
Aussätziges am Weiher,
Wo vor Zeiten
Froh im Nachmittag Liebende geruht.

Oder es läuten die Schritte
Elis' durch den Hain,
Den hyazinthenen,
Wieder verhallend unter Eichen.
O des Knaben Gestalt
Geformt aus kristallenen Tränen
Und nächtigen Schatten.

Anders ahnt die Stirne Vollkommenes,
Die kühle, kindliche,
Wenn über grünendem Hügel
Frühlingsgewitter ertönt.

Above a dead thing
The temple open;
Crystalline view.

Pursuing him on dark paths,
Along walls
Is something which perished.

2

When it has become night
Our stars appear in the sky
Under old olive trees;
Or along dark cypresses
We wander white ways.
Sword-bearing angel:
My brother.
The petrified mouth keeps silent
The dark song of sorrows.

Again a dead thing is met
In white linen
And of the blossoms there
Fall many over the rocky path.

Silver, a sick thing weeps,
Leprous thing at the pond
Where in times past
Loving ones rested joyously in the afternoon.

Or the steps of Elis
Resound through the grove,
The hyacinthlike,
Fading away again under oaks.
O the boy's figure
Formed from crystalline tears
And gloomy shadows.

Differently the brow senses perfection,
The cool, childlike one,
When over the greening hill
The spring storm resounds.

3

So leise sind die grünen Wälder
Unserer Heimat,
Die Sonne sinkt am Hügel
Und wir haben im Schlaf geweint;
Wandern mit weißen Schritten
An der dornigen Hecke hin
Singende im Ährensommer
Und Schmerzgeborene.

Schon reift dem Menschen das Korn,
Die heilige Rebe.
Und in steinernem Zimmer,
Im kühlen, ist bereitet das Mahl.
Auch ist dem Guten
Das Herz versöhnt in grüner Stille
Und Kühle hoher Bäume.
Speise teilt er mit sanften Händen aus.

Vieles ist ein Wachendes
In der sternigen Nacht
Und schön die Bläue,
Schreitend ein Bleiches, Odmendes,
Ein Saitenspiel.

Gelehnt an den Hügel der Bruder
Und Fremdling,
Der menschenverlassene, ihm sanken
Die feuchten Lider
In unsäglicher Schwermut.
Aus schwärzlicher Wolke
Träufelt bitterer Mohn.

Mondesweiß schweigt der Pfad
An jenen Pappeln hin
Und balde
Endet des Menschen Wanderschaft,
Gerechte Duldung.
Auch freut die Stille der Kinder
Die Nähe der Engel
Auf kristallener Wiese.

3

So quiet are the green forests
Of our homeland;
The sun sets at the hill
And we have wept in our sleep.
Wander with white steps
Along thorny hedge,
Singing ones in the ripe-grain summer
And ones born to pain.

Even now grain ripens for man,
The holy vine.
And in stony room,
In its coolness is prepared the supper.
Also, the good man's
Heart makes peace in green repose
And the coolness of tall trees.
With soft hands he allots nourishment.

A waking one is many things
In the starry night
And beautiful the bluishness,
Striding, a pale one, a breathing one,
A lyre.

Leaning against the hill, the brother
And stranger,
Abandoned by man; his moist
Lids drooped
In unutterable dejection.
Out of the blackish cloud
Bitter opium trickled.

Lunar white, the path grows silent
Along those poplars
And soon
Man's journey will end,
Righteous endurance.
The nearness of angels
On crystalline meadow
Also gladdens the children's repose.

4

Ein Knabe mit zerbrochener Brust
Hinstirbt Gesang in der Nacht.
Laß nur stille am Hügel gehn
Unter den Bäumen
Gefolgt vom Schatten des Wilds.
Süß duften die Veilchen im Wiesengrund.

Oder laß treten ins steinerne Haus,
Im gramvollen Schatten der Mutter
Neigen das Haupt.
In feuchter Bläue leuchtet das Lämpchen
Die Nacht lang;
Denn es ruht der Schmerz nicht mehr;

Auch sind die weißen Gestalten
Der Odmenden, die Freunde ferne gegangen;
Gewaltig schweigen die Mauern rings.

5

Wenn es auf der Straße dunkelt
Und es begegnet in blauem Linnen
Ein lange Abgeschiedenes,
O, wie schwanken die tönenden Schritte
Und es schweigt das grünende Haupt.

Groß sind Städte aufgebaut
Und steinern in der Ebene;
Aber es folgt der Heimatlose
Mit offener Stirne dem Wind,
Den Bäumen am Hügel;
Auch ängstet öfter die Abendröte.

Balde rauschen die Wasser
Laut in der Nacht,
Rührt die kristallenen Wangen
Eines Mädchens der Engel,
Ihr blondes Haar,
Beschwert von der Schwester Tränen.

Dieses ist oft Liebe: es rührt

4

A boy with shattered breast,
The song dies away in the night.
Only grant going on the hill,
Under the trees,
Followed by the shadow of the creature.
The violets are sweetly fragrant in the meadowland.

Or grant walking into the stony house,
In the sorrowful shadow of the mother,
Bowing the head.
In blue dampness the lamp glows
Through the night.
For the pain rests no longer.

Even the white shapes
Of the breathing ones, the friends have gone afar.
Powerfully, the walls round about grow silent.

5

When on the street it grows dark
And in blue linen is met
A long departed one,
O, how the resounding steps sway
And the greening head grows silent.

Built up large are cities
And stony on the plain.
But the homeless one follows
The wind with open brow,
The trees on the hill.
Oftentimes, the sunset too is frightening.

Soon the waters will murmur
Loudly in the night.
The angel touches the crystalline cheeks
Of a girl,
Her blond hair
Burdened by the sister's tears.

This is often love: a flowering

Ein blühender Dornenbusch
Die kalten Finger des Fremdlings
Im Vorübergehn;
Und es schwinden die Hütten der Dörfler
In der blauen Nacht.

In kindlicher Stille,
Im Korn, wo sprachlos ein Kreuz ragt,
Erscheint dem Schauenden
Seufzend sein Schatten und Hingang.

Brier touches
The cold fingers of the stranger
In passing.
And the villagers' huts
Vanish in the blue night.

In childlike repose,
In the grain where a cross towers mutely,
Appear to the gazing one,
Sighing, his shadow and departure.

Selected Bibliography

Trakl's Works in German and English

Aus goldenem Kelch: Die Jugenddichtungen. Ed. Erhard Buschbeck. Salzburg: Otto Müller, 1939.

Dichtungen und Briefe. Eds. Walther Killy and Hans Szklenar. 2 vols. Salzburg: Otto Müller, 1969.

Die Dichtungen. Ed. Karl Röck. Leipzig: Kurt Wolff, 1918.

Erinnerung an Georg Trakl: Zeugnisse und Briefe. 2d. ed. Salzburg: Otto Müller, 1959.

Gedichte. Leipzig: Kurt Wolff, 1913.

Georg Trakl in the Red Forest. Trans. Johannes Kaebitzsch. Madison: Red Dove Press, 1973.

Georg Trakl: Nachlaß und Biographie: Gedichte, Briefe, Bilder, Essays. Ed. Wolfgang Schneditz. Salzburg: Otto Müller, 1949. Vol. III.

Georg Trakl: Poems. Trans. Lucia Getsi. Athens, O.: Mundus Artium Press, 1973.

Sebastian im Traum. Leipzig: Kurt Wolff, 1915.

Selected Poems: Georg Trakl. Ed. Christopher Middleton. Trans. Robert Grenier, Michael Hamburger, David Luke, and C. Middleton. London: Cape, 1968.

Twenty Poems of Georg Trakl. Trans. James Wright and Robert Bly. Madison, Minn.: The Sixties Press, 1961.

Literature on Trakl

Bance, Alan Frederick. "The Kaspar Hauser Legend and Its Literary Survival." *German Life and Letters,* NS 28 (1974/75), 199–210.

Basil, Otto. *Georg Trakl in Selbstzeugnissen und Bilddokumenten.* Reinbek bei Hamburg: Rowohlt, 1965.

Bergsten, Gunilla. "Georg Trakls traumatischer Kode." *Studia Neophilologica,* 43 (1971), 333–351.

Blass, Regine. *Die Dichtung Georg Trakls: Von der Trivialsprache zum Kunstwerk*. Berlin: Erich Schmidt, 1968.

Böschenstein, Bernhard. "Wirkungen des französischen Symbolismus auf die deutsche Lyrik der Jahrhundertwende." *Euphorion*, 58 (1964), 375–395.

Brown, Russell E. "Trakl-Bibliographie 1956–1969." *Librarium*, 2 (1970), 120–126, and *Librarium*, 3 (1970), 195–199.

Dietz, Ludwig. *Die lyrische Form Georg Trakls*. Trakl-Studien 5. Salzburg: Otto Müller, 1959.

Doppler, Alfred. "Georg Trakl und Otto Weininger." *Peripherie und Zentrum: Studien zur österreichischen Literatur*. Eds. Gerlinde Weiss and Klaus Zelewitz. Salzburg: Das Bergland-Buch, 1971, pp. 43–54.

Ficker, Ludwig von. "Erinnerungen an Georg Trakl." *Etudes Germaniques*, 15 (1960), 113–119.

____. *Denkzettel und Danksagungen: Aufsätze, Reden*. Ed. Franz Seyr. Munich: Kösel, 1967.

Fiedler, Theodore. "Georg Trakl's 'Abendland': Life as Tragedy." *Wahrheit und Sprache: Festschrift für Bert Nagel zum 65. Geburtstag am 27. August 1972*. Eds. Wilm Pelters, Paul Schimmelpfennig, and Karl Menges. Göppingen: Alfred Kümmerle, 1972, pp. 201–209.

"Georg Trakl." *Text + Kritik: Zeitschrift für Literatur*, 4/4a (1969).

Goldmann, Heinrich. *Katabasis: Eine tiefenpsychologische Studie zur Symbolik der Dichtungen Georg Trakls*. Trakl-Studien 4. Salzburg: Otto Müller, 1957.

Grimm, Reinhold. "Die Sonne: Bemerkungen zu einem Motiv Georg Trakls." *Deutsche Vierteljahrsschrift*, 35 (1961), 224–246.

____. "Georg Trakls Verhältnis zu Rimbaud." *Zur Lyrik-Diskussion*. Ed. Reinhold Grimm. Darmstadt: Wissenschaftliche Buchgesellschaft, 1966, pp. 271–313.

Gumtau, Helmut. *Georg Trakl*. Berlin: Colloquium Verlag, 1975.

Haeckel, Hanns. "Verfall und Verfallenheit: Anläßlich eines Deutungsversuchs an einem Gedicht Georg Trakls." *Zeitschrift für deutsche Philologie*, 78 (1959), 369–394.

Hamburger, Michael. "Georg Trakl." *Reason and Energy: Studies in German Literature*. New York: Grove, 1957, pp. 239–271.

Heidegger, Martin, "Georg Trakl: Eine Erörterung seines Gedichts." *Merkur*, 7 (1953), 226–258.

Hellmich, Albert. *Klang und Erlösung: Das Problem musikalischer Strukturen in der Lyrik Georg Trakls*. Trakl-Studien 8. Salzburg: Otto Müller, 1971.

Hermand, Jost. "Der Knabe Elis: Zum Problem der Existenzstufen bei Georg Trakl." *Monatshefte*, 51 (1959), 225–236.

Heselhaus, Clemens. "Die Elis-Gedichte von Georg Trakl." *Deutsche Vierteljahrsschrift,* 28 (1954), 384–413.

——. "Das metaphorische Gedicht von Georg Trakl." *Deutsche Lyrik der Moderne von Nietzsche bis Ivan Goll: Die Rückkehr zur Bildlichkeit der Sprache.* Dusseldorf: A. Bagel, 1961, pp. 228–257.

Hinze, Diana O. "Wandlungen des Trakl-Bildes: Zur Rezeptionsgeschichte Georg Trakls." Diss. Washington University, 1972.

Höllerer, Walter. "Georg Trakl: Grodek." *Die deutsche Lyrik: Form und Geschichte.* Ed. Benno von Wiese. Dusseldorf: A. Bagel, 1962. Vol. II, 419–424.

Kars, Gustav. "Georg Trakl in wechselnder Deutung." *Literatur und Kritik,* 93 (1975), 132–144.

Kemper, Hans-Georg. *Georg Trakls Entwürfe: Aspekte zu ihrem Verständnis.* Tübingen: Max Niemeyer, 1970.

——. "Gestörter Traum. Georg Trakl: 'Geburt.'" *Expressionismus.* Eds. Silvio Vietta and H. -G. Kemper. Munich: Fink, 1975, pp. 229–285.

——. "Trakl-Forschung der sechziger Jahre: Korrekturen über Korrekturen." *Deutsche Vierteljahrsschrift,* 45, Sonderheft (1971), 496–571.

Killy, Walther. "Der Tränen nächtige Bilder: Trakl und Benn." *Wandlungen des lyrischen Bildes.* 5th expanded ed. Göttingen: Vandenhoeck & Ruprecht, 1967, pp. 116–135.

——. "Nochmals über Trakls 'Passion', mit Rücksicht auf die handschriftliche Überlieferung." *Euphorion,* 52 (1958), 400–413.

——. *Über Georg Trakl.* 3d ed. Göttingen: Vandenhoeck & Ruprecht, 1967.

Kritsch, Erna. "The Synesthetic Metaphors in the Poetry of Georg Trakl." *Monatshefte,* 54 (1962), 69–77.

Kurrik, Maire. *Georg Trakl.* Columbia Essays on Modern Writers, 72. New York: Columbia University Press, 1974.

Lachmann, Eduard. "Georg Trakls herbstliche 'Passion'." *Euphorion,* 52 (1958), 397–399.

——. *Kreuz und Abend: Eine Interpretation der Dichtungen Georg Trakls.* Trakl-Studien 1. Salzburg: Otto Müller, 1954.

Lindenberger, Herbert. "Georg Trakl and Rimbaud: A Study in Influence and Development." *Comparative Literature,* 10 (1958), 21–35.

——. "Georg Trakl's 'Traum und Umnachtung'." *Festschrift für Bernhard Blume: Aufsätze zur deutschen und europäischen Literatur.* Eds. Egon Schwarz, Hunter Hannum, and Edgar Lohner. Göttingen: Vandenhoeck & Ruprecht, 1967, pp. 258–270.

——. *Georg Trakl.* New York: Twayne, 1971.

———. "The Early Poems of Georg Trakl." *Germanic Review*, 32 (1957), 45–61.

Lüders, Detlev. "Abendmuse. Untergang. Anif: Drei Gedichte von Georg Trakl." *Wirkendes Wort*, 11 (1961), 89–102.

Marson, E. L. "Trakl's 'Grodek': Towards an Interpretation." *German Life and Letters*, NS 26 (1972–1973), 32–38.

———. "Whom the Gods Love: A New Look at Trakl's Elis." *German Life and Letters*, NS 29 (1976), 369–381.

Metzner, Ernst Erich. "Die dunkle Klage des Gerechten—Poésie pure?: Rationalität und Intentionalität in Georg Trakls Spätwerk, dargestellt am Beispiel 'Kaspar Hauser Lied.'" *Germanisch-romanische Monatsschrift*, 24 (1974), 446–472.

Neidhart, Hans Konrad. "Georg Trakls 'Helian'." Diss. University of Zurich, 1957.

Neumann, Erich. "Georg Trakl: Person and Mythos." *Der schöpferische Mensch*. Zurich: Rhein, 1959, pp. 247–310.

Palmier, Jean-Michel. *Situation de Georg Trakl*. Paris: Pierre Belfond, 1972.

Philipp, Eckhard. *Die Funktion des Wortes in den Gedichten Georg Trakls: Linguistische Aspekte ihrer Interpretation*. Tübingen: Max Niemeyer, 1971.

Preisendanz, Wolfgang. "Auflösung und Verdinglichung in den Gedichten Georg Trakls." *Immanente Ästhetik/Ästhetische Reflexion: Lyrik als Paradigma der Moderne*. Ed. Wolfgang Iser. Munich: Fink, 1966, pp. 227–261.

Riese, Walther. *Das Sinnesleben eines Dichters: Georg Trakl*. Stuttgart: Julius Püttmann, 1928.

Ritzer, Walter. *Trakl-Bibliographie*. Trakl-Studien 3. Salzburg: Otto Müller, 1956.

Rölleke, Heinz. *Die Stadt bei Stadler, Heym und Trakl*. Berlin: Erich Schmidt, 1966.

Rolleston, James. "The Expressionist Moment: Heym, Trakl and the Problem of the Modern." *Studies in Twentieth Century Literature*, 1 (Fall 1976), 65–90.

Saas, Christa. *Georg Trakl*. Stuttgart: Metzler, 1974.

Salzburger Trakl-Symposion. Eds. Walter Weiss and Hans Weichselbaum. Trakl-Studien 9. Salzburg: Otto Müller, 1978.

Schier, Rudolf D. "Büchner und Trakl: Zum Problem der Anspielungen im Werk Trakls." *PMLA*, 87 (1972), 1052–1064.

———. *Die Sprache Georg Trakls*. Heidelberg: Carl Winter, 1970.

Schlenstedt, Silvia. "Georg Trakl." *Weimarer Beiträge*, 5 (1959), 513–526.

Schneditz, Wolfgang, ed. *Georg Trakl in Zeugnissen der Freunde.* Salzburg: Pallas, 1951.

Schweckendiek, Adolf. "Dichter und Krankheit. Zum Leben und Werk Georg Trakls." *Psychobiologie. Korrespondenz de Psychobiologischen Gesellschaft,* 15 (1967), 69–75.

Spoerri, Theodor. *Georg Trakl: Strukturen in Persönlichkeit und Werk: Eine psychiatrisch-anthropographische Untersuchung.* Bern: Francke, 1954.

Staiger, Emil. "Zu einem Gedicht Georg Trakls." *Euphorion,* 55 (1961), 279–296.

Stinchcombe, J. "Trakl's 'Elis' Poems and E. T. A. Hoffmann's 'Die Bergwerke zu Falun.'" *Modern Language Review,* 59 (1964), 609–615.

Stix, Gottfried. *Trakl und Wassermann.* Rome: Edizioni di Storia e Letteratura, 1968.

Stupp, Johann Adam. "Georg Trakl der Dichter und seine südostdeutsche Abkunft." *Donauschwäbisches Schrifttum,* 14 (1969), 5–27.

———. "Neues über Georg Trakls Lazarettaufenthalte und Tod in Galizien." *Südostdeutsche Semesterblätter,* 19 (1967), 32–39.

———. "Der Vater des Dichters Georg Trakl." *Südostdeutsche Semesterblätter,* 17/18 (1967), 31–41.

Szklenar, Hans. "Beiträge zur Chronologie und Anordnung von Georg Trakls Gedichten auf Grund des Nachlasses von Karl Röck." *Euphorion,* 60 (1966), 222–262.

Thiele, Herbert. "Das Bild des Menschen in den Kaspar-Hauser-Gedichten von Paul Verlaine und Georg Trakl." *Wirkendes Wort,* 14 (1964), 351–356.

Wetzel, Heinz. *Klang und Bild in den Dichtungen Georg Trakls.* Göttingen: Vandenhoeck & Ruprecht, 1968.

———. *Konkordanz zu den Dichtungen Georg Trakls.* Trakl-Studien 7. Salzburg: Otto Müller, 1971.

Cultural and Literary Background

Allen, Roy F. *Literary Life in German Expressionism and the Berlin Circles.* Göppingen: Alfred Kümmerle, 1974.

Benn, Gottfried. "Probleme der Lyrik." *Essays, Reden, Vorträge: Gesammelte Werke in 4 Bänden.* Ed. Dieter Wellershoff. Wiesbaden: Limes, 1959. I, 494–532.

Fowlie, Wallace. *Rimbaud.* Chicago: University of Chicago Press, 1965.

Friedrich, Hugo. *Die Struktur der modernen Lyrik: Von der Mitte des neunzehnten bis zur Mitte des zwanzigsten Jahrhunderts*. 4th ed. Hamburg: Rowohlt, 1971.

Hamburger, Michael. *The Truth of Poetry: Tensions in Modern Poetry from Baudelaire to the 1960s*. New York: Harcourt Brace Jovanovich, 1969.

Hermand, Jost. *Synthetisches Interpretieren: Zur Methodik der Literaturwissenschaft*. Munich: Nymphenburger Verlagshandlung, 1968.

Kassner, Rudolf. *Narciss oder Mythos und Einbildungskraft*. Leipzig: Insel, 1928.

Kraus, Karl. "Aus Redaktion und Irrenhaus." *Die Fackel,* Nos. 781–786 (June 1928), pp. 84–104.

——. *Die Fackel,* Nos. 360–362 (7 November 1912), p. 24.

Raabe, Paul. *Die Zeitschriften und Sammlungen des literarischen Expressionismus: Repertorium der Zeitschriften, Jahrbücher, Anthologien, Sammelwerke, Schriftenreihen und Almanache 1910–1921*. Stuttgart: Metzler, 1964.

Rothe, Wolfgang. "Der grosse Krieg: Geschichtssoziologische Marginalien." *Schriftsteller und totalitäre Welt*. Bern: Francke, 1966, pp. 9–64.

Schmidt, Adalbert. *Dichtung und Dichter Österreichs im 19. und 20. Jahrhundert*. Salzburg: Bergland-Buch, 1964.

Stieg, Gerald. *Der Brenner und die Fackel: Ein Beitrag zur Wirkungsgeschichte von Karl Kraus*. Salzburg: Otto Müller, 1976.

Weininger, Otto. *Geschlecht und Charakter: Eine prinzipielle Untersuchung*. Vienna: Braumüller, 1903.

Wellershoff, Dieter, "Transzendenz und scheinhafter Mehrwert: Zur Kategorie des Poetischen." *Literatur und Lustprinzip: Essays*. Cologne: Kiepenheuer und Witsch, 1973, pp. 38–54.

Williams, C. E. *The Broken Eagle: The Politics of Austrian Literature from Empire to Anschluss*. London: Paul Elek, 1974.

Wright, James. *Collected Poems*. Middletown: Wesleyan University Press, 1971, pp. 179–180.

Wunberg, Gotthart. *Der frühe Hofmannsthal: Schizophrenie als dichterische Struktur*. Stuttgart: W. Kohlhammer, 1965.

Ziolkowski, Theodore. "James Joyces Epiphanie und die Überwindung der empirischen Welt in der modernen deutschen Prosa." *Deutsche Vierteljahrsschrift,* 35 (1961), 594–616.

Zweig, Stefan. *The World of Yesterday: An Autobiography*. New York: Viking, 1943.

On Psychology and Schizophrenia

Arieti, Silvano. *Interpretation of Schizophrenia*. 2d ed. New York: Basic, 1974.

Bateson, Gregory. *Steps to an Ecology of Mind*. New York: Ballantine, 1972.

Binswanger, Ludwig. *Drei Formen mißglückten Daseins: Verstiegenheit, Verschrobenheit, Manieriertheit*. Tübingen: Max Niemeyer, 1956.

Born, Wolfgang. "The Art of the Insane." *Ciba Symposia*, 7 (January 1946), 202–236.

Brzezicki, Eugeniusz. "Über Schizophrenien, die zu einem sozialen Aufstieg führen—I. Mitteilung: Positive Wandlung der ganzen Persönlichkeit." *Confinia psychiatrica*, 5 (1962), 177–187.

Cooper, David. *The Death of the Family*. New York: Vintage, 1971.

——. *Psychiatry and Anti-Psychiatry*. New York: Ballantine, 1971.

Crews, Frederick. *Out of My System: Psychoanalysis, Ideology, and Critical Method*. New York: Oxford University Press, 1975.

Dabrowski, Kazimierz. *Positive Disintegration*. Ed. Jason Aronson. Boston, Little, Brown, 1964.

Deleuze, Gilles, and Félix Guattari. *Anti-Oedipus: Capitalism and Schizophrenia*. Trans. Robert Hurley, Mark Seem, and Helen R. Lane. New York: Viking, 1977.

Esterson, Aaron. *The Leaves of Spring: A Study in the Dialectics of Madness*. Harmondsworth: Penguin, 1972.

Fischer, Roland. "A Cartography of the Ecstatic and Meditative States: The Experimental and Experiential Features of a Perception-Hallucination Continuum Are Considered." *Science*, 174 (1971), 897–904.

Foucault, Michel. *Madness and Civilization: A History of Insanity in the Age of Reason*. Trans. Richard Howard. New York: Vintage, 1973.

Foudraine, Jan. *Not Made of Wood: A Psychiatrist Discovers His Own Profession*. Trans. Hubert H. Hoskins. New York: Macmillan, 1974.

Freud, Sigmund. *Civilization and Its Discontents*. Trans. and ed. James Strachey. New York: Norton, 1961.

——. "On Narcissism: An Introduction." *Collected Papers*. Ed. Ernest Jones. London: Hogarth Press, 1949. Vol. IV, pp. 30–59.

Friedenberg, Edgar Z. *R. D. Laing*. New York: Viking, 1973.

Groeben, Norbert. *Literaturpsychologie: Literaturwissenschaft zwischen Hermeneutik und Empirie*. Stuttgart: Kohlhammer, 1972.

Jaynes, Julian. *The Origin of Consciousness in the Breakdown of the Bicameral Mind.* Boston: Houghton Mifflin, 1976.

Jones, Ernest. *The Life and Work of Sigmund Freud: Years of Maturity, 1909–1919.* New York: Basic, 1957. Vol. II.

Kaplan, Bert, ed. *The Inner World of Mental Illness: A Series of First-Person Accounts of What It Was Like.* New York: Harper & Row, 1964.

Kris, Ernst. *Psychoanalytic Explorations in Art.* New York: Schocken, 1964.

Kudszus, Winfried, ed. *Literatur und Schizophrenie: Theorie und Interpretation eines Grenzgebiets.* Tübingen: Max Niemeyer, 1977.

____. "Reflections on the Double Bind of Literature and Psychopathology." *Sub-Stance,* No. 20 (1978), pp. 19–36.

____. "Versuch einer Heilung: Hölderlins spätere Lyrik." *Hölderlin ohne Mythos.* Ed. Ingrid Riedel. Göttingen: Vandenhoeck & Ruprecht, 1973, pp. 18–33.

Laing, R. D. *The Divided Self: An Existential Study in Sanity and Madness.* Harmondsworth: Penguin, 1971.

____. *Knots.* New York: Pantheon, 1970.

____. *The Politics of Experience.* New York: Ballantine, 1968.

____. *The Politics of the Family and Other Essays.* Rev. ed. New York: Pantheon, 1971.

____. *Self and Others.* Harmondsworth: Penguin, 1971.

____, and Aaron Esterson. *Sanity, Madness and the Family: Families of Schizophrenics.* Harmondsworth: Penguin, 1970.

____, H. Phillipson, and A. R. Lee. *Interpersonal Perception: A Theory and a Method of Research.* New York: Harper & Row, 1972.

Lombroso, Cesare. *The Man of Genius.* London: Scott, 1891.

Marcuse, Herbert. *Eros and Civilization: A Philosophical Inquiry into Freud.* New York: Vintage, 1962.

____. *Five Lectures: Psychoanalysis, Politics, and Utopia.* Trans. Jeremy J. Shapiro and Shierry M. Weber. Boston: Beacon, 1970.

Naumburg, Margaret. *Schizophrenic Art: Its Meaning in Psychotherapy.* New York: Grune & Stratton, 1950.

Navratil, Leo. *a + b leuchten im Klee: Psychopathologische Texte.* Munich: Carl Hanser, 1971.

____. *Schizophrenie und Kunst: Ein Beitrag zur Psychologie des Gestaltens.* 3d. ed. Munich: Deutscher Taschenbuch, 1968.

____. *Schizophrenie und Sprache: Zur Psychologie der Dichtung.* 2d. ed. Munich: Deutscher Taschenbuch, 1968.

Perceval's Narrative: A Patient's Account of His Psychosis 1830–1832. Ed. Gregory Bateson. Stanford: Stanford University Press, 1961.

Rank, Otto. *The Double: A Psychoanalytic Study*. Trans. and ed. with an introduction by Harry Tucker, Jr.. Chapel Hill: University of North Carolina Press, 1971.

———. *Das Inzest-Motiv in Dichtung und Sage: Grundzüge einer Psychologie des dichterischen Schaffens*. Leipzig: Franz Deuticke, 1912.

R. D. Laing and Anti-Psychiatry. Ed. Robert Boyers. New York: Harper & Row, 1971.

Rogers, Robert. *A Psychoanalytic Study of the Double in Literature*. Detroit: Wayne State University Press, 1970.

Sullivan, Harry Stack. *Conceptions of Modern Psychiatry*. New York: Norton, 1953.

Tymms, Ralph. *Doubles in Literary Psychology*. Cambridge: Bowes & Bowes, 1949.

Index

The Poet's Madness

Designed by Richard E. Rosenbaum.
Composed by The Composing Room of Michigan, Inc.
in 10 point Times Roman V.I.P., 3 points leaded,
with display lines in Times Roman.
Printed offset by Thomson/Shore, Inc. on
Warren's Number 66 Antique Offset, 50 pound basis.
Bound by John H. Dekker & Sons, Inc.
in Holliston book cloth
and stamped in All Purpose foil.

Library of Congress Cataloging in Publication Data

Sharp, Francis Michael.
The poet's madness.

Bibliography: p.
Includes index.
1. Trakl, Georg, 1887–1914—Criticism and interpretation. I. Title.
PT2642.R22Z82 831'.912 80-23574
ISBN 0-8014-1297-8